Reframing Business

When the Map Changes the Landscape

Richard Normann

JOHN WILEY & SONS, LTD
Chichester · New York · Weinheim · Brisbane · Singapore · Toronto

Photographs by Bruno Ehrs.

Other Wiley Editorial Offices

John Wiley & Sons, Inc., 605 Third Avenue,
New York, NY 10158-0012, USA

Wiley-VCH Verlag GmbH, Pappelallee 3,
D-69469 Weinheim, Germany

John Wiley & Sons Australia, Ltd, 33 Park Road, Milton,
Queensland 4064, Australia

John Wiley & Sons (Asia) Pte Ltd, 2 Clementi Loop #02-01,
Jin Xing Distripark, Singapore 129809

John Wiley & Sons (Canada) Ltd, 22 Worcester Road,
Rexdale, Ontario M9W 1L1, Canada

British Library Cataloguing in Publication Data

A catalogue record for this book is available from the British Library

ISBN 0-471-48557-8

Typeset in 12/15pt Garamond by Footnote Graphics, Warminster, Wiltshire
Printed and bound in Great Britain by Biddles Ltd, Guildford and King's Lynn.
This book is printed on acid-free paper responsibly manufactured from sustainable forestry,
in which at least two trees are planted for each one used for paper production.

Contents

Foreword

I do not like the word 'guru', which gets bandied about so casually these days. It has an air of superficiality to it – people who provide simple answers to simple questions, five easy steps to every company's problem. Richard Normann is not such a guru. He is better than that.

That Richard asked me to write this Foreword is a great honor for me, because he was a driving force in my own development in this field long before we ever met. Since I am a bit older than Richard, that means he got an early start. He met Eric Rhenman, who created the Scandinavian Institutes for Administrative Research (SIAR), and came under his tutelage. SIAR became a major force in the development of organization theory, at least of a particular form that emanated from Sweden in the 1970s.

SIAR led to a kind of golden age in Swedish management writing, to my mind one of the richest we have ever seen in the field. It stands in especially stark contrast to the pedantic nature of so much of the academic writing on one side today and to the breeziness of so much of the popular writing on the other. While the latter is prone to offer superficial advice without much backup, the former collects masses of data to offer few shreds of theory. SIAR stimulated deep probes into serious and critical issues, offering rich and creative theory. This was induced from intensive experiences – in the case of the SIAR people themselves, consulting contracts, in that of its academic disciples in Scandinavia, detailed case studies. Proponents of this Swedish 'school' of management were not afraid to theorize. As Richard wrote to me earlier this year 'SIAR was a kind of protest movement against academia with [its] traditional methods, and [for] the idea that research and intervention could be united.'

Richard was not just another member of the school. If Eric Rhenman was its great organizer and presence at SIAR, then Richard Normann was the great theorizer, an intellectual presence with about as fertile a mind for inferring concepts from practice as anyone I have read in this field.

A key book by Eric Rhenman, still well worth reading, called *Organization Theory for Long-Range Planning*, published by Wiley in English in 1973, set the tone. It was written by Eric, but Richard, who became Eric's assistant after scoring the best grade in a course he taught at Lund University, made a significant contribution to it as it was finalized in Swedish. Later Richard wrote *Management for Growth*, also published by Wiley, in 1977, another important book.

Richard became Managing Director of SIAR in 1976 after Eric went to Boston to start its activities there. By the end of the decade things had changed and Richard moved on, founding his own consulting group, SMG. But the themes that he addressed in his writings from the beginning, notably innovation and growth, remained central to his concerns (which, to my mind, is a sign of a significant scholar).

So I am delighted to write the Foreword for this book, not least because Richard is at it again! Back he comes to innovation and growth, and forward he goes with the same extraordinary ability to infer wonderfully creative concepts out of his experiences. In this regard, Richard keeps alive what SIAR stood for: using the consulting opportunity to advance general scholarship, namely our understanding of how this world works.

Management writers, to be popular, are supposed to tell managers how to do it better. Consultants are supposed to show them how. I disagree thoroughly with the former and wish to raise questions about the latter too. There is no answer to everyone's problem. Indeed, searching for the answer is the problem. The job of the writer is to bring insight, to open up the reader's mind so that he or she can approach unique problems thoughtfully. The job of the consultant, I believe, should often be likewise. Richard also commented in his correspondence to me earlier this year that 'the role of the social science researcher is to exercise stewardship of a process of evolving language that makes us see the new in the old.' Noble intentions indeed, especially from someone who has been so devoted to practice.

Reframing Business does exactly that. It is enlightening in the best sense of that term. The reader cannot help but marvel at how Richard brings insight to key issues of managing and organization today. Words like 'density', 'prime mover' and 'products' (as 'genetic codes for learning'), take on new meaning, just as does his lovely labeling of three different kinds of actors who trigger the reconfiguration of an industry: Invaders, Path-breakers, and Reframers. ('Love thy invaders!' he urges later.)

One passage captures for me so much of what is now taking place in business: 'The organization which does not reflect and conceptualize what it does but is only geared to encouraging action will become what I think of as "the hysterically hyperactive" organization, with compartmentalization, politics, and lack of aggregation and structuring of knowledge as a result. Frustration and cynicism will ensue, and leadership will lose its legitimacy.' If these words alone were heeded, this book would have an immense impact.

Then we come across: 'A physical product ... is a representation – an accumulation – of past knowledge and activities. It is indeed, frozen knowledge elevated on this platform of the past ... the user can reach higher.' And he or she can reach out too, from economic actors of the past to those of the future, 'My sound reproduction equipment links me to musicians, music managers, record producing companies, friends who love to listen and discuss. And to Beethoven.' How often do we get ideas like this in this literature, let alone expressed so eloquently? Indeed, one has to marvel at how far ahead Richard has been on these issues, and how he is able to weave so many interesting concepts into an integrated frame by which to understand what is going on in business today.

On behalf of the many readers who have already appreciated his wonderful insights, and what should become the many more to appreciate what he offers here, I wish to thank Richard for giving us so much.

Henry Mintzberg
McGill University, Quebec, Canada, May 2001

Ingresso

'And the central point ... is precisely this: a hero has been created who would actually have had all the attributes of freedom, but that nobody remembered to tell him about them, and this man thus remains unaware and incomplete.' (Patrice Chéreau, on Siegfried from Richard Wagner's *Der Ring des Niebelungen*)

As I worked with this book I came to understand that business and other institutions today have to be very skilled at conceptualizing. Today's products and services are more about knowledge and linkages than about steel and mass. Companies are abstractions and value-creating networks more than factories and offices. Today's free flow of information needs to be transformed into unique concepts and frameworks which then focalize action.

In this book I try to deal with the consequences for intellectual processes – *the symbolizing processes of the mind* – of the information- and knowledge-based economy. In the exploding space of reconfiguration options that today's business landscape offers, individual and collective mind processes become crucial. Unless we are able to creatively conceptualize a territory which *a priori* lends itself to any kind of interpretation or any intellectual viewpoint, we will be lost.

And so action orientation and conceptual thinking are two sides of the same coin.

Acknowledgements

The intellectual stimuli and the emotional support that have led to this book are far too numerous to be specified.

My intellectual tradition was established by a string of classical books around the broad subject of organization theory. Philip Selznick, whose seminal work on organizational character would be my desert island book; the Carnegie Tech School with Herbert Simon and James G. March; Burns and Stalker with their incredibly powerful study of innovation in the post-war Scottish electronics industry; Paul Lawrence and Jay Lorsch (who followed up Burns and Stalker); Michel Crozier whose actor perspective and analysis of the mechanisms for seeking power in oganizations have never been equalled; Eric Rhenman who was my mentor and who wrote *Organization Theory for Long Range Planning*; James D. Thompson and Amitai Etzioni who, in different ways, studied the relationship between the inherent logics of value creation and the adequate institutional and leadership requirements (they would probably not have formulated what they did exactly in this way!); Chris Argyris and Donald Schön who illuminated so many of the mechanisms for innovation. And there are thinkers at the borderline to philosophy, like Michael Polanyi with his recognition of tacit knowledge, and Berger and Luckmann with their insights into the interaction between social process and what we perceive as 'reality'; there are West Churchman and Erik Johnsen who started in operations research and ended up in analysis of social process. These influences came to me basically before 1970.

These traditions from the birth of organization theory as a discipline have later been deepened by the work of authors like Henry Mintzberg, Nonaka and Takeuchi, Ghoshal and Bartlett, Prahalad and Hamel, Michael Porter. Humberto Maturana and Francisco Varela have provided a superb complement to our knowledge of knowing and consciousness, and the reader will find how some metaphors from Daniel Dennett have stimulated me. Bruno Latour and others following his tradition have added insights to my quest of inquiring into the relationship between the symbolizing processes of the mind and the shaping of the reality we think of as being 'out there'.

It has been my privilege over the years to work with many clients of great integrity, intellectual curiosity and high ambition, and without their demands and contributions the ideas presented in this book would never have formed.

Some friends and colleagues have been a great general support in numerous discussions over a long period of time. They include Alfredo Ambrosetti, Cathy and Larry Bennigson, Per-Olof Berg, Gordon Best, Rolf H. Carlsson, Claudio Ciborra, Jürgen Gräber, Kees van der Heijden, Erik Johnsen, Martti Kaila, Wally Olins, Gianfranco Piantoni, Lucio Sicca. And special thanks to Margherita Vaglio, who helped me, in a situation of personal distress, to existentially experience the crucial difference and dialectic between identity and different manifestations of identity, which is a key theme of this book.

Among the colleagues I work with practically on a daily basis my deepest thanks must go to Rafael Ramirez. I intuitively employed him in 1987 based on two transatlantic telephone calls to work on a project on new business logics that I was initiating, and I have rarely taken a better decision. That project led to a fundamental reappraisal of well-established management concepts such as the 'value chain', and to the refinement of the idea of co-production and value constellations long before we knew there was such a thing as the Internet; apart from many limited-circulation publications several years earlier these ideas were first published in a *Harvard Business Review* article in 1993.

Elisabet Annell, Bert Levin, Lennart Nordfors, Carl-Olof Olsson, Eskil Ullberg and Johan Wallin are among those many colleagues who have, in recent years, made valuable intellectual contributions. Ulf Mannervik has a very special place in that group since (with assistance from Johan Jyllnor) he also helped me to visualize several of the ideas into images finally captured through the lens of photographer Bruno Ehrs. This would not have been possible for him without his grasp of the essence of the book. Torvald Normann pushed me to understand more of the

Internet world, and also contributed material for some of the cases referred to in this book.

I also want to extend my deep thanks to Diane Taylor from John Wiley & Sons. Her broad knowledge of what goes on in the general area makes her a most valuable discussion partner. But, even more important, she has this remarkable ability to make her interlocutors listen to their inner voices and bring them out.

Kristina Boman, who worked as my secretary and personal assistant for many years, put in tremendous work on the book, and apart from myself is the only person who has seen it emerge. Christin Berglöf took over in the final stages and miraculously managed to meet the final deadline.

The five most recent books I published were all written together with colleagues. I came to realize that it had simply become too comfortable for me to have others do much of the work. The time had come to do it all on my own. This probably has caused the book to be weaker than it might have been in some areas, but at least it has forced me to have a real workout session.

So while I am totally responsible for the results I want to extend my gratitude for all the support I received.

Richard Normann
La Celle Saint Cloud, France, May 2001

Introduction: We Have to Change in Order to be the Same[1]

THE DUAL NATURE OF INSTITUTIONS

Organizations are the embodiments of our achievements of the past, and they are endowed with our ambitions. They are the springboards linking the past to the future. They are often blamed for imprisoning us in our history. In a more optimistic vein they are the platforms that liberate us from the past and enable us to move into the future. Both views are valid.

The most important institutions of the past were the nation-state and the Church. The twentieth century has seen the business corporation emerging as probably the most significant species of institution. Coca-Cola and McDonald's arguably are the best-known brands in the world. Event-based or temporary institutions like the Olympic Games (which reappears regularly) and the organization created for the Kosovo war (which hopefully doesn't) can also move to the centre of global attention.

The business corporation as it is known today was an invention of the beginning of the industrial era. Of course, business had been conducted before. The idea of the limited company probably stems from Venice in the twelfth century. The oldest existing limited company is said to be Stora, of Sweden – 700 years old (now merged with Enso).

More important than the age of the corporation is what it stands for. The most dramatically successful business institutions until now were the car-producing companies – 'the machine that changed the world'. The whole industrial era has been characterized by the metaphor of 'Fordism'.

Such companies were 'Prime Movers' in their time. They were not only dominant. They set the rules by which others had to play. And in so doing they developed not only themselves but also the business landscape

– the whole 'ecology' of value-creating institutions – around them. They brought about 'ecogenesis'.

Microsoft was created in the last quarter of the twentieth century. At the end of the century – according to *Business Week*'s top thousand of 1999 – the market value of Microsoft was roughly equal to that of the world's total car companies. What does this reflect? It does not necessarily say anything about the staying power of Microsoft (or Intel, or Cisco, to name but a few companies which have soared in the last few years). But it does indicate that whatever Microsoft does is remarkably relevant for this moment. Whether Microsoft will be on that list 75 years from now (as Ford would have been if that list had existed 75 years ago) is another matter. This distinction will be dealt with later in this book. But the rise of companies like Microsoft, as compared to the industrial giants of yester-day, illustrates the extent to which business institutions are changing in the face of new technology and other developments now taking place.

Institutions are instruments for collective, purposeful action. They are based on formal law but also on social contract and a level of trust. Insti-tutions in that sense certainly exist in the animal world, but they have been taken to a much more advanced state by human beings, and they continue to evolve. Using strands of popular stories – for example, from a well-researched novelist like Michael Crichton and from Carl Sagan – the crucial first steps of the emergence of a society of humans might be thus envisioned:

> The dinosaurs were gone, and the pre-human mammals dared come down from the trees (that period is still with us in our dreams when we have evocations of the terrible idea of falling down, and of snakes and other reptile monsters).
>
>   To watch above the high grass some of them developed the habit of rising on their hind legs. This freed their front legs to use sticks and other tools. Doing so made their brains (and thumbs) evolve, and the brain grew bigger. But bigger brains meant bigger heads, and difficult births, which had to take place at an earlier age to protect the mother. Offspring which were relatively helpless over a long period had to be taken care of in order to survive. This could best be done in a collect-ivity based on long-term contracts and differentiation of roles and tasks. This, in turn, allowed the process of specialization and innovation of tools to continue. Success of the species and gradual pre-eminence within the ecosystem lead us to . . . today's world.

To perform collectively, beings must communicate. They do so by oral and visual signs which gradually become language. Subjective experiences become shared. Interaction and collaboration, facilitated by language, develop into certain predictable patterns and rules and roles and contracted expectations, which become embedded as a social web. Institutions then take on an existence partly independent of, and transcending those of the individuals. They span beyond the moment, spinning threads between the past and the future.

Institutions that have proved to be functional must also take measures to defend themselves against disturbances and hostility. They develop defence systems to ensure their continued existence. At an existential level, they become invested with meaning and purpose by symbols and by overriding theories and 'stories'.

LEADERSHIP AS ENACTING A REALITY

In an earlier book, *Management for Growth*, I particularly explored the difference between the logic of exploiting a 'business idea' within a formulated *paradigm*, and the creation of novelty which requires new frames of reference.[2] The fundamental process of leadership is that of interpreting a (continuously evolving) context, formulating our notions of our own identity and the emerging new contextual logic into a set of 'dominating ideas' which are both descriptive and normative, and then translate these dominating ideas into various realms of action.

As change increasingly comes to characterize the world around us, more often than not the problem is that the dominating ideas reflect a 'reality' of the past, not the 'reality' of the present nor of the future. And sometimes dominating ideas may have been so successful that they are adhered to even though they should really have been abandoned and replaced. Thus, 'the failure of success'. Such misfits between the dominating ideas and an evolving context are often easy to see with hindsight, but we should bear in mind that *every* reality is open to innumerable interpretations and descriptions, and that in the heat of the moment there are always good reasons for defending many such sets of dominating ideas (as management guru entertainers who sarcastically tell stories about the wrongdoings of managers of earlier eras tend to forget). 'History is nicely ordered, the present is always a blur', as David Hockney said.

It is not the purpose of this book to introduce to the reader the marvellous idea that we are moving into a new era. Endless numbers of books have done so, and several of them well. But to understand the mind-set and the value creation logics that are required today it is useful to take a look at how we got here, since we have necessarily been influenced by the path we have covered. I therefore propose a brief historical overview.

RECONFIGURATION AND REFRAMING

So institutions are the manifestations of a dialectic process. They are based on subjective mental processes that respond to a context of constraints, threats and opportunities and that then become intersubjective – shared and social. They link with other institutions and unities in a web of communication and interaction. They manifest the identity and the actions that worked in the past in symbolic and concrete artefacts. These stimulate actions for the future which may lead to new developments, and sometimes to their own destruction.

And so institutions are doomed to be, always, in defence of whatever allowed them to be successful in the first place. But they are also geared to give way to change forces from the environment, from their own actions, and from the will of actors within them. This book is about the dialectic of this dual role. It is about co-aligning two lines of thought. On the one hand, it strives to look at the changing logic of today's business context and *logic of value creation*, expressed in opportunities for dramatic *reconfiguration* of business systems. On the other, it investigates *the mental, symbolizing processes of the collective mind* which allow institutions to change themselves and function in this new context. This counterpoint in the mental realm of reconfiguration process taking place in the business realm will be called *reframing*.

THE MYTH OF THE SIMPLE RECIPE

The Emperor Hadrian, Niccolò Machiavelli, and Karl von Clausewitz are examples of early thinkers (and practitioners) from different eras who have thought deeply about principles for effective organization and strategy. But the birth of modern organization theory as we know it has its roots in the early twentieth century and the Industrial Revolution.

Henry Fayol formulated general principles about 'good organization', such as optimum span of control, hierarchical levels, clarity of chain of command. Frederic Taylor – after whom the famous concept of 'Taylorism' has been coined – used a 'scientific method' to study how workers performed tasks in industry and then formulated normative principles supposedly leading to optimal efficiency.

Even today, management literature sometimes seems obsessed with the tradition of proposing the optimal solutions, 'the one best way'. Bookshelves are flooded with quick-fix 'how to' literature. (Lovers of such books should stop reading here.)

Herbert Simon, who later won the Nobel Prize in economics, was one of the first to challenge the search for 'the one best way' in his book *Administrative Behaviour* (1947). He could do so on practical as well as on purely logical grounds: For example, the proposition to keep the number of levels in the hierarchy as low as possible contradicted the principle of keeping the span of control reasonably small. His argument opened the way for the great movement of organization theory in the 1960s, the 'contingency school'. Burns and Stalker (1961) brilliantly showed how organizations in fast-changing environments required entirely different modes of organization, interaction, and leadership, than organizations in relatively stable environments. (It is somewhat amusing to find many of today's theorists rediscover the same principles, launching them as if they represented something new and radical!). The Tavistock School, J. D. Thomson, Amitai Etzioni, Igor Ansoff, Eric Rhenman, Erik Johnsen, and many others showed that the nature of the task, the nature of the technology, the strategic situation, the position in the life cycle of a product or business, the nature of the goals and the stakeholders of the organization, and other factors, have a profound influence on what is a 'good' organization, 'good' strategy, and 'good' leadership.

Some researchers even observed that it was perhaps not even desirable to have clear principles; that perhaps contradiction and dialectics was an important ingredient in healthy organizational life, at least in some situations. For example, Lawrence and Lorsch found that innovative organizations were characterized by *both* differentiation *and* integration. Churchman, in an essay on *Prediction and Optimal Decision*, found that he had to abandon the search for universal principles leading to optimum rationality, and that probably the only overriding principle that could be searched for was – to paraphrase – the quality of social process in resolving dilemmas. Henry Mintzberg has articulated and developed such ideas more than anybody else lately.

Thus, the theory of organization and strategy moved from its quest for 'the one best way' to a recognition that 'it depends', and – at least the germs were there – from a belief in rational decision making stemming from a Newtonian view of the world as a rational mechanism, to the first steps of belief in social process, learning, and 'emergence'.

THE DISPOSITION OF THE BOOK

The book reflects its purpose of co-aligning two conceptual realms: On the one hand, a 'business' frame of reference related to the new context of value creation, the new patterns of *reconfiguration of business* that results from it, and the business logics of players required to successfully play in this new field. This realm is about the 'business landscape'. And, on the other hand, how human minds – individual and collective within and across institutions – conduct *the mental processes of reframing* that better enable them to live within – and, indeed, enact – the new realities and trigger more effective action given today's context. This realm is about the process of perceiving patterns in the 'landscape', thus creating 'maps' which, when enacted, can change the territory.

The book starts, in Chapter 1, with an investigation into the evolution of strategic paradigms, reflecting historical changes in the technological–financial–political context in which business and other institutions function. I identify three such stages. The story is temporarily interrupted (Chapters 2 and 3) by an exploration of the reasons for and patterns of present-day reconfiguration. The 'opportunity space' for value creation, opened up by current driving forces in technology, globalization, deregulation, new values, etc., is analysed. Then the story of the evolution of strategic paradigms is finished in Chapters 4–6 by looking at the logics of today's successful organizations – 'Prime Movers'.[3]

Chapters 7–9 deepen the argument in important areas. It is proposed, in Chapter 7, that today's value-creating context allows a much more 'dense' packaging together of various actors into different patterns of 'co-production' of value. Chapter 7 suggests that we need to think of business companies not as producers of products or services, but as designers of tools which enable such dense and effective co-production.

A particular type of actor in the new economy which is different from the global, volatile new business companies is briefly scrutinized in Appendix 1: Territorial actors. If the rules of the new economic game mean that companies become global networks, this does not mean that nations or – particularly – regions and local communities necessarily become less important as actors. On the contrary. But they have to learn how to play the global game with both feet attached to the ground.

After some search for theoretical underpinnings in Chapters 10 and 11 (Part IV), Chapters 12–15 then take us into the second of our main territories, that of the symbolizing processes of the collective mind. Using different strands from theories of learning and creation, from chaos and complexity theory, from cognition and constructionist theory, I attempt to build a 'tool' – called a 'crane' for reasons to be explained – which satisfied a number of structure and process criteria to produce mental reframing leading to powerful business reconfiguration.

In Part VI I then try to evolve a framework of different levels of knowledge development processes that lead to different types of outcomes in terms of the definition of an organization's identity and role in a value-creating ecology context. An attempt to identify the capabilities necessary for different levels of change is made. Finally, some implications for leadership finish the book.

A NOTE ON VALUE AND VALUE CREATION

I use the term 'value' in a very broad sense. We may think of value in realms such as economics, justice, aesthetics, social equity and fairness, or ethics, to take some obvious examples. When I speak about value creation in this book I generally have a focus on value that can be measured in economic terms, without excluding the others. 'Economics', of course, is *not* the science of money but the science of effective use and allocation of resources.

In recent years it has often been claimed that we have entered a 'new economy', particularly in the USA. If I have understood it correctly, the argument is that because of new technological breakthroughs it will now be possible to have growth without business cycles, and full employment without inflation.

When I speak about the new economy I do not refer to these ideas which I don't believe in for a moment, except as a transitory phenomenon. As far as I am concerned they may well have been invented by asset managers whose wealth depends on their ability to influence investors' belief in a bright future. But what is clear is that new technology breakthroughs together with some associated driving forces are making new patterns and a new elevated level of value creation possible. We are able to create more value and wealth, and in new ways.

The concept of value I will use here is closely related to the notion of economic (though not necessarily monetarized) productivity. Productivity is a measure of the relationship between output and input. Traditionally, we measure productivity related to people, 'workers'. It makes basic good sense to think of productivity related to the input of people, since the concept of wealth (the result of economic value-creating activities) is meaningful primarily in terms of how much of it is available to people. The more output a person/'worker' can create per cost of input, the higher the productivity, and the more wealth potentially available to the person.

Productivity gains historically have been achieved by more efficient deployment of resources, leading to more wealth to distribute between stakeholders. In the 'developed economies' we have chosen to exploit increases in productivity by taking out higher salaries, which have allowed us to 'consume' more, but we have also chosen to use less of our time for salaried 'work'.

Formal figures about GNP per capita do not tell us whether we are more clever, better educated, or have greater aesthetic experiences. Growth of formal per capita GNP figures reflects two trends: One is a trend of change (presumably and hopefully positive development) of 'real', perceived 'value'. The other is a trend of bringing more transactions into the formal, monetarized economy. The latter, in turn, is the result of several trends which will be highlighted in this and other chapters, particularly the shattering of old value-creating institutions (for example, families where activities such as child care took place without formal monetary transactions between the family and the environment) or manufacturing companies (where cleaning, strategizing, or engineering used to take place inside the company by permanently employed personnel). Today, many such activities have been 'outsourced', resulting in a proliferation of formalized, monetarized transactions and a seemingly enormous but partly illusory growth explosion particularly registered as 'services'. Such 'outsourcing', however, liberates assets in the longer term. In many stale, regulated, protected, integrated structures assets have become combined and imprisoned in such a way that, for a period of time, the most relevant way to look at value may be in terms of what context the assets would work best in. This justifies a temporary focus on shareholders as the key stakeholders. In the long term, though, shareholder value is, of course, generated by the creation of customer value. I happen to believe that in most situations the most relevant stakeholder group to focus on is customers.

The Industrial Revolution brought a breakthrough in productivity and thus greatly increased economic value (or 'wealth', which is the normal term for economic value). If I now focus on the concept of value creation this is because the opportunity space for obtaining highly productive systems has taken another big jump, presently propelled particularly by information technology.

Such an explosion of the available opportunity space creates a vacuum that will inevitably be filled by economic actors, bringing about a race, a game with new rules and new requirements. This race will see more new winners than those who were successful in the era when industrial logic prevailed. A new strategic logic is inevitable. Any institution today must fully explore the new design space for value creation.

There is, of course, another major reason for today's focus on 'shareholder value'. With global, volatile, capital markets, with deregulation and privatization and outsourcing, with more and more individuals feeling that they have to take care of their own future (rather than relying on governments), gigantic amounts of money have gone into equity markets, and the main criterion in these markets for evaluating corporate managements is whether they can deliver economic value to the shareholders/ investors. Under the circumstances shareholder value focus is logical and rational. It goes without saying that the opportunities to deliver shareholder value are highly related to corporate managements' ability to take advantage of the new opportunity space for value creation (in the broader sense) mentioned above.

So there is no basic inconsistency between the concept of value creation as I use it and the focus on shareholder value.[4] Ultimately, however, delivering shareholder value depends on the ability to use the new opportunities to create value for customers.

The new strategic logic means that managers need to be good at *mobilizing, managing,* and *using* resources rather than at formally *acquiring* and necessarily *owning* resources. The ability to reconfigure, to use resources inside and particularly outside the boundaries of the traditional corporation more effectively, becomes a mandatory skill for managements. Shareholder value reflects (or is supposed to reflect) the application of these skills. It is not the only measure, but it is not in principle a bad measure. Having said this, my main preoccupation in this book will not so much be the *distribution* of the value that is created as the *creation* of the value itself in terms of better deployment of resources.

Part I
The Map and the Landscape

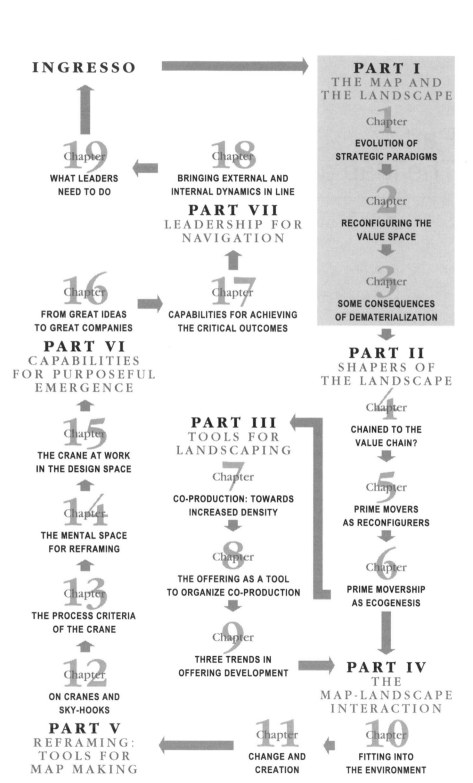

INGRESSO

PART I
THE MAP AND
THE LANDSCAPE

Chapter 1
EVOLUTION OF
STRATEGIC PARADIGMS

Chapter 2
RECONFIGURING THE
VALUE SPACE

Chapter 3
SOME CONSEQUENCES
OF DEMATERIALIZATION

Chapter 19
WHAT LEADERS
NEED TO DO

Chapter 18
BRINGING EXTERNAL AND
INTERNAL DYNAMICS IN LINE

PART VII
LEADERSHIP FOR
NAVIGATION

Chapter 16
FROM GREAT IDEAS
TO GREAT COMPANIES

Chapter 17
CAPABILITIES FOR ACHIEVING
THE CRITICAL OUTCOMES

PART VI
CAPABILITIES
FOR PURPOSEFUL
EMERGENCE

PART II
SHAPERS OF
THE LANDSCAPE

Chapter 4
CHAINED TO THE
VALUE CHAIN?

Chapter 15
THE CRANE AT WORK
IN THE DESIGN SPACE

PART III
TOOLS FOR
LANDSCAPING

Chapter 5
PRIME MOVERS
AS RECONFIGURERS

Chapter 14
THE MENTAL SPACE
FOR REFRAMING

Chapter 7
CO-PRODUCTION: TOWARDS
INCREASED DENSITY

Chapter 6
PRIME MOVERSHIP
AS ECOGENESIS

Chapter 13
THE PROCESS CRITERIA
OF THE CRANE

Chapter 8
THE OFFERING AS A TOOL
TO ORGANIZE CO-PRODUCTION

Chapter 12
ON CRANES AND
SKY-HOOKS

Chapter 9
THREE TRENDS IN
OFFERING DEVELOPMENT

PART IV
THE
MAP-LANDSCAPE
INTERACTION

PART V
REFRAMING:
TOOLS FOR
MAP MAKING

Chapter 11
CHANGE AND
CREATION

Chapter 10
FITTING INTO
THE ENVIRONMENT

Evolution of Strategic Paradigms

1

THE INDUSTRIAL PARADIGM: PRODUCTION AT THE CORE

Most businesses originally were based on dominance of some asset. Even as I – the son of a farmer – went to school in the 1950s I was continuously reminded that those who owned land were secure, and that a country which possessed iron ore (I lived in Sweden at the time) would always be wealthy, since steel would always be needed.

The asset could also be a geographical position (such as that of the city of Venice, between East and West), or it could be based on negotiated or coercively maintained privilege. Banks, for example, until recently based their position on a quasi-monopoly to collect deposits from the public. Enormous sectors of economic activity in the European welfare states, such as most of health care, savings for retirement, large sectors of transportation, and education, are still based on such negotiated and law-enforced privileges.

With the coming of industrialism, the centre of gravity of the critical assets shifted from natural resources, negotiated privilege, and geography to mastery of production technology and capital to back it up. Newton's theories had become translated into mechanical (and later electromechanical) technology. We were a step closer to the perfect, engineerable world. The invention of the engine liberated production from the site of the source of energy. Craft production could turn into mass production with standardized, specialized tasks.

It was probably in the production of guns for the American Army, and later on in Singer – the sewing machine manufacturer – where the industrial model was first applied. But the archetypical symbol is Ford, and therefore many speak of this paradigm as 'Fordism'. Belief in rationality and in the opportunities of technology was almost limitless. People were seen more or less as substitutes for not-yet-invented machines, and 'Taylorism' was a way to make people behave as machinelike and predictably as possible. Thinking and doing were seen as separate realms of activity, each with their place in the organizational structure, not to be mixed up with each other. The Japanese were to change our ideas about that later on.

'Industrialism' thinking also applied to what happened outside the factory. An example is Tetra Pak and Åkerlund & Rausing (the company in which Tetra Pak was born):

> Å & R's packaging systems made it possible to transport more rationally....
>
> Everywhere in the chain goods handling became less expensive. Afterwards many ... have described the radical change of goods distribution as equally important as the industrial revolution.
>
> An important step was when the company managed to get several bakeries to package their bread according to the Perinex method, developed by Å & R. ...
>
> The bread was wrapped in waxed paper already in the bakery, giving the bread longer life and making it easier to transport. The company also made the textile industry deliver clothes in decorated packages. ... (Andersson and Larsson, 1998; my translation)

Production engineers were clearly at the top of the power hierarchy. Although the goods produced had to be sold and distributed much of the language even of today's business schools reminds us that this was seen as a subsidiary activity to production. When I started my studies in business administration in Lund, Sweden, in 1963 there was a department specialized in 'distribution' – now a logistics term – rather than in 'marketing' as it would now be called. The equivalent department at the Copenhagen Business School is still – in 2000 – called 'Institut for afsætningøkonomi', literally 'Institute of disposal economics'. Not that content has not changed or that advanced thinking is not taking place – but there are still gremlins in words!

Customers were – and basically still are – described in economic theory as an abstract congregation called 'the market'. They were the recipients at the end of a chain which moved raw materials, which gradually had 'value' added to them, until they reached the buyers.

But already in the early industrial era we can see more of a power shift to the market – to customers. In Alfred P. Sloan's classical *My Years With*

General Motors we learn how Ford's stubborn adherence to an old formula of a uniform product to a 'mass market' finally led to General Motors taking over dominance in the industry. Sloan's predecessor, Durant, had bought a number of different car manufacturers, most of them in difficulty, and Sloan restructured along three principles. Bring 'industrialism' and standardization to the product lines for efficiency, but maintain a diversity of product lines as distinctive product brands appealing to different segments of the market; and allocate responsibility and accountability to these units.

Thus was born the idea of *product differentiation* and *market segmentation*, which was a first step towards a new paradigm. But it was an adjustment within the old paradigm, in which the product remained in focus, in which the critical competence was production, and in which the customer was seen as the receiver at the end of a 'value chain'.

The movement from craft to industrialism was based on a thorough rethinking of the task at hand. It meant, first, unbundling the whole into parts. Instead of looking at, say, a sewing-machine as one project (and the next sewing-machine as another project), the sewing-machine was now analysed in all its details and sub-components. By standardizing each component and allocating its production to a unit specialized in performing this – and only this – particular task, identical for every specimen of the component, economies of scale were gained. There was no longer any need for a craftsman to have a broad set of skills. And since any wheel would fit any car only the designers of the total system were required to have a knowledge of the whole.

Having broken down the whole into standardized parts it was possible to reassemble those parts into a new, standardized whole.

This way of analytically dividing the whole into parts, standardizing the parts, and allocating the production of each part to highly but narrowly specialized structures created a great surplus of productivity – a 'value added' – compared to craft technology. 'The one best way' could now uncompromisingly be searched for every task. The surplus or value added meant greater total wealth. As is well known, it also had a great impact on the way corporations were managed and on the way society came to be organized.

Much later – in the 1960s and 1970s – the same principles were applied to services. Levitt (1972) vividly described the benefits of the industrialization of services in a famous article. 'McDonaldization' made its mark. But when these principles were applied to certain types of services the results were sometimes absurd. Thus, in the heyday of the Swedish national healthcare system a rule was introduced to the effect that it was purely coincidental what particular doctor (within the same clinic, we have to recognize!) a patient would see when making regular new visits for the same illness. This rendered production scheduling much easier, as all physicians were supposed to be equally good or good enough for any patient on any visit. The significance of factors such as patient history, mutual learning, trust, and tacit knowledge were forgotten or wished away. Fortunately, it was later discovered that doctors and patients are not quite the equivalents of wheels and chassis in car production, and the principle was (albeit not without resistance) at least partly abandoned.

'Fordism' had a deep influence on all realms of life. After American technology and production power had been decisive for winning the Second World War, a shattered Europe was remarkably quickly rebuilt. Cars and television sets – in fact both of them 'machines that changed the world' – became integrated parts of people's lives. Optimism was great. And when the new social contracts and the European welfare states took shape after the war, 'public services' were greatly expanded and patterned on the industrial model.

The 1950s and 1960s saw 4 per cent annual growth in the OECD countries, something that gradually came to be seen as normal, and so governments in particular came to discount future growth. Rationality reigned supreme. EDP – Electronic Data Processing – appeared as a curious new subject at business schools, and promised to create growth of productivity in administrative tasks similar to what Taylorism had created within production. Operations analysis and integrated control models for companies seemed to promise almost unlimited future growth and rationality.

'IF YOU DON'T TAKE CARE OF YOUR CUSTOMERS, SOMEBODY ELSE WILL': OUTSIDE-IN

But the seeds of change were already there. And the coming of a new era was announced by three phenomena: the demanding customer, Japan, and the oil crisis.

The first oil crisis (in 1974) probably became the catalyst, or a trigger, for what was an inexorable development. The euphoria of the post-war period with its belief in the industrial model was followed by a period of greater uncertainty and complexity. Economic growth in the OECD countries decreased and came back to the historically 'normal' 2 per cent figure. In many West European countries the industrial growth machine had come to be taken completely for granted. Values of entrepreneurship and of doing business were at their lowest. The state-run welfare sectors had been expanded and were now very large parts of the economies. Future growth had been discounted just when it stopped.

In the mid-1970s a new concept starts to grow in management theory: service management. The development of this theory emerged in parallel from a number of groups, particularly in the Nordic countries, France, and the USA. With colleagues in SIAR (Scandinavian Institutes for Administrative Research) I started a large multi-client project on successful management of service business with primarily Swedish but also Danish and Finnish participants in 1976–7.[5]

It was certainly not a coincidence that the concept of service management emerged at this point of time. Of course, the so-called 'service sector' as it used to be defined in national accounting had already been dominating in society for quite some time – typically 60 per cent in the 1960s. But this cannot be the only explanation. Rather it was the lack of growth and therefore a new competitive climate which created a need for new frames of reference in business economics.

Another important contributing factor to the new competitive climate was the Japanese export offensive. In the mid-1970s it dawned on the Western economies that the Japanese had revolutionized manufacturing, and their products – no longer just cheap imitations but of high quality and sometimes quite innovative – were ready to flood the markets of the Western world. So in the very moment when the rate of growth stopped there was a distinct increase in global supply capacity.

With growing personal wealth, the advent of new media, and new habits of international travel, customers had changed their world view. They had become more active, more demanding, more aware of alternatives. True, there was still a long time until they would be able to choose between different suppliers of services in areas such as telecommunications, health care, savings for retirement, transportation, etc., but the change had started. Companies found that customers were no longer captive; they had to be seduced. Relationships had to be based on loyalty, not on captivity. In the wake of the Paris events in May 1968 and the Vietnam war, many customers not only began to question the idea of mass consumption, but actually began to doubt the legitimacy of institutionalized authority, including that of larger corporations.

Companies also discovered that their cost structures had changed. A distinctly larger relative share of investments were now in distribution, marketing, branding, research and development, as opposed to production as such. In fact, costs and investments now strongly reflected the importance of customer relationships. And since investments in customer relationships were so large, simple business calculations proved the importance of achieving *a financial return on customer relationships*, partly by ensuring the customer's loyalty (coming back to buy the next time and the next time and the next time...), partly by broadening the assortment supplied to every customer ('share of customer's wallet'). And in many 'mature' markets with products which were difficult to differentiate from each other companies discovered that differentiation came from 'software' and 'service'. The customer looked at more than the pure product as such.

With the metaphor 'the moment of truth', introduced in *Service Management* (and publications preceding that book from 1977 onwards), I suggested that the analysis of a company ought to start from the interface between customer and company, not from the production or the product. This metaphor also implied a social, interactive dimension in the customer relationship. The interaction also had to serve the purpose of enhancing each customer's urge to differentiate his or her identity. Brands emerge as a strong factor in business. The customer became much more than a 'receiver' (a theme which will be elaborated in Chapter 5).

The most fundamental way to interpret the new phenomenon was to look at business in a totally new perspective. Business did not come from the assets of the company, but was generated by the customer relationship. The customer relationship, not the factory, represented the decisive business potential. *The key flow was not from the factory outbound, but from the customer inbound.* Skilful utilization of the customer relationship was the key.

The difference can also be found in the changing language of business: the notion of the 'market', consisting of an anonymous mass, was being replaced by the notion of 'customers'. Customers had faces, they became individuals. Instead of talking about a 'market', we speak of a 'customer base'. Market share is no longer (only) calculated in terms of number of customers but in terms of *share of the business of each individual customer*.

Also the business company's critical competence changed from being related to production to the competence of *handling customer relationships and the business potential of the customer base* as such. 'Service management', 'loyalty programmes', 'customer clubs', 'plastic cards' linked to 'customer data bases', 'relationship marketing', 'quality programmes' – such were the new words of honour in business theory.

'Value added' of various activities by a company were measured not only in traditional production-related terms but also in terms of how activities affected the customers' loyalty to the company, and of how much the company had increased its likelihood to increase the 'share of wallet' of each customer. Measures of performance in traditional terms in the P/L statement were complemented with 'balanced scorecards' including customer satisfaction.

> For example, when working with a well-known advertising agency we found that two large branches with similar size and profitability had achieved their results in very different ways. In one of them customers were very appreciative and employees full of energy and enthusiasm. In the other several key account customers were highly critical and were looking at alternatives, and two leading 'creative' people had just left and others were highly critical of local management.

All this represents a radical shift of strategy and business model archetype compared to the industrial paradigm. Instead of seeing the business as a flow of materials to which value is continuously added and *ending* with the customer, we now see business *starting* from the customer and flowing to the company. The perspective changes from inside-out to outside-in. The *market as a sink* is replaced by *the customer as a source*.

In practice the two views – the customer as a sink versus the customer as a source – are often complementary and mixed, but intellectually they are quite different. This difference has not always been well understood. This is so also because the idea of customer orientation and service implies so many perspectives – anywhere from a marginal refinement of the traditional industrial paradigm to this fundamentally changed perspective of seeing the business as resulting from a competent handling of the customer relationship. The old models were rarely abandoned. (Nor, of course, do I mean that they were irrelevant.) While some companies gradually acquired the new view as their fundamental paradigm, the majority of companies tried to extend the old, industrial paradigm.

As an example, we had the common notion of 'product plus'. Manufacturing companies typically try to extend the definition of a product, adding to it various forms of 'software'/'service' to better adapt it to the customer and increase the customer's loyalty. A complementary approach from production companies was their rediscovered focus on of what they love to call 'after-market service'. The expression as such is telling. It clearly indicates that the 'original product' was the key, but that complements, spare parts, and maintenance can be useful, necessary, and indeed quite profitable.

But a major line of theoretical development during this era was the exploration of the 'service logic' as such, as something different and distinct from the manufacturing logic. Service was seen as the production of the intangible. It was recognized that service was produced 'in the field', in interaction with the client. Service-producing companies were often very spread out, exactly for this reason: 'Service delivery ' (or 'servuction', as Eiglier and Langeard (1987) coined it to paraphrase 'service production') had to take place where the customers were. This type of business logic emphasizes the role of the people out there in the customer relationship – 'the front line' (an expression I believe was created by Jan Carlzon, then CEO of Scandinavian Airlines). The packaging and transfer of knowledge across the organization, visionary and motivating and communicating leadership, empowerment and education of human resources became prominent in business theory and business practice. To many, the concept of 'service management' meant a management technique in which one clearly defined the strategy and business idea and service concept of the company, communicated these through the whole company, delegated as much power as possible to the 'front-line', and then supported customer- and concept-driven behaviour among the whole personnel with technology, quality systems, reward systems, and performance-recognition systems. The role model of leadership becomes that of the visionary communicator, creating energy and identification with a meaningful vision and service concept.

In this endeavour to bring more of the operating people into the whole picture (or bringing the whole picture into the operating people!) this era made a sharp break with the industrial management paradigm. It was not that specialization was no longer valid. But it was recognized that narrow specialization and blind obedience to authority – 'management by instructions' – was no longer in accordance with the times, with the new emerging social character and values of people. Second, there was a recognition – perhaps easier to arrive at in people-to-people relationships in a service business than in traditional manufacturing – that handling the task might not be completely predictable and might consist of situations that vary and need to be handled individually to some extent, therefore requiring a broader outlook and broader skills. Clearly, since it had been recognized that customer relationships represented a crucial asset it was worth while putting in some extra investment at the customer interface.

To summarize: the view of the customer changes radically in this new business logic. Companies now are seen as having *customer bases* in which *customers are individuals* (institutions or persons) and representing *sources* of business; they are no longer anonymous markets and receivers/sinks. And the critical competence moves from production competence to *relationship competence*. *Relationships* as such transcend and frame *transactions*. Both technological (such as plastic cards and customer relationship management systems) and emotional (such as branding) methods to create and manifest relationships come into the forefront of management.

The result was a new strategic paradigm which we can call *customer base management*. Its mental model is quite distinct from that of the industrial paradigm, and it is important to recognize it as a strategic archetype. In practice most business companies for a period came to live with a mix of the industrial paradigm and the customer base management paradigm, some essentially departing from the first of them, others from the second. And, clearly, in many cases this unreflected fusion – the adding on of some elements of a new paradigm but essentially staying with the old – resulted in a great deal of confusion and lost opportunities.

I will briefly explore some aspects of customer base management in a later chapter.

THE ECONOMY OF RECONFIGURATION: THE CONTEXT FOR A NEW STRATEGIC LOGIC

The last few years once again have brought a shift into a new era leading to a new strategy paradigm. As in the Industrial Revolution, the driving force again is new technology, notably – so far – information technology. In the next chapter I will describe this shift as a very deep change in the opportunities to create value.

Out of these opportunities emerges a new archetype of the organization: The business company as *an organizer of value creation*. The crucial competence of business companies today is exactly this: the competence to organize value creation. This does not mean that production competence or relationship competence are unimportant, but such competences are now increasingly being 'framed' by the overriding competence of *organizing value creation* far beyond their formal boundaries. In some cases this goes so far that business companies literally become 'virtual', i.e. organizers of other economic actors and little else. But in most cases business companies still retain within their own legal boundaries certain productive activities, relationship activities and – particularly – business concept design activities.

The new paradigm – which for the moment I will call *reconfiguration of value-creating systems* – also implies a dramatic conceptual change and a

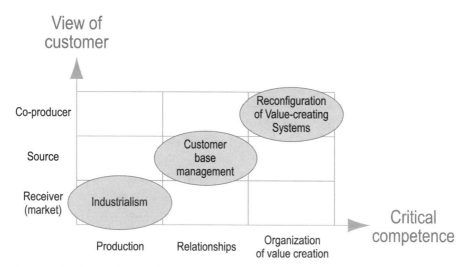

Figure 1.1 The evolution of strategic paradigms.

very real shift in how we view customers. The customer is no longer just a receiver, no longer just a source of business, but now actually a *co-producer*, and a co-designer, of value creation.

The three stages of strategy logic depicted in this chapter are summarized in Figure 1.1. For the companies and other institutions which are able to organize value creation beyond their own boundaries, thereby setting the rules for others by effectively creating not only new products and services but shaping a new business context (what I will term 'ecogenesis') I reserve the term Prime Movers.

In the next chapter I will investigate the mechanisms at work in the new game of reconfiguration. Then I will consider the anatomy of Prime Movers.

Reconfiguring the Value Space

2

THE DENSITY PRINCIPLE

Some years ago I received an offer from American Express:

> If I went to a particular shop in Stockholm (and paid with my card), it said, I could have two suits and a certain number of shirts made to measure for me, at a very advantageous price – and with a couple of silk ties thrown in. Since I often visited Stockholm, since I happened to need new suits, and since I realized that as a resident of France I could even deduct the value added tax (this was before Sweden's entry into the European Union) I decided to try it out.
>
> To my surprise, the shop was a very small one – but they had samples of cloth, drawings of designs, a couple of computers, and people with ideas. I ordered four suits.
>
> A few weeks later I came back. My suits were there, made to my body measurements in Germany from cloth of a famous French brand fabricated in Italy. The shirts had been made to measure from Swiss cotton in British Hong Kong. The silk ties – not made to measure – were again of another famous French brand but also made in Italy.

This seemingly naive little story contains much of the essence of today's economy. Literally, a global system was mobilized. Activities went on in real time and in parallel, all coordinated by information technology – and by the shape of my body. The final result combined the competences of some of the best designers and manufacturers in the world (at least given the financial constraints of the transaction). And American Express and the shop made a barter deal: the shop got access to the (attractive) customer base of American Express cardholders in exchange for giving them a discount, which was perceived by the cardholders as a special benefit from American Express, enhancing cardholder ('member') loyalty.

What is illustrated here I think of as the 'principle of *density*'. The best combination of resources is mobilized for a particular situation – e.g. for a customer at a given time in a given place – independent of location, to create the optimum value/cost result. *'Density' expresses the degree to which such mobilization of resources for a 'time/space/actor' unit can take place.* Offerings can be ever more individualized. Internet brings information – more than we can handle – to us. The mobile phone frees us to choose whatever time/space unit that fits us to communicate and trade. The symphony orchestra can be brought into our home – or our car.

In the new economy there are liquid markets for virtually all possible resources. These markets are based on dematerialized information and are global. The resources and assets include raw materials, components, manufactured products, services, information, financial services, risks, . . .

What used to be bundles of activities put together within one legal structure and in one geographical position are now being exploded. Activity sets are being taken apart, and each part is allocated along the global, liquid markets, to the most suitable actor in the most suitable place to be performed at the most suitable time. And then activities are again being recombined – rebundled – with the business company and ultimately (and increasingly) with the final customer as the actor and coordinator.

With this comes an increase in 'density'. The ultimate expression of the density principle would mean that any economic actor at any time would have more or less a whole world of specialist knowledge and specialized assets at his or her disposal.

THE EFFECTS OF TECHNOLOGY: LOOSENING OF CONSTRAINTS

The effect of technology is – and always has been – to loosen constraints. As a result of technological development, what was not possible becomes possible. Or what was not economically feasible becomes so.

Eras of progress in the history of mankind generally have been associated with technological development. Many of them were related to the art of warfare, which allowed more effective exercise of power. Much of the power of the Roman Empire was due to innovations in transportation and communication. The Renaissance saw significant change in transportation technology (it now became possible to sail to India, or America as it turned out), and – probably even more significant for the long term – in the diffusion of information and knowledge through the invention of book printing. *Time* Magazine made Johannes Gutenberg man of the millennium.

Perhaps the most notable invention of the Industrial Revolution was that of the engine, which literally meant the liberation of energy: it was now possible to apply large amounts of energy far away from the energy sources. Energy no longer had to come from humans, the nearby waterfall, or animals. Electricity later made energy omnipresent, as if by magic.

Production of the necessities of life, such as food, housing, clothes, could now be specialized and came to take up only a smaller portion of society's resources. Specialization of economic activities was rapid. A necessary corollary to this was the dramatic development of transportation – of goods, people, and information. Specialization requires more linkages and networks than an economy of self-sufficient units. Equally necessary was the parallel development of transaction infrastructures. According to Rachline (1992), 'bank' as a concept existed prior to the concept of 'enterprise'.

Today's new technology – and here I stick conservatively to information technology without speculating about what possible new dimensions genetic technology and other round-the-corner breakthroughs might bring – liberates us from constraints particularly in terms of:

- Time   *When* things can be done
- Place   *Where* things can be done
- Actor   *Who* can do what
- Constellation   *With whom* it can be done.

By way of a simple illustration:

> In *The Economist*, March 1994, the magazine attempted an analysis of the future of medicine. One scenario, 'Surgery 2010', depicted a patient in Sofia (Bulgaria) in a mobile operating room, being operated on by a surgeon from St Louis (USA), assisted by a consultant from New Delhi (India), with a simulation of the operation taking place anywhere. All these activities, taking place in real time, were linked together by satellite technology and – of course – electromechanical technology coordinating the various activities of the actors and translating their intentions into physical action.

What we see here is again a global system in which the best and most competent resources for the purpose can be mobilized in real time to act in a unique, case-oriented way, on a particular subject. When – by way of illustration – I mentioned this example to some world-class surgeons in a university hospital recently their comment was: 'Yes, this is all fine, but take away ten years or so from 2010.'

All this adds up, cumulatively, to the issue of *what* can be done. Many more illustrations will follow. Together, the elimination of constraints along all these dimensions open up a new, much larger *opportunity space* of reconfiguration. Some economic actors will be quicker and more comprehensive in seizing the potential and thereby occupying the space. They are Prime Movers.

DRIVERS PROMOTING DENSITY

The density opportunity is driven primarily by new technology, but also to a great extent by our imagination and our mind-sets. The major thrust of today's new technological break-throughs is in the opportunities to re-structure activity sets – or 'reconfigure' them – in ways that were hitherto impossible. Such restructuring implies two basic processes. The first is achieved by shattering activity sets and assets which used to be closely linked to each other, and the second comes from being able to re-link activities and assets that used to be impossible or difficult or very time consuming or too expensive to put together. The first of this set of driving forces, thus, is related to the ability to 'break up', or to *unbundle*; the second to the ability to 'link', and 'put together' or to *rebundle*. An overview of the forces that lead to density is found in Figure 2.1.

Dematerialization and liquification

A car is not just a heap of steel and plastic. It is also an information carrier. It bears information about the existence of a factory, about research and development work, about dealer networks. It tells us something about history (it has been conceived produced, moved, etc.). It also suggests to the knowledgeable observer possibilities for future use.

The more we are interested in the *utilization* of an asset, the more we need to know how it fits into a context of future production and value

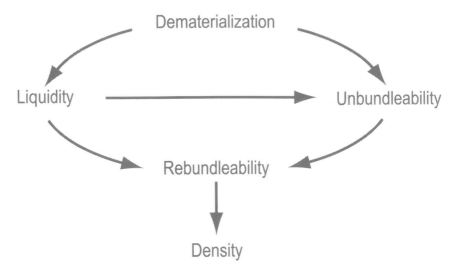

Figure 2.1 Drivers promoting density – overview.

creation. Thus, the more interested we are in *information* about its performance and characteristics, its position in time/space related to other assets. Such information also enables us to evaluate the competence requirements for use, as well as an appreciation of the risks involved. For the action (or deliberate non-action) we take related to an asset, *information about the 'asset-in-context'* and not only the asset itself is critical to us.

No wonder that political, military and economic actors throughout history have been anxious to have information about what they could not immediately and physically see and sense! Man has always striven to make information travel lighter and faster than the physical assets it pertained to. Road systems and postal systems for messengers, semaphore systems, telegraph systems, have been installed for competitive advantage since far back in history. It has been said that the real breakthrough of the Rothschild family was based on their advance knowledge of the outcome of the Battle of Waterloo, thanks to their carrier pigeon system. Pigeons have also served in other contexts:

1898 Carrier Pigeons
PARIS – The transatlantic Steamship Company is organizing a carrier-pigeon service for its Atlantic liners, and it is hoped that these birds will be useful in informing people on land of the breakdown of machinery or other accidents which may happen in mid-ocean. The

recent accident to the vessel Champagne induced the company to take this step (*International Herald Tribune*, 1998).

On the other hand, history is also full of stories about the vagaries of information travelling slowly. In Tolstoy's *War and Peace* there is a famous description of the situation of General Kutuzov at the Battle of Borodino. Because of smoke and dust and noise it soon becomes impossible for the general to visually appreciate what is going on; messengers die as they try to dart between him and the various scenes of the battle; even when this does not happen the situation of the local battle scene would likely have changed appreciably at their arrival. The information upon which decisions are based is not reliable, no longer representative of the change of the physical world, not coordinated.

Even if it had been possible to find technologies for making information travel faster, it was not until the breakthrough of information technology and digitalization that information became totally *dematerialized* and able to travel with infinite speed, in principle existing everywhere in real time.

The ability to *separate the information aspect from the physical world* is the most important driver of today's technological revolution. The separation requires a special infrastructure based on digital technology, but once that infrastructure is in place information is free to flow in real time. It has been dematerialized – the information no longer requires a physical object, not even pigeons, to carry it.

As we are now well aware, this complete separation of dematerialized information can create a world in itself, a virtual world as opposed to a physical world. The virtual world takes on a life of its own. Yet, paradoxically, the most interesting aspect of this separation of the physical world from the dematerialized virtual world consists of the opportunities it gives to re-link the two in new ways.

In the euphoria of digital technology infrastructures we may forget that dematerialization is not a new phenomenon. The world of finance and payment systems provides us with a centuries-old and fascinating example of dematerialization. And now, with that old but very modern system combining with digital technology, the world's largest market for commercial transactions by far has emerged: about 95 per cent of all the international commercial transactions taking place today are transactions around dematerialized, financial assets rather than physical assets!

The dematerialization of financial assets is deeply intertwined with the growth of trade and with specialization. In primitive societies people swapped physical assets: a fish for a piece of flintstone. But to enable more transactions a new neutral, symbolic 'currency' was required, and so (after local experiments with shells and other objects) the general concept of 'money' was invented. This built on the notion that the 'value' of something could be separated from the 'something', so that different 'somethings' could be neutrally compared and exchanged. A system of markets, and of market-making institutions, went along with this development.

However, the unbundling of the neutral 'value' from the asset itself did not yet mean dematerialization. Shells and copper plates are still physical objects and had to be carried about; the same goes for paper bills. The financial system has hesitated for a long time before it took major steps to dematerialize money. The USA abandoned the gold parity system in 1933.

The banking system had abandoned the distinction between the physical world and the world of capital much earlier, namely with the introduction of credit. Credit is truly dematerialized. Commerce with credits is commerce moved into the realm of the future. Credit builds on trust, and the belief that actors will perform in the future. As we know, if we all go to our banks to ask for our money in physical form we will hardly get anything and the whole system will collapse.

The dematerialization of money depended on contextual information. Somebody who wanted to trade with unknown interlocutors in another country used his or her bank, which used a correspondent bank that had local networks and knowledge about local actors, and an impeccable track record.

Sometimes that dematerialization may be much more complex than we think. An obvious example is knowledge. It is popular to say that knowledge is now available everywhere, that there is a global market for it. In fact, this is a dangerous misunderstanding. Resurrected old theories about knowledge (from Jung to Polanyi to Nonaka and Takeuchi) tell us that much knowledge is 'tacit'. It has not been explicitly coded, but it exists in the unconscious or subconscious of individuals. Therefore it cannot easily be unbundled from those individuals; some complex knowledge cannot be separated from its physical carriers. To make it even more complex and inseparable knowledge is not only embedded as 'tacit' in individuals, but in cultures and established social systems. Knowledge exists in language and 'concepts' which are culture-embedded (shared between individuals and extending over generations) and the transfer of which depend on the context and on gestures and body language. It is often only in interactive social processes within a given context, with a given cultural background and expectations network, and through procedures which in themselves may not have been coded and made explicit, that the tacit knowledge may express itself through action. So while it is true that there is an explosively growing virtual information world it is also true that the dematerialization of *knowledge* does not at all keep pace relative to many other dematerialization processes.

Still, with digitalization we have taken by far the greatest single step towards dematerialization of information in the history of mankind. This creates the foundation for the expanding value space.

An immediate effect of dematerialization (once information infrastructures are in place) is *liquification*, meaning that what has been dematerialized can easily be moved about. Since it is now possible to dematerialize information about literally any assets, and since this information is highly liquid, new effective global markets for physical assets, for information, and for information about information (and we can go on!) have been created.

The great strength of digitalization is not that information becomes dematerialized (this happened with the telegraph), but the *versatility* of the digital format. Once something has been digitalized it is possible to move it and to remanifest it physically in many different shapes (which was not the case with analogue information).

Yet another effect of this is the opportunity for increased *specialization*. Specialization implies a continuation of opportunities to 'outsource', or more generally to *relieve* actors from performing tasks which can be better performed by more specialized actors elsewhere. Relieving in this sense was one of the main thrusts behind the Industrial Revolution, and it is inherently linked to specialization.

Unbundleability

For a simple but effective example of unbundling of activities hitherto well defined and held together in time and place and by actor, consider

IKEA[6], the world's leader in home furnishing. The following represents an excerpt from their catalogue (my translation):

This is done by IKEA:	*This is done by the customer:*
Design and develop the products	You check, choose and pick up the goods yourself
Wrap in flat packages	You transport the furniture to your home
Manufacture and purchase large volumes	You assemble the furniture
Check the quality and the functions	You tighten the screws

Together we save money!

What is interesting about this is that it presents the very idea of a company in terms of two role descriptions: what is the role of the company, and what is the role of the customer. (What IKEA does not do in this catalogue – of course, designated for the customer – is to point out the roles of other economic actors such as various producers around the world. IKEA outsources most of their manufacturing to factories in many different countries, and they also use external economic actors for several activities including design and transportation.)

We can see that IKEA has unbundled the activities involved in home furnishing and reallocated them along the dimensions mentioned earlier:

- In *place*, by moving assembly from a factory to the customer's living-room, thus better utilizing available space already paid for
- In *time*, by moving assembly from before to after purchase
- By *actor*, enabling the customer to assemble, therefore relieving factory workers from doing it

The above analysis pertains only to the assembly activity. We will return to some less obvious but more subtle and intriguing aspects of the case later.

There is nothing new in allocating certain activities to the customer. After all, if General Motors or Volvo or Fiat produce cars, the customers drive them. *The novelty is in the way the total activity clusters, not just some pieces traditionally thought of as being 'at the end' in the system of value creation, are unbundled and reallocated to different actors*, and most notably to the customers in the IKEA example.

Why has IKEA been successful? And why are so many new players redefining many industries today? Exactly because they know how to 'unbundle' the total set of activities required to create value, and then reallocate them to different economic actors, yet ensure that they are all tied together by an overall concept, and that they are all leveraged towards the final determining factor of whether value has been created – the customer.

A special case of unbundleability should be mentioned, namely the notion of *risk*. Dematerialization has resulted in ever more refined tools to understand risks (as well as to handle risks), and this in itself is a crucial development. As Peter Bernstein (1996) has said in his book *Against the Gods*: 'The revolutionary idea that defines the boundary between modern times and the past is the mastery of risk. The notion that the future is more than a whim of the gods and that men and women are not passive before nature.' Thus, 'the fall into the future' (Rachline) – the notion that the perspective of actors should and can be moved from the past and the present to value creation in the future – is highly related to this notion of understanding and managing risk better; a crucial aspect of the service economy with its focus on performance rather than production and product.

Rebundleability

Just as dematerialization and unfreezing and liquification make unbundleability possible, they also promote *rebundleability*. Rebundling of assets and activity sets is helped by *connectivity*, and especially real-time connectivity that leads to *interactivity* and *reciprocity* between economic actors.

The 'Surgery 2010' example illustrates the notion of rebundleability of activity sets. The operation can be divided into its various necessary activities, and the most effective resources can then be mobilized for each of them, independent of place. By linking them together through the concept-based knowledge of the particular type of operation and enabling them to interactively communicate with each other (and to transfer physical movements in one place to another through robot technology) these dispersed resources re-emerge as one focused and coordinated whole.

Also, just as the new technologies make increased relieving possible they also make more *enabling* possible. If 'relieving' means that 'I can do this for you since I am more specialized and I can do it better', 'enabling' means 'I can help you do things yourself that you were never able to do before by empowering you with more capabilities and assets that you did not have access to'.

The notion of 'enabling' reminds us of one of the most interesting find-ings and intellectual pathways of the 'service management era', namely that of the customer not as a 'consumer', but as a 'co-producer' and 'par-ticipator'. If the notion of value creation and the scope of the 'Value-creating System' that a company needs to keep in mind, is extended from the production of a product to the value creation that will take place in the future in the client system, focus also will move to *the capabilities of the customer as a value creator*. I will develop this theme later.

One more strong source of rebundleability should be mentioned, namely that of the use of *'barter currencies'* in addition to monetary curren-cies for transactions and for longer-term relationships. It would be a mistake to believe that, even in modern times, the whole economy is monetarized. In fact, many transactions and relationships take place by exchange of barter currencies between actors. For example, American Express gets hotels, shops, restaurants etc. as distribution outlets for their services in exchange for bringing their strong customer base to the same places. Companies such as EF Education and JC Decaux (more about them later) to a great extent build their whole businesses on the way they manage to link various actors who have something to barter with each other. Customer communities form over the Internet based on barter of knowledge and experiences. Cooperative organizations re-emerge in different and often complex shapes, also based on transactions and relationships which go far beyond money. The innovative use of barter currencies makes it possible to link actors with each other, each having complementary resources (such as time, competence, information, etc.), therefore increasing the capacity and density of a value-creating system and process.

Technological linkages, backed up by concepts, by pedagogical en-abling and by an understanding of the stakes that actors (potentially) have to work together are all instruments that can be used to 'rebundle' resources and mobilize them in a coordinated way to form a new, more effective cluster of value-creating activities.

Some Consequences of Dematerialization 3

COST STRUCTURES, VALUE, AND PRICE

The driving forces mentioned change the relative availability and costs of assets and therefore force companies to rethink their business models. An obvious example is the relationship between average cost and marginal cost. The development or mobilization of any asset requires an up-front cost which has to be retrieved either as such or by adding a share of that up-front cost to every specimen sold – this is the essence of economies of scale.

Infrastructures, also for today's information systems, are expensive (and not seldom risky to build). While there may be a tendency for *up-front costs* to increase, there is certainly a sharp drop in the *reproduction cost* for dematerialized assets. Therefore, the *relationship between average cost and marginal cost* dramatically increases in the immaterial world compared to the physical world. As a result, in many areas the economies of scale, and the incentives to large size, increase even more than in the 'industrial' world. But to complicate matters it may be quite difficult for an economic actor to raise the price much above the marginal cost.

Economics attributes 'transactional value' or 'market value' to assets, goods and services. As is well known from the failed planned economy experiments, it is not easy for any single actor to set the suitable transactional value. A 'market', with all its intriguing and impenetrable ways to handle enormous complexity, is required for that. However, it is possible to say something in principle about the range within which the market value will be, or can be, established. The value is no higher than what buyers are prepared to pay, and no lower than sellers are prepared to sell for.

Sellers usually look at their costs (including a risk and entrepreneurship premium) as the minimum transaction value they will accept, but they may also calculate the value of possible future transactions into the price. That is, they may consider the transaction or part of it as an investment. In fact, this is becoming more and more common, as witnessed by companies giving out software, valuable information content, mobile phones, or consulting services 'for free'. Such pricing represents a shift of focus on behalf of the seller from trying to recover historically generated cost from the transaction to *seeing the transaction as an investment in a future revenue-generating relationship*. The phenomenon is a strong indicator of the validity of the trend from the industrial strategic logic towards higher logics such as the customer base management logic, as described in the previous chapter. A later chapter on offerings will develop the issue of the relationship between what is the real customer offering and what the price tag is put on.

Buyers will consider what the acquired asset (product or service) will help them achieve in considering the price they are willing to pay. They, too, may and often will give a look to the future and consider at least part of the transaction an investment. In principle, they would be willing to pay almost as much as the discounted net additional revenue stream (or value stream measured in some other possibly more subjective way) that will result from acquiring the product or service. This we can call the *leverage value* of the offering.

In principle, yes! Because there is another limiting factor which is called competition. I know of books which I have read, and speeches I have listened to, which by this logic I would have been fully prepared to pay tens of thousands of dollars for, since they really have contributed as much and more to my professional activities. But as long as there are publishers who are prepared to sell me fantastic books at $50 – why should I pay $10 000? Or maybe I could borrow my colleague's book which he paid $10 000 for, paying him a fee which he would welcome. And there would be a strong incentive to borrow the $10 000 book and illegally copy it for $10. Competition also defines the price level; leverage value is not allowed to reign.

In any case, the market price will end up somewhere in the range indicated by this reasoning. I am happy the market mechanism determines the price, so I don't have to. And I am positive that valuations get more and more complex as we move from the industrial business logic (where the market price was essentially 'historical cost plus') to the newer logics which are oriented towards future revenue streams for both sellers and buyers, with risk management and appreciation of uncertainty as inherent elements of offering design and pricing. In the new economy transactions tend to deal relatively more with future value-creation expectations than in the old economy.

The above will induce companies to search for new strategies to reflect the new logic. For example, dematerialized assets such as information about economic actors may be used for many different purposes. The versatility of such assets (as opposed to the specialized ways of using, say, an excavator) renders them suitable for many kinds of packaging and re-packaging, with strong incentives to search for *economies of scope* as well as *economies of scale*. The very dematerialization and removal from physical constraints of an asset increases its flexibility.

DEMATERIALIZATION AND INCREASED EFFICIENCY OF PHYSICAL PROCESSES

Dematerialized assets can be used to greatly increase the use of material assets. Markets for physical products and physical asset-dependent services (such as those of an airline) can be made much more efficient if more actors can be brought to the market through the virtual world. Moreover, the physical products may not have to be brought to a physical market at all, since many of the actors' decision-making processes can be made without having the product at hand (particularly if it is commoditized). Global, virtual auction houses now function with success. By and large those airlines which developed reservation systems, helping them to understand and relate to their customer bases and distribution channels better, came out as the winners of the turmoil of the post-deregulation US airline industry. During the months when this is written the world finally seems to have gone through a rapid awakening to the idea that there might be some useful linkages between the physical and the virtual world. The currently expanding interest in IT-application areas such as data warehousing and data mining largely reflects the expectations that business companies have of making better use of and moving their physical assets more effectively by having better and more versatile information about them and about their customers.

Singapore managed to become the South-east Asia centre of shipping transportation (a business of physical assets transporting physical assets) by introducing an elaborate strategic information system enabling more effective movements and matching of physical assets with each other. A rapidly increasing proportion of all people now use the Internet for some part of the process of buying a car. My conclusion from working with pharmacies on e-business strategy recently was that fears that dotcom drugstores will take over the business are largely unfounded – but that unless pharmacies can create much better information about customers and use of pharmaceutical products and use this information in multiple ways they will be in trouble.

DEMATERIALIZATION AND THE PREVALENCE OF SERVICES

The dematerialized world of immaterial assets now often tends to *lead*, rather than follow, the development of the material world. It is now knowledge-intensive 'services', not 'manufacturing', that lead the economy. Without those services, manufacturing will flounder.

In his book *De zéro à epsilon* (1992) François Rachline makes the observation that the word for 'bank' (banque) seems to stem from 1458, whereas 'enterprise' (entreprise in French) as a concept and word was born in 1530. However, 'entreprise' at that time denoted a company carrying out organized trade, whereas the current meaning of 'entreprise' as a business company involved in organized production of goods or services for commercial purposes was forged only towards the end of the eighteenth century. (Rachline, 1992, p. 203) It was, according to Rachline, the actions of the banks in the immaterial world, the extension of credit, the establishment of trustful relationships, which created the infrastructure and paved the way for the material, industrialized world. In the same vein one could certainly draw parallels with the leading role of software companies and knowledge institutions in today's world. As Richard Holbrooke has reportedly said: 'The competitive advantage of the US is neither its political and military force nor our business companies. It is our universities.'

FROM A VERTICAL TO A HORIZONTAL LOGIC

Napoleon Bonaparte allegedly said: 'Trade unites people. Everything that unites them makes them cooperate. Trade therefore is essentially harmful to authority.'

He had a point. The institutions that he represented and fought for were essentially territorial and vertical in their control logics, namely the nation-states. The new logic of value creation is essentially horizontal, boundaryless, not tied to physical territory, network-like rather than hierarchical. How this is reflected in the structure and functioning of business organizations will be explored later in this book. So will the idea that for the individual actor, at least, the horizontal processes need to be organized in such a way as to create 'conceptual nodes' which are vertical in nature.

There is no question that the inexorable shift of the underlying logic of value creation from a geographically concentrated focus on physical processes to a global virtual world-driven logic implies a tremendous power shift between institutions. The archetype vertical control logic, geographical boundary delineated institution – the nation-state – finds that its traditional means of control no longer function; the horizontal flows and liquid assets simply escape its traditional modes of exercising power. However, geography still matters. Physical meeting places matter; culture matters (and therefore history and geography). To take any company from Silicon Valley and put it in, say, Lille in France or Nairobi in Kenya would dramatically influence it. So geography matters, but perhaps not necessarily geography as defined by nation-state boundaries.

OPPORTUNITY BECOMES IMPERATIVE

The separation of information from the physical world is at the core of the gigantic 'unbundling' process we already described: The shattering of clusters of assets and activities which were physically linked and geographically localized. The change of logic is illustrated Figure 3.1.

We no longer live by the old constraints. The opportunity is there to dematerialize and to globalize. In physics, the 'vacuum principle' tells us that there are strong forces for vacuums to be filled. We could make a travesty and talk about *the vacuum principle of business and value creation*. Since opportunities to dematerialize, liquify, and globalize exist, there are strong incentives to take them, because the rewards for economic actors who do so are potentially so great.

If your company doesn't use the opportunity to fill the value space vacuum, somebody else will.

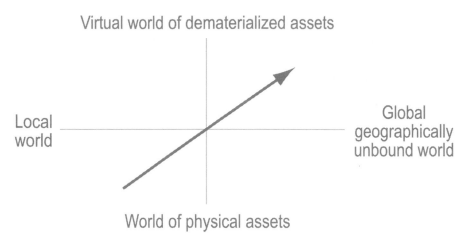

Figure 3.1 Repositioning of the leading actors.

Our hypothesis, strongly supported by empirical observations, is that the leading actors of today in business are the ones who understand how to take advantage of this new opportunity space. They function according to a logic which has moved from the lower left-hand corner to the upper right-hand corner of Figure 3.1. And this move corresponds to the move from the industrial to the reconfiguration strategic logic. Underlying change forces make the change in strategic logic inevitable. Leading actors in today's value-creating ecology and the new economy must seize the opportunities.

This is not to say that everybody must become a globalized software company: on the contrary. Perhaps it is a cheap point to say that we don't satisfy our hunger with items of information. Clearly, there is the opportunity for any economic actor to specialize and perform a limited number of activities, but the ecology of total activities must be in some state of (dynamic) equilibrium or reasonably non-chaotic disequilibrium. While some companies may live more or less totally in the physical world and in a predominantly local world, others may live primarily in the virtual and perhaps global world. But for the majority of business companies and other economic actors the point of the new economy is to use the shift of logic not only to do business in the virtual domain, *but to link the exploding opportunities of the virtual domain with the physical and geographically limited domain*. This is the challenge to the key economic actors.

In other words, the reconfiguration vacuum by the dematerialization – liquification – unbundling process that inevitably takes place creates opportunities for *rebundling the virtual and the physical domains in new and unique ways*.

NEW ARCHETYPAL ACTORS

The new economy brings a new set of archetypal actors, each operating with different and perhaps gradually complementary logics within the total ecology of value creation. In no particular order, they are:

- *Market makers for new infrastructures.* Financial service organizations, software companies, and media companies are examples of businesses largely in this domain. Microsoft, America On-Line, Oracle, Nokia, Crédit Suisse First Boston, American Express, Visa are examples.
- *Large corporations.* These will be analysed later in this book, but they increasingly function according to the third overall strategic paradigm briefly described earlier. This means that they function essentially according to a horizontal, boundaryless logic, and *they use dematerialized assets and their infrastructures for rebundling different parts of the physical world on a global basis*. They are often organizers of value creation rather than producers in a traditional sense – Prime Movers, as we will call them.
- *The small entrepreneurs.* While it is true that the new logic of value creation creates even more incentives to scale than the industrial world it is also true that barriers to entry and the opportunities not only to find but to define niches and new markets increase. Therefore we see an abundance of entrepreneurs who specialize in some small area of the value-creation ecology, naturally, of course, taking advantage of the area where most is happening: the dematerialized world. The new world, paradoxically, favours both the large and the small.
- *Territorial actors.* The world will never be without geographical boundaries. The nation-state is not the most favoured concept in the New World. It is enough to take any geographical map and look at where the national boundaries are; they reflect the nature of military territorial defence more than anything else. Nation-states which continue to function according to the old logic of control will find their

efforts futile. Not that nation-states are unimportant. If they don't have the control possibilities of old, at least they can do a lot to create trouble for themselves and their citizens.

However, another type of territorial organization is becoming increasingly important, namely cities and regions. They tend to represent much more of natural value-creating networks – an interesting 'ecology of value creation' – than nation-states. They are small enough to ensure the physical closeness that is crucial for today's knowledge economy. Yet, they have to live in the global economy, and they have even fewer formal means than the nation-state to exercise vertical power and are therefore extremely vulnerable to the dominating horizontal logic. Their great opportunity lies in taking advantage of the horizontal logic, and somehow link several horizontal logics into a vertical geographical fusion. Cities and regions are among the most fascinating actors and 'institutions' in today's world, with enormous opportunities and stakes. Some experiences from working with such actors can be found in Appendix 1.

SUMMARY

The implications of the development of the causal chain of *dematerialization – unbundleability – asset liquidity – rebundleability – density* are fundamental for understanding strategy and business in the new economy. It profoundly changes the way that value can be created. It opens a value space vacuum.

But does it have to be like this? Do we want it? Will business companies use the opportunities?

The answer is yes. It is like the physical principle of the vacuum. Nature fills vacuums. Opportunities will be exploited, for the simple reason that they are there. And for the simple reason that unbundleability, liquidity, rebundleability, and density lead to great new opportunities to create wealth and certainly value.

The question is not whether the vacuum will be filled. The question is who will reconfigure value creation to fill it. This I will discuss in next chapter on Prime Movers.

Part II
Shapers of the Landscape

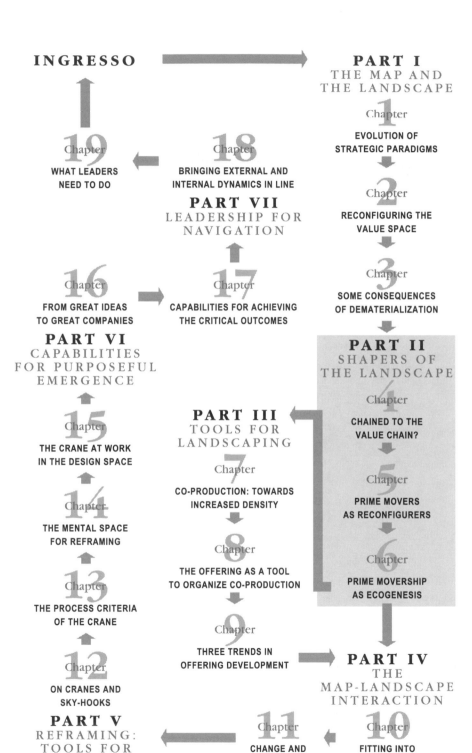

INGRESSO

PART I
THE MAP AND
THE LANDSCAPE

Chapter **1**
EVOLUTION OF
STRATEGIC PARADIGMS

Chapter **2**
RECONFIGURING THE
VALUE SPACE

Chapter **3**
SOME CONSEQUENCES
OF DEMATERIALIZATION

Chapter **19**
WHAT LEADERS
NEED TO DO

Chapter **18**
BRINGING EXTERNAL AND
INTERNAL DYNAMICS IN LINE

PART VII
LEADERSHIP FOR
NAVIGATION

Chapter **16**
FROM GREAT IDEAS
TO GREAT COMPANIES

Chapter **17**
CAPABILITIES FOR ACHIEVING
THE CRITICAL OUTCOMES

PART VI
CAPABILITIES
FOR PURPOSEFUL
EMERGENCE

PART III
TOOLS FOR
LANDSCAPING

PART II
SHAPERS OF
THE LANDSCAPE

Chapter **4**
CHAINED TO THE
VALUE CHAIN?

Chapter **15**
THE CRANE AT WORK
IN THE DESIGN SPACE

Chapter **7**
CO-PRODUCTION: TOWARDS
INCREASED DENSITY

Chapter **5**
PRIME MOVERS
AS RECONFIGURERS

Chapter **14**
THE MENTAL SPACE
FOR REFRAMING

Chapter **8**
THE OFFERING AS A TOOL
TO ORGANIZE CO-PRODUCTION

Chapter **6**
PRIME MOVERSHIP
AS ECOGENESIS

Chapter **13**
THE PROCESS CRITERIA
OF THE CRANE

Chapter **9**
THREE TRENDS IN
OFFERING DEVELOPMENT

PART IV
THE
MAP-LANDSCAPE
INTERACTION

Chapter **12**
ON CRANES AND
SKY-HOOKS

PART V
REFRAMING:
TOOLS FOR
MAP MAKING

Chapter **11**
CHANGE AND
CREATION

Chapter **10**
FITTING INTO
THE ENVIRONMENT

Chained to the Value Chain?

4

Donald Schön, in his foreword to *Designing Interactive Strategy* by Normann and Ramirez (1994/1998), said that 'It might very well have been sub-titled. Against Porter'. I would say that was both to the point and an exaggeration. Porter, in his classical work on competitive strategy, built the concept of the 'value chain' according to which various economic actors working in a sequential, chain-like configuration 'add value' all the way until the customer is finally reached. Porter duly and clearly recognized that a company's position in this 'chain' may be challenged not only by its traditional competitors but also by actors representing substitute technology, by suppliers, and by customers themselves. And in his work on the competitiveness of nations Porter, with his 'cluster' theories, begins to develop notions of actor systems which can only fit the value chain model more or less by forcing them to do so.

The notion of the value chain has become one of the most powerful models of corporate strategy and the dominating one (the domination today being challenged by asset- and competence-based strategies as represented by Prahalad and Hamel) since the diversification and portfolio models of Ansoff and of the Boston Consulting Group from the 1960s. Clearly, the value chain as a metaphor owes much to the traditional concept of industry, in which materials move through various stages in a process, 'value' being added to them at every stage. Indeed, it is the core model of the first strategic paradigm described in Chapter 1. Since physical materials can flow basically only in one direction, and since a piece of material can be only in one place at one and the same time, one has no difficulty in seeing the power and relevance of the chain metaphor. Yet, today's business game is a very different one and therefore some of the old models and metaphors lose their power in favour of new ones.

Dematerialized assets such as information and capital are almost completely liquid and can be at almost any place at any time, or can be in more or less all places at one and the same time. And the vastly increased reconfigurability of value creation means that traditional chain-like patterns can be dissolved and shattered by very unexpected players. For example, a truck maker found that 'their' value chain was reconfigured by a financial services player who reframed trucks into a part of transportation and logistics, and also therefore raised the relevant level of decision making from purchasing departments to top management groups among their customers. Conversely, many financial services companies today find that their business is being reconfigured by industrial companies who break up their value chains and reconfigure them with financial services, such as General Electric.

In fact, today's market game is much more about *who can most creatively design framebreaking systemic solutions* than about who can position himself in a 'chain'.

The value chain was a stronger metaphor in a production- and materials-based economy than in a knowledge- and service-based one. While brilliant in its time, it now fails to evoke the complexity and multidimensionality of reconfiguration opportunities – of the new business system design space. It represents a valid and strong analytical framework but it constrains the view.

RECONFIGURE OR BE RECONFIGURED

Some time ago I was asked, at a conference, what it would take to be a good airline in today's world. My answer was that one would need three things: a brand, an integrated customer offering design unit, and a reservation system (linking the customers, travel agencies, a database, and perhaps a plastic card system with each other). Apart from a slim management structure, everything else (and, for that matter, the reservation system) can be outsourced, i.e. owned by others but managed as an integrated system under a brand and according to a business concept. There are other ways to do it, but these would be the three minimum critical requirements.

The vacuum principle – i.e. that emerging opportunities will be utilized by somebody – results in a *reorganization of value creation*, as activities are reshuffled into new time slots, between places, and between economic actors, resulting in new configurations and actor constellations. The new technologies engender the opportunity to unfreeze old structures – well beyond the boundaries of the individual corporation – and to put new ones in place. Not that the new ones will be forever – they will be exposed to attacks. But in the transition between the old and the new paradigms there is nevertheless a shakeout, with some actors more powerful and swift than others to reconfigure into a basic new pattern.

We may call the emerging class of actors who take advantage of the new opportunities 'Prime Movers'. They obey the call of business today: *reconfigure or be reconfigured.*

They realize that the key to the leading positions in the new economy is in creatively using the dematerialized assets and flows (as opposed to focusing on the physical processes). They see the handling of these de-materialized flows as their core processes. They transform information into knowledge which allows them influence over physical processes and ex-tended actor systems. And, as a consequence, they look beyond the boundaries of the local, taking advantage of the global. They escape the boundaries of the legal entities they have been founded as, vastly extending the scope of assets, they view as part of their action space. The *conceptual* organization they try to *manage* is much larger than their legal bound-aries, and the *contextual domain* they try to *appreciate and influence* is larger still. Briefly, they function more freely than the others in horizontal logic (Figure 4.1).

The consequence of reconfiguration is that whole business systems – not just individual companies or products – are reorganized into new patterns; I will later refer to this as 'ecogenesis'. In many cases borderlines between what used to be thought of as 'industries' are erased, so that established industry definitions become superfluous. This puts great strain on industry associations, bureaux of statistics, and politicians, as well as on economists who may end up using irrelevant data based on old categories.

THE EXPLODED COMPANY

When I went to business school all the company cases we worked on seem – in retrospect – to have been from the same mould: materials flowed in, feeding various production lines populated by more or less dili-

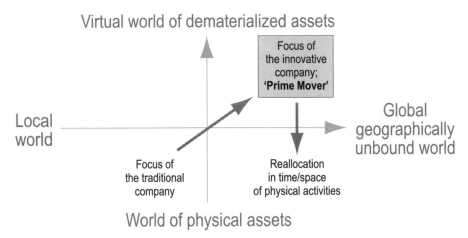

Figure 4.1 The path of Prime Movers.

gent and motivated workers supervised by managers mentally governed by either theory X or theory Y (roughly, assuming, respectively, that people must be completely governed and controlled, or that they are able to learn and participate and co-govern) (McGregor, 1960). Finished products were 'distributed' to customers. Everything was duly recorded by clerks using double-entry book-keeping (invented in Italy in 1492). If it was a progressive company they were probably already into using computers. Large-scale mechanical production machinery was implied, and one could certainly sense that smoke was coming out of the factory chimney although nobody worried about it – Rachel Carson's *Silent Spring* (1962/1993) had appeared only a few years earlier.

The company's core process was almost always implied to be a physical production flow, and then there was an auxiliary but necessary 'administrative system' to ensure appropriate control of this core process and its adaptation to the environment.

This dominating image of the business company has changed. Not only are the 'products' and therefore the 'production' processes different. The dominating part of the economy is now in so-called services as opposed to goods production. It has been said that the US GNP now weighs the same as 100 years ago but has twenty times the value in real terms. But it is in the way the corporation is configured that a more radical difference exists.

Outsourcing to specialists

In the book *The Machine That Changed The World* Womack *et al.* (1990) made the already classical comparison between Toyota and General Motors. For example, whereas General Motors produced about 70 per cent of the components that went into the car themselves and bought 30 per cent from the outside, Toyota had the opposite proportion. The image that finally comes across is that Toyota is seen much more as a management and design entity than General Motors, which focused on physical production as the key source of 'value added'.

Toyota, then, in this example had gone much further into 'unbundling' of different functional activities and their associated assets than General Motors. The general idea was that Toyota was so much more effective and efficient by considering the information- and knowledge-intensive activities as their core process, and that therefore they had structured their company accordingly. These core processes were used to 'manage' assets and economic actors which to a very great extent were located outside the formal and legal Toyota system.

In the public services sector much the same effects were striven for by 'privatization' and outsourcing contracts, although much of what was privatized or outsourced was specified and regulated in such detail that desirable reconfiguration was hindered rather than promoted.

Today there are rumours – no doubt to be considered seriously – that some car companies are thinking about outsourcing manufacturing completely. Pharmaceutical companies now increasingly 'outsource' much of their research and development, certainly a core function in that business. Why? Because scale and scope advantages in specialized areas of R&D take on dimensions which even the giants cannot match. And – perhaps even more important – because talent often tends to flow more easily to the independent units with more versatile tasks and networks and less perceived elephantiasis and bureaucracy. And, finally and perhaps heretically, because the critical knowledge for success in, say, pharmaceutical companies may in some cases be moving towards other realms such as the understanding and management of diseases and customers.

Long before the outsourcing trend, companies had discovered that manufacturing could often beneficially be relocated to places where production factors were more advantageous (which in that case usually could be interpreted as 'less expensive'). European textile industry relocated manufacturing to Portugal; Nike put much of its production in Asia. The outsourcing trend and the relocating trend together began to thoroughly reshape our perception of what a business company looks like.

According to – paradoxically – the same logic companies today also relocate certain functional activities to places where the key production factors are *more* expensive than elsewhere – simply because they are crucial and the best. What IT-related company in the world today can be without a unit in Silicon Valley? Silicon Valley is 'where it happens', so that is where one has to be to gain time, to get access to the latest ideas and trends, to be attractive to the best people.

Emancipating imprisoned assets

The general discovery and notion that assets could be asleep, imprisoned into paralysis within large structures, explained many of the business trends of the 1980s. Corporate raiders acquired companies and then chopped them up and sold the various pieces, placing each of them in contexts where their *positional* value would be higher than their *substance* value. Thus unbundled, the sum of the parts often proved to be much larger than the old whole, making raiders and investment bankers rich. The driving force was very much to identify economies of scope, not just of scale.

For example, the high level of technological excellence in technologies related to sports cars design and production developed by Porsche was very expensive and had to be paid for by a comparatively very small number of cars. However, it had potential uses for many other companies. By selling technological know-how to other companies – such as SEAT, Volvo, Lindhe – the limited economies of scale allowed by Porsche's own car production could be compensated for by economies of scope, finding other use applications for the assets.

A related principle was applied by managers such as Jack Welch of General Electric and Percy Barnevik of Asea Brown Boveri. Barnevik put two highly integrated, sleeping giants together and then chopped them up into about 5000 profit centres with – typically – 50 people and $10 million turnover in each. There was no longer any possibility for any person or asset to hide in the large structure. Each part had to prove itself in the marketplace, and to do so had to make itself useful in internal and external partnerships to achieve the necessary combination of competence and marketing clout. When each part was forced to prove itself and design its own partnership context the sum of the parts generally proved to be higher than the old bundled whole. Each asset had to search for all possible economies of scope as well as of scale.

Moving towards less commoditized areas of value creation

Other companies found that they could beneficially unbundle large parts of their structure since old synergies were gone and since they were no longer competitive in certain areas. For example, KF – the consumers' cooperative (one of Scandinavia's largest companies in the 1970s) – found that their integrated structure with production companies and retail business was no longer competitive. The in-house production companies could no longer compete with the best in cost efficiency, quality, or brand recognition. The retail part seriously lagged behind its competitors. In the end it was decided to disinvest the production companies and to bring the retail business up to a state-of-the-art level. KF focused on the area closest to the owners/members/customers.

Such trends cascaded a whole range of business truths such as 'back to the core business' (whatever 'core business' was in a new world), 'stick to your knitting' (as if it were self-evident what 'the knitting' was), 'organize around core competences' (creating the most curious and infinitely long lists and definitions of core competences in some companies).

The accumulation of trends

All these trends, which are all different manifestations of the same force field, have led to the emergence of the exploded, unbundled organization (Figure 4.2). And the resulting 'virtual' organization, in the eyes of traditional industrialists who see manufacturing as the key, and in the eyes of politicians who see corporations entering a 'horizontal' logic escaping the nation-state's vertical, territorial logic, sometimes has been described as hollow and as a symbol of nasty de-industrialization. At the time of writing, protests are going on against 'globalization', perceived as promoted by the World Trade Organization, putting power over jobs into

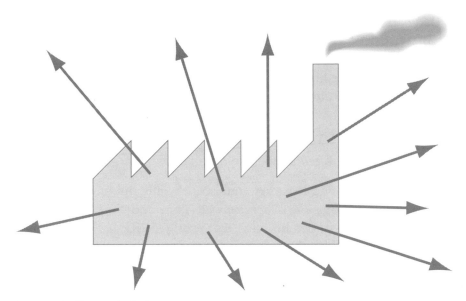

Figure 4.2: The exploded company.

the hands of large corporations whereas it used to be with trade unions and national policies.

Good or bad? Good for the corporations and the customers, if well done. Bad for nation-states and territorial organizations who do not know how to make themselves competitive. And for employment? Outsourcing and other forms of liberation of assets are certainly good, in that they create entrepreneurship and development of a rich fauna of specialized competences with their own dynamics. Relocation is bad for employment if the territorial units try to resist change rather than see it as an opportunity for flexible redeployment of resources into areas of higher productivity and knowledge-intensive value creation, thus following the path of higher productivity and greater wealth through 'creative destruction' that history has proven to be the valid one.

But the point is that the trend is inexorable, since it follows elementary economic laws of how to create more productivity and therefore value and wealth. The vacuum principle functions: it is now possible, and it is beneficial, so it will be done. Opportunity turns into imperative.

There are essentially three kinds of actors who trigger reconfiguration. They are, respectively, imperfection-based invaders, technology path-breakers, and reframers. While the borderlines between them are not necessarily distinct we will focus on the third category, after taking a brief look at the first two.

IMPERFECTION-BASED VERSUS COMPETENCE-BASED RECONFIGURERS

In business terms, deregulation tends to have the same effect as technological breakthroughs: it makes possible what was not before possible, thus creating a virgin space for the astute actors. Every discontinuity, whether resulting from technology or deregulation, creates new action strategies and new players.

In the wake of deregulatory measures in certain industries, such as airlines and financial services, I made a study of developments in the financial services industry in 1984-5.[7] During the previous years I and colleagues had developed a whole set of concepts related to customer-oriented strategies. When we set out for this study of financial services there was no doubt that we had expected to find 'winning strategies' characterized by customer orientation and the systematic building of competences to leverage the value of acquired customer bases. To our surprise we found that this was not nearly the whole truth and we publicly recognized that we had been wrong.

True, there were a number of major corporations which struggled to thoroughly transform themselves along the lines we had expected, such as – at the time – Citibank and Svenska Handelsbanken. But there were others, including some very new players, who were much more dramatically and instantly successful. Our archetypal example of this became the Norwegian Oslobanken, founded in 1984.

> Oslobanken established itself in a patrician villa in the outskirts of Oslo, where initially less than 50 people were employed. Their publicity was simple and effective and was based on describing their offering. They published a small 4-page folder the front cover of which compared the interest rate on deposits paid by the major Norwegian banks and by Oslobanken. The curves were telling: Oslobanken paid 2 percentage points more than the other banks (2 percentage points meaning a price premium in the order of 25%). Their message basically was: 'Deposit your money with us and we will give you 2 percentage points higher deposit interest. Borrow money

> from us and we will give you a competitive market rate. Communicate with us over telephone and by letter. Use checks and some other services from our bank, but remember that over a certain limit we will charge you a fee for doing so. And, by the way, we are not as greedy as other banks – we don't think you should necessarily gather all your business with us, so you can keep your old bank relationship. And what should you use that old bank relationship for? Well, to buy all the services that your old bank provides for free.'

Oslobanken became an instant, enormous success. We found a multitude of similar strategies. They could also be found in other industries under deregulation – an example in the airline industry was People Express.

Leaders of companies such as Oslobanken and People Express were hailed as heroes, as the new generation of businessmen. But neither of those companies now exists. Both started to make mistakes. Both over-expanded. Perhaps the outside world was instrumental in this by asking for too many interviews and giving them hubris. Anyway, they and many others disappeared from the map (though not without having left traces of their presence which still remain).

There may be, and certainly are, a number of different explanations for their disappearance, but one that is quite clear is that there was often a failure to understand the basis of success of these companies. Deregulation revealed accumulated market imperfections – high cost structures, gentlemen's clubs, high cross-subsidies between products, cross-subsidization between customer groups. Companies which had been opaque black boxes now became transparent, and new 'invaders' (Normann *et al.*, 1989) were able to unbundle products/services and give better deals to customer groups which had been mishandled or exploited outright.

As markets become transparent and 'unbundleable' there is always the opportunity for a gold rush. And it tends to be the quick and simple strategies which win. But such strategies are imperfection based, they are primarily neither competence based nor customer orientation based. As these successful players gain from the imperfections they contribute to eliminating them. And while, for a period of time, they eat deeply into the positions and profitability of the established players some of these will adapt, innovate, and reconquer positions.

If financial services and airlines were among the most talked-about industries in which these phenomena could be observed some years ago, this is now true of virtually every business. The old telecom incumbents are among the most visible victims. Information technology now also in fact serves as a 'deregulator', creating transparency and unbundleability. And established companies, fearing to be left behind and not always understanding very well what is going on, spend hugely on information technology, creating immensely profitable markets for suppliers of hardware, systems, and consultants in that field.

But much of this certainly is temporary. Many of the companies that now figure in interviews and whose instant success leaders are encouraged to express their wise principles fail to see the truth. They are successful because they were astute enough to seize the opportunity of the transparent imperfections, and they acted – often with admirable skill and power – to create riches for themselves and happy shareholders. But if we confuse the real reasons for success with the sophisticated leadership and management and business principles they are encouraged to advocate we are cheating ourselves.

In fact, for such imperfection- and correction-based quick success stories there are three options. One is to cash in and get out of the business while there is still time (as many of the 'dotcoms' failed to do). Another is to sell out to anxiety-ridden established players. The third is to consolidate their positions by realizing that the imperfections that made them successful will not persist and have to be replaced by systematic, long-term strategies building new capabilities and consolidating relationships including with customers. Some will succeed.

Much as I admire today's business entrepreneurs *per se* (especially before they have gurus write books about them – almost always a sure sign that things will deteriorate) we should at least be clear that the leadership qualities required for imperfection-based successes are much more akin to what we usually think of as an astute 'business nose' and streetsmartness than to leadership in the sense of navigating an organization through a structurally changing context. It is primarily the latter kind of leadership which is a subject of this book.

TECHNOLOGY PATH-BREAKERS AS RECONFIGURERS

A technological breakthrough in itself may be enough to trigger reconfiguration. The original Macintosh created reconfiguration of, among other areas, the graphical industry: with desktop publishing much of it moved to the individual user's desk. To follow up on the same line, when I recently talked to the CEO of a major data services and consulting company he said, without having been provoked:

> We are moving the printing press into our servers. And we have moved the delivery van into our networks.

Nobody can dispute the incredible reconfiguration power of a new technological infrastructure such as the Internet. It, and many of the technology 'products' associated with it, serve to reconfigure businesses even without any particular overall plan or intent to reframe according to a certain pattern. The reconfiguration becomes as inevitable once the technology system is there as was once the case with the invention of railways or the wireless or the combustion engine.

Frankly, with only a slight exaggeration I would say that many of the new technology companies hailed as the drivers of today's business revolution are among the least customer oriented-companies and have the lowest awareness of what they are doing at a conceptual level that I have ever met. But they happen to have the right product at the right time, which then opens up for other companies which do conscious reframing and reconfiguration, based on the opportunities created by the new technological products and infrastructures.

Many such 'option-opening product'-led companies realize that they cannot expect to continue for ever along this path. To invent a next groundbreaking, option-opening product is at best a highly risky venture which can hardly be programmed. It takes dramatically different skills and capabilities to be a reconfigurer by being a reframer once the power of a path-breaking, option-opening technological invention has evaporated. Intel, Xerox, Oracle, Sun Microsystems and Microsoft are examples of companies struggling with this transition as this is written, building the bridges between the technological path-breaker stage and the new era of Prime Mover reconfiguration by reframing and designing Value-creating Systems.

In these cases the power of a technological breakthrough must be replaced by the power to envision a new, reconfigured business system. This vision must then be embodied in new competences and organization and management systems. Many will succeed; many will also stumble as they try to cross that road. They are all attempting to be Prime Movers.

Prime Movers as Reconfigurers

5

I will reserve the term 'Prime Movers' for reconfigurers who do not just base themselves on a historical economic imperfection, and where the reconfiguration does not only come about as a result of technological breakthroughs. Such reconfigurations mainly thrive from the effects that a technological breakthrough or deregulation have on shattering old business systems. Prime Movers reintegrate and rebundle as well as disintegrate and unbundle, though the latter is generally a prerequisite for the former.

Prime Movers create cases of reconfiguration which seem to stem from a new design vision of an 'industry' or broader system of value creation. The design vision seldom is clear-cut from the start; rather, it has emergent characteristics. Prime Movers tend to envision a broader Value-creating System (as opposed to a technological innovation, a new product, or the simple exploitation of an economic imperfection) as the outcome of their strategy. The results tend to be boundary breaking, redefining the roles of different economic actors (as well as excluding some and bringing in new ones) and setting new rules of the game. Let us look at some examples.

IKEA

In Chapter 2 we introduced IKEA, the world's leading home furnishing company, as an illustration of the third strategic paradigm. Surely, there was no detailed blueprint of the IKEA system from the start. There was, however, a strong sense of mission, based on dissatisfaction with and discovery of inefficiencies among the actors of existing furniture supply system. Ingvar Kamprad, the founder, strongly felt that there must be much better ways to ensure that the ordinary, low- and medium-income household could have a better living environment at home.

The design of the business system, with sales by mail-order, was radical enough from the start, but nowhere near as elaborate in concept as it would gradually become. To a great extent, the 'final' design emerged from facing and handling adversity. For example, since the existing furniture supply system in Sweden effectively and successfully threatened any furniture manufacturers who produced for IKEA Mr Kamprad had to go to foreign manufacturers, thus discovering the benefits of subcontracting and of systematically allocating activities to low-cost production contexts. And, so the story goes, at the opening of the first warehouse outside Stockholm the line of impatient and expectant customers outside was so long that IKEA lost control and the customers stormed into the warehouse to pick up furniture themselves. This event was then creatively reinterpreted, and led to the systematic shifting of activities over to customers.

As we saw in the previous chapter, in their catalogue IKEA today introduces its business idea in terms of a specific division of work between the company and the customer.

Apple and Microsoft
The story (or stories) of Apple and Microsoft (who cooperated to create the Office package in the early days of the companies) is a telling tale about reconfiguration. One might argue that this story is all about high tech, but that would be to underestimate the actors. When the Apple Macintosh computer came out it was no more high tech than the IBM personal computer, rather the opposite. The difference was not in the technology but in the sense of mission and the vision that emerged.

The movie that advertised the original Macintosh painted a fabulous and intriguing vision of power shifting to the users. It was a tale of deepened democracy and escape from centralized, authoritarian control, about the individual and humanism conquering against an Orwellian world. It was not about the benefits of a new product but about a new mode of being, with new relationships between man and machine and between the individual and the system.

Apple then failed to capitalize on this tremendous initial success because the company did not fully realize the magnitude of the shift of business logic for itself that moving from the industrial (and customer base-oriented) paradigm to the value-creating paradigm implied. They tried too hard to contain the key to success, which was their operating system and their software including the customer interface, in their own grey boxes. They could not make up their mind about what paradigm they were in. Paradoxically, time would soon show that the leading company in the world of personal computers would be one which did not manufacture and sell computers at all, namely Microsoft.

The Microsoft story, in its turn, has of course not ended. Nor has the story of Apple. But what is absolutely certain is that Microsoft achieved a level of Prime Movership that few, if any, companies before in the world have stood for. They realized that they could use their software – their more or less dematerialized assets – to mobilize and manage hardware and physical manufacturing and product development. They created a new ecosystem for computing and communication.

Shahal

Shahal Medical Services Ltd is an Israel-based company (which has also created a unit for international expansion of its system). At the time of writing – early 2000 – it has 55 000 members in Israel, representing primarily cardiac, hypertensive and respiratory illnesses, but also elderly people and healthy people with a high level of health awareness.

The company uses online services and is based on telemedicine brought to the end-customer's home (or wherever the customer is, via mobile communication). Customers make measurements of body signals which are sent to monitoring centres open 24 hours a day. This is linked to immediate consultation and advice, based on symptoms, medical history, and real-time measurements.

The system is designed around proprietary software modules, a broad range of advanced end-user devices, and protocols for the set-up and management of homecare telemedicine systems.

The system creates new linkages between end-customers/patients, the monitoring centre, physicians, public authorities, and a mobile intensive care unit. The latter consists of a fleet of intensive-care ambulances, each unit staffed by a physician, paramedic, and driver-medic, as well as with extensive equipment for emergency treatment and medication.

Shahal's offerings consist of

- The Shahal Monitoring Center, communicating with the members
- A number of disease focused tele-medicine solutions
- Online services
- The mobile intensive-care unit.

The system, which is summarized in Figure 5.1, clearly reconfigures health care. For one thing, it is explicitly based on shifting more activities, knowledge, control, and power to the end-customer/patient by the use of enabling technology.

Ryder Systems

When I worked with a major international heavy truck producer some years ago we found that significant changes had come to the marketplace. The

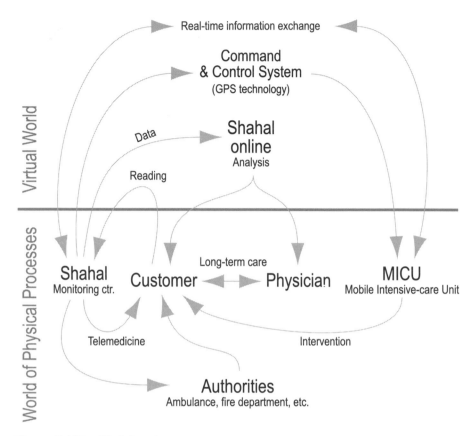

Figure 5.1 The Shalal system.

producer found that an increasing number of its trucks – and by then a very large proportion – was no longer sold directly to the traditional end-customers as represented by industrial firms with transportation needs, and truck transportation companies. Instead, these trucks were sold to companies packaging them together with other services and offering the end-customers – particularly industrial companies, retailers, etc. – overall logistics system solutions. Foremost of these new companies was Ryder Systems.

Coming from the leasing business, Ryder had gradually developed this business in a number of steps. It had offered to lease out trucks (and then whole fleets of trucks) to its customers. It had developed special knowledge in handling the rather special personnel category that truck drivers consists of. It had offered its customers to paint their trucks with the customers' colours and logos.

But gradually it had also developed complex and extensive logistics solutions to end-customers, going deeply into the operations and even manufacturing and supply chain strategies of these. For example, it had come to manage the integrated logistics of General Motors, the largest industrial company of the USA.

This reconfiguration had not been immediately apparent to the truck companies, since they continued to sell as many trucks as before – but now many of them to Ryder rather than directly to the end-customers. But they were worried about what would happen to their margins. And they discovered that the new 'invaders' had set up their own repair shops, that they encouraged non-proprietary spare parts, and that they shifted various services around the truck from the truck producers (and its dealers) to themselves. And, perhaps worst of all, while Ryder Systems was in continuous discussions with top managements of the client companies since they dealt with strategic issues of logistics strategy, the truck producers had traditionally sold to people lower down in the hierarchy within client companies. Ryder had managed to reframe the offering, outconfiguring the traditional players and attributing the role of subcontractors to them.

Åkerlund & Rausing/Tetrapak
When new packaging solutions were introduced by Åkerlund & Rausing – already referred to in Chapter 1 – the consequences were not just a change of package for food products. It enabled a redesign of factories and processes in food-producing companies, made possible new integrated distribution systems, and led to a redesign of the retail shops.

In my book *Service Management* I analysed other interesting reconfigurers (although I did not call them so at the time). Cases such as EF Education and JC Decaux (described later in this book) demonstrate that vision rather than new or high technology may be at the source of radical reconfiguration. These companies reconfigured old resources and tasks into a new framework.

RULE BREAKERS WITH A VISION

Prime Movers of the reframing kind tend to fall squarely into the third strategic paradigm. One characteristic is that they move away from focusing on the competences required to manufacture and sell a product to a focus on the much broader set of competences related to the *design and functioning of a Value-creating System.* This may seem like a strange statement in an era when we continuously hear the war cries of 'focus on core competences' and 'back to basics'. Nevertheless, empirical observations strongly support the statement.

It seems that the dilemma can be thus resolved. The Prime Movers listen to the war cries and live up to them in the sense that they have only a limited number of competences and activities inside themselves. Instead, they develop another specific competence, namely the competence to mobilize and manage external actors and their competences which are outside the Prime Mover company.

IKEA has mobilized the assets and competences of manufacturers globally, designers, and – in particular, and in an unusually systematic way – the customers. Microsoft integrates actors such as computer manufacturers, software writers, and chip makers. Healtheon/Web MD in healthcare, EF Education in the language education area and JC Decaux in municipal information services all link sets of previously unconnected players to form a completely new pattern, enabling new value creation. While retaining and nurturing their own specific generic competences which they add to the totality of the Value-creating System, each of these Prime Movers adds a unique competence to the whole: *a vision-based network pattern*, and the ability to actually *bring players with disparate assets and competences together* into forming a new, functioning Value-creating System.

The end result is that Prime Movers move from focusing on a traditional and narrow (often production- and commodity-based) set of competences to a much broader and partly new set of competences and assets, which they are able to mobilize and coordinate (but not necessarily or even generally own) so that the result becomes a shift of focus from a product or service to a Value-creating System. The *design vision* which this requires often originates in a strong sense of mission based on dissatisfaction and inefficiencies in the existing system. An example of a strong such mission-based vision founded in ideas about moral justice and equality was the creation of KF, the Swedish consumer cooperative, in 1899.

The result of these efforts is a system which does not obey the existing rules of the game but breaks the old patterns and creates new rules. When the established furniture industry began to see the danger of IKEA

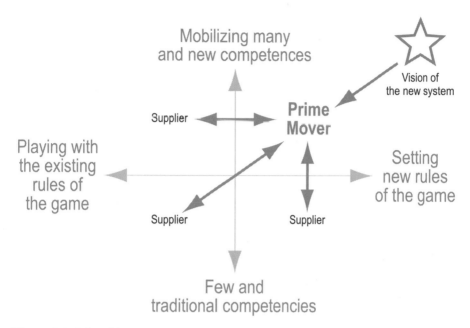

Figure 5.2 Prime Mover – How do we recognize one?

they used advertising to remind the public that 'IKEA is not a real furniture company' (I imagine that Mr Kamprad must have been the first to agree, probably with a satisfied smile).

Is IKEA a furnishing company, a retail company, a mail order company? Is it in manufacturing or services? Is JC Decaux in advertising, city transportation, traffic control, or what? Is Ryder in trucking, in transportation, in logistics, in asset management? Is EF in education, the travel business, the entertainment business, the experience business? And is Microsoft in the computer business – and redefining it by not being into computers!

Prime Movers, by reconfiguring, draw new boundaries thereby erasing old system definitions. Thus, we find that Prime Movers can be defined as depicted in Figure 5.2, moving from narrow and traditional competences to mobilizing broader (and developing new) competences, and from accepting the existing business definitions and rules of the game to imposing new rules of the game that transcend traditional industry boundaries and business system definitions.

THE RECONFIGURED

What happens to those who don't reconfigure? Typically they have to adapt to the new rules of the game. Truck makers found their bargaining position and profit margins seriously squeezed as Ryder pushed them into the corner as sub-contractors, taking over much of the customer relationship. PC makers find themselves in a commodity market unless they, in their turn, find ways to redefine their business and become Prime Movers (at the expense of other players).

In other words, the reconfiguration game caused by the new opportunities for value creation will, according to the vacuum principle, tend to divide economic actors into those who reconfigure and those who are reconfigured. The former are Prime Movers, the latter tend to become sub-contractors and work in commodity markets with tough margins.

But will this mean that we will end up with one or a handful of Prime Movers who dictate everything in a global business system? This is a scenario, and one that is much feared by many (cf. Nordfors and Levin, 1998). But it is not the only scenario, and it is not one very likely to happen.

There are two reasons for this. The first is that while success may breed success, and Prime Movership may reinforce itself, the new opportunities for value creation also favour small players and invaders. The dominant players, the Prime Movers, can never feel safe; they will be sure to be attacked from all angles, and their mistakes will be exploited not only by a few main competitors but by thousands of little players. The likelihood of a static equilibrium is small. As is often the case, this may not result in the death and disappearance of the big players, but it may result either in their loss of dominance (and perhaps, later on, ultimate destruction and disintegration) or in their continued reconfiguration, competence building, and maintained Prime Movership. Moreover, as Christensen (1997) has demonstrated so well, established players have difficulties handling innovators with 'disruptive technologies'.

The other reason is that the world is full of opportunities to reconfigure and reframe one's business. The game is not lost for Compaq or Dell or Apple because Microsoft has become such a formidable Prime Mover. AOL, Linux, IBM, Oracle, Nokia, Sun Microsystems and many others (the list will have changed and expanded as this is printed, and again as the reader reads it) are nibbling on Microsoft's position. Truck makers like Volvo and Mercedes-Benz can develop strategies of their own, different from that of Ryder, to counter Ryder's Prime Movership position. Others may find ways to directly challenge the rules of the game imposed by Microsoft and Ryder, or they may creatively define other areas of activity in which they accept the Prime Movership of the others, but achieve their own Prime Movership and impose their rules of the game in a business area co-existing with, and even thriving on, the systems developed by Microsoft and Ryder.

PRIME MOVERSHIP AS A MIND-SET OF VALUE CREATION

Prime Movership is much more than skin deep. The more I have worked with these matters, the more I have come to think about Prime Movership not only as a set of objective, observable behaviours, but also *as a mode of being, a mind-set*. Whether and how this mode of being can be preconditioned is the topic of later parts of this book.

However, some observable types of behaviour and action seem to characterize Prime Movers.

Identification with Value-creating Systems: upframing

Companies with a strong identification with their product (or production process) rarely become reframing Prime Movers although it is not uncommon for them to think of themselves as such. Those who do typically have a mental orientation more related to a broader notion of value creation. They look at the overall functioning and the larger, overall system in which they themselves are a part. We will refer to this as *upframing*.

This is the case even if the physical output of the company might seem to be a narrow product. For example, Intel – a chip maker – spends a great deal of effort to understand the context in which their chips function. Seeing the personal computer, in which the chip is a key component, as the possible and desirable core tool for the value creation of users, Intel is highly concerned with strengthening and promoting the role and usage scope of the PC. This is manifested in, for example, Intel's involvement in strategic joint ventures and alliances with some of the world's leading companies in areas such as entertainment, digital photography, etc., as well as in venture capital business related to the promotion of software which can enhance the competitiveness of the personal computer. Thus, while the dominating *realm of operations* may seem quite narrow and related to chips, the *intellectual realm* in which Intel is active is much broader and involves forward-looking interaction with a wide range of leading actors who together promote the general context of value creation in which chips form a part. Recently, as a result of this distinction between the operational and intellectual realms, the former has moved into new directions such as setting up service centres for medium- and smaller-sized businesses wanting to go into e-commerce. Whether this and other actions will take Intel far enough into reconfiguration of what risks becoming a commodity business the future will tell.

A company that wants to expand its notion of the Value-creating System in which it works may start by systematically looking at the *life cycles of the products* and the *total value-creation contexts of the customers* with which it works. The car industry, which doubtless now stands before an accelerating rate of change in the concept of what it stands for, is a case in point. For one thing, it increasingly has become forced to look at the car from design to recycling of the materials, incorporating the technological and financial aspects of recycling already in the design of the car. Second, it creates structures and procedures to ensure the effective deployment and marketing of used cars (Volvo was an innovator here in the late 1970s). Third, it looks at the life cycle and the corresponding needs of the customer by providing a set of cars each suitable for different stages of the customer's evolution. Fourth, the car industry – although one might think it is amazingly late! – now begins to look more at the totality of the customer's transportation situation. An example is the launch of the Mercedes-Benz' Smart car, which is a two-seater for use primarily in cities, and where the customer offering is complemented by a special offer (together with partners such as a car rental company) to Smart car buyers enabling them to rent cars at extremely favourable rates for occasions when the needs of the customer extend beyond what the Smart car can provide – such as weekend trips, vacation trips, etc.[8] Note that this is a different concept from the extended offering around the car itself – financing, discounts on petrol, various packages for service and repair, leasing – that many car companies have already offered. The new idea allegedly is a *customer*-related *mobility offering*, not a car-related extension of the offering.

Then, again, perhaps some car or other company may come up with a different reframing and reconfiguration strategy, proving that 'mobility' wasn't such a powerful concept after all!

Into the customer's business

A particularly fruitful way of reframing, in our experience, is to focus on the customer of the company as the major stakeholder, and to mentally frame oneself as *part of the customer's business.* Many pay lip service to this idea; a few take it to their hearts. A major conceptual implication of doing so is to move away from the traditional industrial view of the customer offering as an *output* of one's production system to a view in which the customer offering is seen as an *input* in the customer's value creating process. This requires the company to understand the customer's business and value-creating process and use that as the basic framework within which one defines one's business.

Understanding the customer's business implies that one must look at the customer's major stakes – and they generally are in the customer's relationship to his or her customers. Therefore, true customer orientation means that one has to go beyond the direct relationship between oneself and one's customers to understand the relationship between the customers and the customers' customers – from the 'first' to the 'second level customer relationship' (Figure 5.3).[9] The primary, long-term measure of

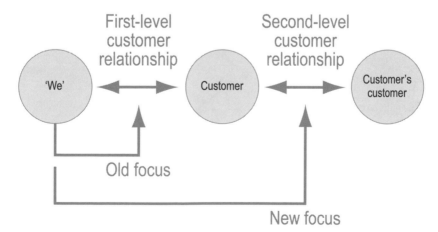

Figure 5.3 From first- to second-level customer relationship.

success is not how much we get out of each customer, but *how our customer fares in relation to his or her market* – his customers – in terms of competitiveness (market share, profitability, customers' customers' loyalty, and so forth). One's own efforts should then be evaluated based on how they contribute to the customer's positioning in these respects.

The 'value star'

A second implication of looking at our customer offering as an input into the customer's value creation rather than as an output of our own system is that we must look at other inputs on the customer side. In fact, we find that any company should consider more or less the totality of inputs of the customer's into their value creating processes, as depicted in Figure 5.4. Because of the graphical configuration we may characterize this set of inputs as the customer's 'value star'.[10]

The Ryder case was a good example of how important it is to look beyond one's own input to the customer's value-creation process. The truck makers tended to see only a 'value chain' consisting of the truck and truck support-related items and services. Ryder, who talked to customers about finances and about their totality of business issues, came to perceive how the truck was positioned as but one possible element in the total context of the customers' logistics.

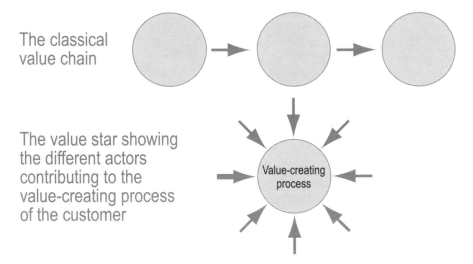

The classical value chain

The value star showing the different actors contributing to the value-creating process of the customer

Value-creating process

Figure 5.4 From value chain to value star.

The customer's efficiency versus his effectiveness

Seeing the offering to the customer as an input in the customer's value-creating process it is often useful to distinguish between two types of effect. The first is related to the customer's *internal efficiency*, mainly as manifested in the customer's cost structure. If the cost of various inputs to the customer's process can be made lower, or if we can create inputs which make the customer's internal processes more efficient, the customer will have the benefit of a cost advantage as a result of our intervention.

However, there is also the possibility that the input we provide to the customer has a direct effect on the customer's *own* customer offering, i.e. the offering to our customer's customers. In this case our intervention will be directly visible (although not necessarily possible to directly attribute to our intervention) to the customer's customer. Our customer's ability to develop his market position as a result of offering innovation will be enhanced. We may say that his *external effectiveness* has been enhanced.

To illustrate the difference, many of the resource-optimization systems now offered by software companies serve mainly to increase the cost efficiency by better co-aligning various resources within and outside the customer system (for example, in the supply chain). On the other hand, many relationship databases (data warehousing and data mining systems), call centre solutions, Internet-related solutions, etc. will have a direct impact on how, say, a bank or a retail company will be seen by its customers and what it can offer them. Thus, they may assist the customer in. reframing and reconfiguring *his* business. These two dimensions are illustrated in Figure 5.5, with examples from graphics industry.

Relieving and enabling

The two dimensions have a certain kinship with the concepts of 're-lieving' versus 'enabling'. Very often a 'supplier' can *'relieve'* its customers from doing certain things, since the supplier can do them better, perhaps because of more experience or scale advantages. Thus, certain value-creating activities are *reconfigured from the customer system to the supplier system*. On the other hand, the 'supplier' may provide offerings which

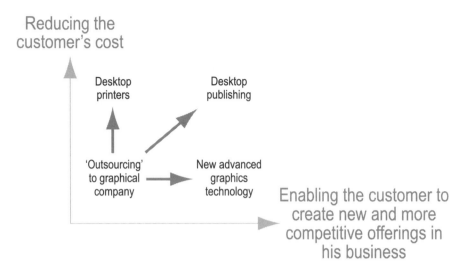

Figure 5.5 Two dimensions of customer value.

'enable' the customer to do things that the customer was not able to do before. In this case activities that could be performed by the supplier or other actors – or by nobody! – can be seen as *reconfigured to the customer*. It is often the case that the supplier provides offerings which, together with competences and tools that already existed in the customer system, enable the latter to do things which neither the supplier nor the customer were able to do before on their own.

Winning the access channel battle

Since, according to the second strategic paradigm of Chapter 1, the customer relationship is (and continues to be) a strategic asset we can expect companies to go to great efforts to hang onto and cement their customer relationships while we can expect their competitors to do their best to cut off and take over those relationships. The 'access channel battle' is raging. The proliferation of new access channels such as media and the Internet, the raised knowledge and activity levels of customers who, themselves, actively search for the best partners, the tendency towards decreased loyalty of customers – these factors and others all contribute.

The customer may view the relationship with a particular company (because we are in the co-productive age I hesitate to say 'supplier'!) as a matter of pure efficiency and more or less operational routine, or it may be strategic, having a bearing on the customer's opportunities to do business on his own. In the previous section we mentioned how Ryder managed to bring up the issue of truck purchasing from that of an operational purchasing decision to a strategic configuration decision. While truck companies try to sell an efficient truck surrounded by good maintenance services, Ryder offered a new logistics and even manufacturing strategy configuration. The decision was lifted from the table of the factory manager or purchasing manager to that of the company management board. Similarly, companies offering commoditized services such as cleaning and maintenance now meet stronger competition from companies offering 'facility management'. 'Systems integrators' threaten even the most technologically advanced component manufacturers in the information technology business.

In the early Internet days most companies saw their website as a marginal addition to their advertising budget. Later on it became part of the marketing strategy and consequently came under the responsibility of the marketing manager. Today it is distinctly on the desk of the CEO in the 'transformation to an e-business' file.

The relationship between company and customer, and therefore the access strategy, typically also has both a *physical*, an *intellectual/rational*, and an *emotional* aspect.

Silvio Berlusconi, the Italian media tycoon, set up a television network which was exceedingly successful as an alternative to the Italian state television. Another way for his group Fininvest to reach the customers was via the acquisition of Standa, one of the major retail chains (although this mode of physically reaching the customers proved to be less important in the total strategy). He then gained access to the emotions of all Italians by acquiring Milan AC and building it into the world's most successful soccer team over a period of years. With such a combination of access strategies it was perhaps not a surprise that Mr Berlusconi became prime minister of Italy just a few months after announcing that he was going into politics. (The example is used to illustrate the importance of the access channel battle, but not to comment on what you actually do when you have acquired the access.)

The turnaround of IBM under Louis Gerstner is an example of skilful access-based strategy. As is well known, IBM had seriously lagged behind as a number of 'invaders' reconfigured the 'industry'. Probably the most common advice to Gerstner as he became the new CEO was to copy the competitors: cut up IBM (ABB-wise) into small units, let each of them battle it out, bet on the emergence of a new entrepreneurial spirit, flexibility, and rapidity. But Gerstner recognized that this would be a copying strategy in which IBM would have no particular competitive advantage against the invaders who had invented that game, and also that it would not capitalize on the two major assets of IBM: the enormous breadth of competences, and the incredible worldwide customer base and long-standing technological interdependences between customers and IBM as well as the personal relationships between IBM people and customers. So, instead, IBM rebuilt itself from those strengths, leveraging on its customer access but reframing the customer relationship from 'technology push' to more of solutions provision and service, where IBM could use its breadth of competences.

This framework for thinking about customer access can be summarized in Figure 5.6.

A note on branding as access strategy

The World Cup soccer final between France and Brazil on 12 July 1998, was reportedly watched by 1.7 billion people via television. Disney World's *The Lion King*, a very successful movie, was first shown in over 50 countries. Nearly 200 items of merchandise related to the movie were

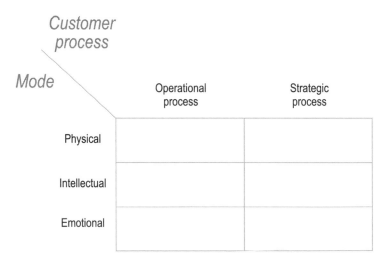

Figure 5.6 Modes of access and levels of access.

licensed and sold, to capitalize on the Lion King image. A year after the movie a Broadway version was shown; the only way to get out from that show was through a shop in which Lion King-related merchandise was sold.

On the day when this chapter was drafted it was announced that the Swedish chewing gum, Toy, is going to be discontinued. Toy as a concept has been an integrated part of the lives of at least a couple of generations of Swedes, based on the image of victorious, gum-chewing post-war Americans and an incredibly successful advertising campaign featuring Alice Babs, a beloved singer. But the volume of Toy chewed by Swedes had gone down to 20 per cent of what it used to be a generation ago, and it can no longer compete with the big international brands. Building and maintaining a brand is so expensive that the cost must be balanced by very considerable scale and scope economies.

As I bought ice-cream in the two local shops on my summer island in the Finnish archipelago I found that the products available in the summer of 1998 were quite different from what had been offered in previous years. There were still a few local brands, but now I could buy Carte d'Or and other brands which I can also buy at home in La Celle St Cloud outside Paris. The visual image was the same, with a small addition of the trademark of GB, a well-known and trusted Swedish ice-cream brand (but one year later this trademark was gone as well). A close study of the package informed me that Carte d'Or is a brand of Van den Bergh, an Italian Unilever company, and that the ice-cream had been manufactured in Denmark. Thus: a typical example of globalization, with different geographical sources for various functions such as manufacturing and concept, but everything held together by one brand.

These are simple, everyday examples of the importance of branding as an access and customer relationship strategy, resulting from the enormous effects of economies of scale and scope related to the dematerialization of information. They illustrate how the dematerialized processes have become the primary processes which now control and shape the physical world, rather than the other way around.

A brand must have a basic content, but this basic content can then gradually manifest itself in different shapes – different products, different events, etc. The brand and its power will suffer if the manifestations are incongruent between themselves and if they do not all live up to certain quality criteria. Companies with incredibly strong brands, such as Gucci and Ferrari, have had painful experiences of overstretching and using their brands for products which did not fulfil basic quality criteria, with serious setbacks as a result; at the time of writing both have successfully corrected their strategy. The brand can be communicated in multiple ways – newspapers, television, movies, Internet, sports events, video, shops, theme parks, ...

A brand strategy therefore means that the fundamental content and concept is extracted and abstracted from basic assets, so that it can be linked – in its dematerialized form – to customers. The result is that one can capitalize on the basic concept by reaching *many customers* on *many occasions* in *many customer value-creating processes* with *many price carriers* (see Chapter 8). If this dematerialized message can be transformed into multiple, price-carrying, materialized manifestations, enormous scope and scale advantages have been reached.

In the new value-creation logic as depicted in Chapter 2 branding in this respect is an inescapable element of any access channel strategy and any offering. It is also noticeable that branding is no longer just a matter of consumer business, but also of business to business.

SUMMARY: PRIME MOVERS AS REFRAMERS

As happened in the Industrial Revolution, the opportunities offered by new technology, globalization, and deregulation create the space for the emergence of new, dominating players. The 'vacuum principle', which works in business as well as in nature, ensures that the opportunities for reconfiguration will be used. I have called the actors who take these opportunities 'Prime Movers'.

This concept, which I and colleagues have used since the second half of the 1980s, can be related to many other concepts in business literature today. New organization types have been described as, for example, 'virtual' or 'imaginary'. Such concepts recognize that they may be geographically spread and perhaps that they may focus on conceptual functions such as design.

To me, Prime Movers are much more than players who are 'virtual' and who 'outsource' activities. They are – or at some stage become – driven by visions of a redefined, more effective larger system. They strive to reorganize activities and other institutions so that this larger system can come into being. Their critical competence is in the combination of envisioning this more effective larger system and in organizing other players to co-produce so as to jointly enact the more efficient larger system. This ability may, from the outset, be based primarily on technological innovations, or it may arise from intellectual and conceptual innovations which then enable themselves and others to co-align and focus their activities.

Prime Movership that redefines a Value-creating System is a way to escape the trap of commoditized products and services in transparent markets. This focus on the larger system means that the outcome of the efforts of Prime Movers tends to be 'ecogenesis' rather than just a new product or service. The notion of ecogenesis will be discussed later.

'Prime' does not necessarily mean 'first'. It is, of course, true that in many instances the first mover also will become the Prime Mover, if the first mover is able to play on the positive feedback and network effects often claimed to constitute the cornerstone of the new economy. But first movers do not always become those who set the scene for the slightly longer term, and therefore I prefer the more general concept of 'Prime'.

I am often asked whether this notion of Prime Movers means that we will see power move to only a few dominating actors in the world economy. While it undoubtedly seems that there are currently tendencies towards concentration towards many 'global' players I would not jump to such a conclusion.

First, many of these global players that we see today emerge from defensive moves, rather than creative or aggressive strategies. The established gather their forces against the reconfigurers. They become larger, but they do not necessarily reconfigure. Such tendencies can now, around the turn of the century, be seen in areas such as financial services, media, pharmaceutical industry, and others.

Second, new technology makes it ever more possible for small players to intrude and nibble at even the most innovative Prime Movers. Nobody is secure.

Third, and changing the argument to a slightly different realm, I would strongly advocate the view that Prime Movership is more a state of mind than something that can readily be observed from the outside. I would argue that *every economic player* can, and probably should, strive for

Prime Movership *relative to the existing position of that player*. Every actor must take care to understand the larger context of actors and value creation of its business. Every actor must try to envision the future of that larger system. If one's current *operational* position can be clearly defined, one's *intellectual* position must be much wider and must imply the continuous questioning of the operational position against the background of greater forces impinging on the larger context.

One does not have to be a Microsoft, a Nokia, or an Oracle to be a Prime Mover. The effort to be a Prime Mover can start from any position of any modest actor, and may end up in something that may not at all look dramatic to the outside observer, even though there may have been no lack of drama to the actor or actors involved. Prime Movership, above all, is an intellectual stand, a mind-set.

How processes and capabilities that develop such a mind-set can be set up is the topic of much of what remains of this book.

Prime Movership as Ecogenesis   6

BEYOND CONTINUOUS IMPROVEMENT AND ADAPTATION

We generally hear that organizations must adapt to changing conditions. They must obey to the forces of stakeholders. They must cater to changing needs of their customers.

Yet, in reality the picture is less clear-cut. The process of adaptation does not always follow a one-way road. In his book *Organization Theory For Long-range Planning* Eric Rhenman (1973) distinguished between four types of organizations, depending on – first – whether they possess a 'strategic management' (which can create freedom of action for them and – second – whether they have 'external goals' (ambitions about the state of the environment) or only 'internal goals' (goals related to their own performance). In his classification, 'appendix organizations' try to fulfil the desires of their masters; 'marginal organizations' have no other option but to adapt and be flexible; 'institutions' measure their success in terms of how much they are able to influence the external environment; and 'corporations' try to optimize their own performance but generally do so thanks to their power to 'dominate' and 'homogenize' at least certain territories of the external environment.

Thus the large and really successful organizations – 'corporations' and 'institutions' in Rhenman's terminology – rarely seem only to adapt passively and reactively. Nor can they, at one stroke, design the outside world and impose their definition of it. In the battle for Prime Movership, captured by the 'reconfigure or be reconfigured' expression, they try to reconfigure. Obviously, reconfiguration implies more than a passive adaptation on behalf of the focal organization. It also implies something less than total dominance. The process is one in which a business system is co-created which changes the context of several organizations but where still somebody usually is the focal actor and Prime Mover.

Change can be described along many dimensions. It can take place through *continuous improvement*, or through more radical *rethinking and renewal* of the business model. Some – in all likelihood most – change processes are essentially *reactive–adaptive outside-in processes* (accepting that the environment has changed and that we have to change to reflect the new environment), but a few are *proactive inside-out* (so that the focal organization creatively imposes itself and structures the external environment in line with some overall contextual driving forces). The dimensions are illustrated in Figure 6.1.

The battle for Prime Movership now taking place – in the wake or rather in the midst of technological revolutions – forces us to look at the upper-right-hand corner of Figure 6.1. It is not only products and services ('offerings') that are renewed today. What we see is the reshaping of whole *business systems* in which successful Prime Movers organize actors in the environment far outside their own legal domain. Continuous improvement often becomes a trap from the inside of which companies fail to see that the rules of the game are changing faster than the company, or that the game has changed altogether. On the other hand, the idea that an almighty designer (read CEO or corporate board of directors) can act

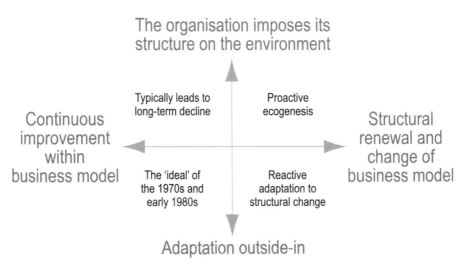

Figure 6.1 Four strategies to achieve fit with the environment.

like the classical Newtonian clock-maker and design everything as if it were a machine that can be conceived in one place, once and for all is false.[11]

Since we are talking about *changing a whole business landscape* and re-defining the rules of the game (and all this generally in collaboration although often with a 'Prime Mover' player in a leading role) I will refer to this process of establishing Prime Movership as that of accomplishing *ecogenesis* (perhaps best translated as 'birth of a context for co-dwelling').

PHYSICAL ECOGENESIS INFRASTRUCTURES

In this sense Prime Movership can often be metaphorically described as the process of establishing an *'infrastructure'* for a larger system (Normann and Ramirez, 1994/1998), which then will influence the strategies and actions and interactions of other actors in that system.

Such design and provision of infrastructures has often been the task of the state or public organizations. Two comparatively recent examples from France are the TGV (Train à Grande Vitesse, high-speed train) system and the Minitel system. Minitel is a non-interactive videotext system which gained a very high penetration of households since the terminal was given away for free, and since tens of thousands of services became available, further enhancing the initial usability. Minitel is to the Internet what the steam engine was to rocket science, but since people came to get attached to it, Internet penetration had a slow start in France. Both systems were infrastructures which, once in place, created new sets of linkages and new behaviour patterns for many, many actors. Governments have also been highly involved in setting standards and creating regulations in media such as broadcasting and television. But many media battles have been fought out in the private domain. The video standard battle between Betamax and VHS was won by the fastest mover – the VHS adherents managed to create large volumes of software and hardware quickly, so that when the allegedly technologically superior Betamax system was ready enough actors had already made their investment.

Many ecogenetic strategies are, of course, technology based. Even so, it takes great skill to bring a sufficient number of actors into agreement so that they line up with a particular system, perhaps modifying it in the process. Sony and Philips succeeded with this at the introduction of the

Compact Disc (but at the time of writing may yet fail with the next generation launched at the turn of the century, since their new SACD standard has a competitor in the DVD disc). Apple Computers had the most brilliant and obvious candidate for a new industry infrastructure – and therefore for a tremendous Prime Mover strategy based on ecogenesis – in their customer interface and operating system, but failed to see the need to bring in other computer makers to make sure the system was installed in a sufficient number of places. By insisting on selling the system in their own boxes they slowed penetration, encouraged the competition and lost momentum, and were finally overtaken by Microsoft – which used a totally different strategy and therefore became the new standard in spite of (in my humble opinion and that of many others) inferior technology and user-oriented vision.

The power of this kind of ecogenesis which builds on creating a new 'infrastructure' standard can be inferred from the stability that often results after the standard or system has become established, even if better alternatives might exist or appear. We live with VHS and not Betamax and with Microsoft instead of Apple; we have had to live with Compact Disc even though it (and the associated replay equipment) produced vastly inferior sound to a well-designed and well-maintained vinyl system during the first ten to fifteen years of its life-cycle (at least to the ears of this writer who is a music and hi-fi addict); we live with the QWERTY layout of our typewriter and computer keyboards even though the system was once consciously developed to be slower than necessary in the age of mechanical typewriters so as not to clog the mechanism; the existence of the Minitel system has made the normally technologically advanced French nation a late starter in Internet use.

CONCEPT- AND SYMBOL-BASED ECOGENESIS

Ecogenetic strategies do not, however, have to be technology based. Sometimes they start out more or less as *concept based* though the concept will usually have to be backed up with technology.

For example, Tetra Pak – a company born in the university city of Lund in southern Sweden which has made its owner family one of the very richest in the world – is generally associated with a milk package. But the idea was much broader than that. From the beginning there was in fact the vision of a wholly reconfigured system of milk distribution, from processes in the dairies to transportation to rationalization of grocery stores and of the handling of milk in the consumers' homes. Åkerlund & Rausing, the company in which Tetra Pak was born, had already pioneered looking at packaging not as a way to sell packages but as a means to rationalize production in bakeries, textile factories, etc., thus reconfiguring the whole classical 'value chain' from production to the end customer (Andersson and Larsson, 1998, p. 74).

The change process in Xerox Corporation, from being 'the copying machine company' to becoming the 'document company', is similarly concept based. Both Tetra Pak and Xerox established visions of a more effective larger system, spanning resources and processes much broader than their own realm of activities. Based on such an analysis they then evolved visionary concepts as well as – gradually but perhaps not quickly enough – the supporting hard technology and services to embody these concepts. The insight that the technology had to be developed, and that some of it was probably already there, existed from the start, but the momentum of the processes in both cases came from this *vision of the concept*. And the vision was based on understanding a larger, external context.

In Appendix 1 we find examples of ecogenetic strategies which were at the outset based more on concepts than on hard realities. The Olympic Games 1992 induced actors in Barcelona to begin to envision the city as a Prime Mover in a much larger region (which has come to encompass not only Barcelona but also Catalonia and cities in southern France). The Olympic Games became the catalyst for articulating – 'externalizing', to use the terms of Berger and Luckmann – this concept, gradually giving it more content. The Games became an artefact 'transitional object'. As the vision of an identity for Barcelona emerged – a role in transforming and enhancing the region, in improving the transportation system of Europe, etc. – the physical manifestations of this identity were also invented and put in place: transportation infrastructures, urban planning projects, developments in industrial location schemes and in education systems, and so forth.

Also, in the case of Öresund, the Copenhagen–Malmö area in Denmark and southern Sweden, the process now goes on. The physical phenomenon of the bridge has revitalized an old but thoroughly sleepy *idea* to regard the area as a genuine region – an actor with a strategy, a mission, and the means to fulfil it. The bridge across the strait of Öresund (a *physical* artefact which became a *symbolic* and catalysing artefact long before its opening in the year 2000) gave new life to the *concept of the region* – another mental or symbolic artefact. This mental concept now stimulates interaction and imagination; the resulting structural patterns and interactions lead to concrete initiatives and physical changes, and the process may now have the dynamic momentum that is necessary so that the concept becomes self-realizing. But the physical bridge is not enough.

CHARACTERISTICS OF ECOGENETIC STRATEGIES

We can tentatively begin to identify successful ecogenesis strategies in terms of some of their characteristics.

- Ecogenesis tends to come about as a dialectic interaction between 'hard' technology/infrastructure and 'soft' concepts. It may start with either one or the other, but the ecogenetic process is likely to lose momentum unless concepts can trigger actions leading to physical manifestations, and unless technology and infrastructures can trigger concepts – and so on in a growing spiral.
- Ecogenesis strategies are often linked to the now famous 'increasing returns' economy (Kelly, 1997). 'Infrastructure' concepts and 'network' concepts typically yield such increasing returns, at least up to a point. Mathematical models demonstrate how the opportunity to create linkages between elements in a system can lead to a complete change of the nature of the system. The strategy of achieving ecogenesis therefore often has a couple of *phases*, as described by complexity theory: a first stage in which the seeds are sown and planted, and a second stage when they are linked to each other so that a movement and a snowball effect can be expected.
- The focal actor – the Prime Mover – tends to be successful if it can identify and mobilize sleeping resources that can take on more value based on a concept and a systemic view (i.e. positional value) and if linkages can be created by new infrastructures or by other means of 'market making' of non-monetary currencies. These ideas will be developed later in this book.

- Except on rare occasions based on negotiated monopoly or really unique technology Prime Movers do not become such by being arrogant. To become a Prime Mover and to achieve ecogenesis requires the exercise of power, but successful Prime Movers tend to think of power as 'power with' or possibly 'power to' rather than as 'power over'. They design plus sum games and make sure that everyone or enough players win; another theme which will be developed further.

- Prime Movership and ecogenesis involve the creation of a social reality, 'bringing forth *a* world', to use Maturana-Varela language. As Callon and Latour (1981) have shown, actors may 'macro structure' reality in such ways that it comes to be taken for granted by a sufficiently large number of actors. This can be done both by developing technological relationships (between things) and social relationships (between people). The authors use the metaphor of 'black boxes', which can be used by (in our language) the focal actor or Prime Mover (or ecogenesis wannabe) to 'define' certain arguments by keeping them out of scrutiny or by otherwise making them non-discussible.

In working with the Swedish healthcare system we found that the (easily acceptable and positive) idea of 'equal care for everybody' had led to almost total undiscussibility of the fact that people have increasingly diverse life and health styles, so that 'identical care' actually has come closer in practice to 'inappropriate and unfair care for everybody'.

The consumer cooperative which will be described more in detail later had come to see 'cooperation' as 'ownership by the consumers', instead of interpreting cooperation in a broader sense more relevant to an era in which capital is no longer such a scarce resource. This 'boxing in' of the concept made a reinterpretation of the company's strengths and a recognition of its new growth opportunities more difficult.

These are examples of how weak or traditional arguments can be at least seemingly irreversibly put into a 'black box' and be excluded from scrutiny, and how therefore a definition of reality can be so. We continuously see similar strategies of arguments and lines of reasoning and theories which are advanced by actors as-if-obviously-and-unquestionably-true-and-descriptive-of-reality. Part of the Prime Mover's task is to find the arguments – even the rhetoric – to make such boxes transparent.

VALUES AND VALUE IN ECOGENETIC STRATEGIES

Today's very complex business and social world forces us to look far beyond the individual organization when we discuss change. In their classical paper 'The Causal Texture of Organizational Environments' – one of the most significant contributions ever to organizational and strategic thinking – Emery and Trist (1965) distinguished between four types of environment. The fourth, which they called 'turbulent', has become the normal state today. In such an environment, turbulence and change forces come not only from individual actors and competitors *but also from characteristics of the force field itself*. (Their argument sounds very much like complexity theory before that concept was formulated.)

In less complex environments an individual actor, by sheer force of their concepts and technology, may impose itself on the environment. Such steamrollering strategies have been, and still are, possible. Many would characterize the American 'culture industry', with front runners such as Disney World, Hollywood, McDonald's, Coca-Cola, and a few others, as prime examples. They create a new landscape which becomes imprinted with their technology and their ideas. In this sense their strategies are ecogenetic: they do not adapt, they shape.

Microsoft is another example of this phenomenon. But the events occurring around Microsoft for some time (this is written in the spring of 2000) also show the limitations. Emery and Trist point out that very turbulent environments, to be liveable and productive, require some overriding values and 'an institutional matrix' allowing organizations to effectively co-exist and – to use our terminology – co-produce. As value constellations (again, to use our terminology) become the rule rather than the exception, *values as an infrastructure for value creation* become prominent. There is a strong interrelationship between *values* and *value*.[12]

This actually means that the notion of ecogenesis can take on another, higher dimension than that of steamrolling by force. In their analysis, Emery and Trist quote Selznick (1957), who says:

> ... The default of leadership shows itself in an acute form when *organizational* achievement or survival is confounded with *institutional* success (1957, page 27). ... The executive becomes a statesman as he makes the transition from administrative management to institutional leadership (p. 154).

Institutional leadership, in this context, should be taken to denote a concern with the longer-term functioning of the larger system, not only with the economic success of the individual organization. This issue, and this higher level of ecogenesis and Prime Movership as well as of leadership, will be addressed again in the final chapters of this book.

Part III
Tools for Landscaping

INGRESSO ➡️ **PART I**
THE MAP AND
THE LANDSCAPE

Chapter 1
EVOLUTION OF
STRATEGIC PARADIGMS

Chapter 19
WHAT LEADERS
NEED TO DO

⬅️ *Chapter* 18
BRINGING EXTERNAL AND
INTERNAL DYNAMICS IN LINE

PART VII
LEADERSHIP FOR
NAVIGATION

Chapter 2
RECONFIGURING THE
VALUE SPACE

Chapter 16
FROM GREAT IDEAS
TO GREAT COMPANIES

➡️ *Chapter* 17
CAPABILITIES FOR ACHIEVING
THE CRITICAL OUTCOMES

Chapter 3
SOME CONSEQUENCES
OF DEMATERIALIZATION

PART VI
CAPABILITIES
FOR PURPOSEFUL
EMERGENCE

PART II
SHAPERS OF
THE LANDSCAPE

Chapter 4
CHAINED TO THE
VALUE CHAIN?

Chapter 15
THE CRANE AT WORK
IN THE DESIGN SPACE

PART III
TOOLS FOR
LANDSCAPING

Chapter 7
CO-PRODUCTION: TOWARDS
INCREASED DENSITY

Chapter 5
PRIME MOVERS
AS RECONFIGURERS

Chapter 14
THE MENTAL SPACE
FOR REFRAMING

Chapter 8
THE OFFERING AS A TOOL
TO ORGANIZE CO-PRODUCTION

Chapter 6
PRIME MOVERSHIP
AS ECOGENESIS

Chapter 13
THE PROCESS CRITERIA
OF THE CRANE

Chapter 9
THREE TRENDS IN
OFFERING DEVELOPMENT

PART IV
THE
MAP-LANDSCAPE
INTERACTION

Chapter 12
ON CRANES AND
SKY-HOOKS

PART V
REFRAMING:
TOOLS FOR
MAP MAKING

⬅️ *Chapter* 11
CHANGE AND
CREATION

⬅️ *Chapter* 10
FITTING INTO
THE ENVIRONMENT

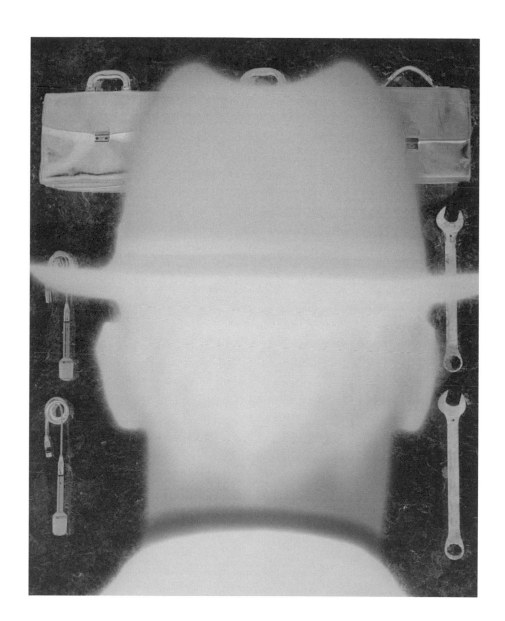

Co-production: Towards Increased Density   7

WHY CO-PRODUCTION?

Coordinated efforts by different actors towards a common whole is not new. The economy has proceeded through an ever more complex role differentiation between economic actors, rendering them different and interdependent rather than similar and autonomous. Economics describes the logic leading to complementary specialization as that of 'comparative advantage'.

Bosch develops the engine management system; Mercedes-Benz assembles it together with other components. Mercedes-Benz conceives and produces the car; I drive it. Of course this is co-production.

What is new is not co-production but the way it now expresses itself in terms of role patterns and modes of interactivity. The characteristics of today's economy naturally reshape co-productive roles and patterns. The distinction between 'producer' and 'consumer', or 'provider' and 'customer' is ever less clear as the business landscape takes on more of a 'service' mode (Normann, 1984/2000; Eiglier and Langeard, 1987, Sasser *et al.*, 1978). The new role patterns within what used to be thought of as 'industries' defy classification in simple 'value chain' terms and in 'competitor' versus 'partner' terms (Normann and Ramirez, 1993, 1994; Moore, 1996; Davis and Meyer, 1998, Ramirez and Wallin, 2000).

THE CO-PRODUCTION OPPORTUNITY

The driving forces influencing value creation in the new economy explode and cascade our options to have co-production. At a high level of aggregation these forces manifest themselves in globalization, in the increasing differentiation and then re-integration between the dematerialized, 'virtual' economy and the tangible world of mass and physical activities (one would wish that more investors could realize that there must also be a connection between the two!), in 'convergence' between 'industries'. Reallocation of activities in time/space and between actors enable the formation of a more complex and differentiated web. Not only does the differentiation between economic actors increase, but each actor tends to manifest himself in *multiple roles*. And as the web becomes ever more complex, the growing multitude of relationships and types of transactions and risks gives rise to new opportunities and new services and – again – new players and new roles.

Relationships and positions in Value-creating Systems, not individual objects, become crucial. Information about objects and information about relationships become the valuable assets. *Knowledge* about how to create relationhips and patterns of co-production is an even more valuable asset.

Co-productive relationships change with reference to both *time* and *space*. From being primarily sequential in time they tend – as a result of connectivity and interactivity – to become *simultaneous, synchronous,* and *reciprocal*. By this process we can compress time – we can, in fact, literally *create time* since we can package activities more densely into given time slots, thus liberating other time slots for other activities. And we can also proceed by occupying time slots that used to be 'unproductive'. The ATM or the telephone bank or the Internet bank is open 24 hours a day, and wherever I am; it is not just open from 10 to 4 and it does not require me to be in a particular street. Large corporations now set up research and development units in Europe, the United States, and Asia, so that a project can follow the sun and liberate itself from the rotation of the earth, using the 24 hours of the day rather than '9 to 5'.

Thus, there are 'hard', driving forces that allow this liberation from previous time/space barriers, resulting in the opportunity for closer and more differentiated coupling between actors and a total rethinking of the boundaries between them.

But the pursuit of co-production requires good thinking, not just good technology. Many breakthroughs in business have (if not by intention of the actors at the time at least in retrospective analysis) been the results of creative co-production, often completely unaided by any sort of advanced communication technology. Since the world is flooded by books on what information technology can do I will emphasize these more fundamental aspects – business creativity and social innovation rather than just the technological aspect – of co-production in what follows.

In this chapter I will explore three dimensions of co-production which open up new opportunities to create density: *customer participation, customer cooperation,* and *value constellations.*

CUSTOMER PARTICIPATION: THE FIRST CO-PRODUCTION DIMENSION

The 'service logic' experience

The Latin language has two words for 'consume'. They, and their meaning remain in the English language (but not in German or my native Swedish). 'Consume', according to my dictionary means 'destroy', 'use up', 'waste'. 'Consummate' means 'complete', 'perfect' (as verbs). It is the 'use up' meaning that has come to dominate how we think about consumption and consumers, and I am sure that many with me – conditioned by a Protestant ethic culture – have been urged to move the meaning of the word 'consume' close to the 'destroy' and 'waste' meanings. To consume is nice, but we should feel a little guilt and shame since we are enjoying and destroying!

But looking at consumption as more than destruction, and particularly at the consumer as more than somebody who uses up, has still been a theme of some importance among economists and business theorists. Alvin Toffler (1980) used the telling expression 'prosumer' to denote that the customer could fill the dual roles of producer and consumer, and Gershuny and Miles (1983) noticed a strong trend towards 'self-service' in society. They saw the increasing emphasis on the consumer's role as a producer primarily as a tool for increased productivity and as a result of the increase of the relative cost of labour. Instead of buying other people's *time* (more and more expensive) to perform services the consumer buys *tools* (less and less expensive) with which he or she performs self-service. For example, a vacuum cleaner plus the time committed to using it constitute a substitute system for servants. In spite of the growth of the 'service sector' there is therefore a strong trend towards substituting capital plus own work for the buying of services.

This line of reasoning already brings us to an interesting twist, namely the notion of *'barter currencies'*: Instead of a transaction which involves a product and service in one direction and money (and information) in the other, the customer puts some (but less) money on the table, plus time, plus skill, plus perhaps other assets that he or she already possesses. This line of thought can be further elaborated, as we shall see. *Self-service is about barter!*

But it was with the advent of 'service management' as a discipline, and with the analysis of a service (as opposed to 'manufacturing') logic that the notion of the customer as much more than a consumer really picked up speed in business theory. It was noted that the production and the consumption of a service typically strongly overlap time-wise and location-wise. Our hair is getting cut as it is being cut, and so far – unfortunately, I often think – nobody has been able to design a system for this particular service by which the customer can be absent from the act (the mountain must come to Mohammed, or Mohammed to the mountain). An analysis of the service logic highlights the difference between a sequential process between actors separated from each other and a simultaneous, synchronous, and reciprocal process in which the roles of producer versus consumer naturally begin to blur.

I have to admit that I have come to stop using the word 'consumer', not only because of its connotations of resource wasting and environmentally harmful 'mass consumption', but because the word in the traditional, narrow sense implies a whole system of thought which intellectually constrains us and which prevents us from seeing opportunities to innovate. I push myself to think of the customer as a *value creator* rather than a value destroyer.

While I was intellectually wrong about doing so much out of the distinction between service (as opposed to the manufacturing) *sector* (Normann, 1984/2000) I must give myself some credit for switching to the notion of the service *logic*. It forces us to shift our attention *from production to utilization, from product to process, from transaction to relationship*. It enhances our sensitivity to the complexity of roles and actor systems. In this sense the service logic clearly *frames* a manufacturing logic rather than replaces it. Creative business thinking comes from applying the service logic mode of thought, recognizing that within that overriding logic there are islands of a manufacturing logic. In other words, the service logic encourages us to think in terms of value creation and Value-creating Systems. It moves us from the oversimplified view that 'producers' satisfy needs and desires of 'customers' to the much richer but more complex view that they together form a Value-creating System. Within that system the provider has to find a way to position himself, and enhance and leverage the value creating process of the customer. It helps us move from the traditional industrial notion of products as *outputs* to the value-creation economy notion that offerings should be seen as *inputs* in a value-creating process.

Modes and functions of customer participation

The scope for involving the customer in value creation is endless. For simplicity, let me borrow a figure from my book *Service Management* (Figure 7.1).

The customer can participate in all phases of the business process:

Figure 7.1 Modes and functions of customer participation.

research and development, specification of the individual customer offering or 'product', actual 'production' work, quality control. Customers can be turned into a crucial marketing force for the provider. They can certainly play a critical role in maintaining and reinforcing the ethos and spirit of a company. I will never forget the SAS airline hostess who, when a few months after the dramatic turnaround of SAS in 1981–2, answered my question how come that the attitudes of SAS personnel had changed so quickly with:

> No, we have not changed, we have always been like that. But, you see, it is unbelievable how much our customers have changed!

Customers can do physical work, intellectual work, and they can also become emotionally involved (no doubt very much the case in the example quoted above!).

There is more. The customer has assets that can be put to productive tasks. These assets may be intangibles such as time, involvement and emotions, competences, information, etc. They may also be very tangible, such as one's house or apartment (which becomes the *workplace* for distance workers, the *hospital* for homecare patients, the *assembly factory* for IKEA customers, the *shopping place* for Internet shoppers, or the *prison* for electronically controlled prisoners).

A striking example of consciously designing for co-production, illustrating many of the above points, is provided by the previously introduced example of IKEA. The way IKEA presents itself to customers in the catalogue is all about co-production, about how activities have been reallocated between provider and customer. A more hi-tech-oriented example of reconfiguration based on increased customer participation is represented by Shahal, but the list is endless.

Relieving and enabling revisited

Seeing the customer as a producer and co-producer of value brings us back to the important distinction between two philosophies that a company can apply to reconfigure business, namely relieving versus enabling.

The reader will recall that *relieving* means that the specialized provider does things for the customer which the provider can do better. Relieving is the idea behind outsourcing: we are better at doing certain things that you now do yourself, so outsource them to us, and you can concentrate more on your 'core business' and what you do better. Relieving implies a shift – a reconfiguration – of activities from the customer context to a provider context. The customer may save costs and time as well as get rid of complexity.

Enabling, in contrast, is deliberately aimed at *expanding the scope of what a customer can do* (as opposed to just liberating him from having to do something he did before). It visibly changes what value the customer can create in his business, or his value-creating process in general. It endows him with new competences and market opportunities. An enabling proposition can transform the customer into his own physician, his own interior designer, his own securities trader, his own furniture assembly-line worker, his own desktop publisher.

The offerings implied in many customer relationships contain elements of both relieving and enabling. For example, national healthcare systems or health maintenance organizations (HMOs) will typically both relieve customers (as in the case of acute illness) and try to enable them (such as by informing them about what is a healthy life style, about preventive care, about self-care, about post-surgery rehabilitation). A bank or an insurance company may relieve its customers of certain risks and transactions, while trying to enable them to lead safer lives and to plan their personal financial situation better. Ferrari will relieve you from building your own mechanical monster but will also offer to enable you to become a better driver by offering you education in driving (as well as make you feel good and – if you wish – show off).

Still, one of the two philosophies typically is the dominating one and it usually is relieving, by far the dominating logic of the industrial era. Healthcare systems are typically designed to primarily relieve customers in case of manifest needs to heal acute illness. One senses the influence of the value chain model with the customer as a passive receiver at the end, receiving a 'healing' or 'repair' product. Yet a very high proportion of the 'consumption' of health care services depends on actions and decisions that the individual takes on his own. Furthermore, even in the case of acute illness as well as post-acute illness treatment it is obvious that actions of the 'customer' (and persons forming part of the 'customer's' day-to-day environment) have a great influence on costs as well as on ultimate success. In such a situation it would be highly justified to ask what an overall enabling logic as opposed to the predominant relieving logic would mean. A healthcare system applying an enabling logic would ask itself what it could do to support the customer's processes to *create health* rather than what it can do to *cure illness*. Of course, such a system would still contain large elements and islands of relieving, but my guess is that it would mean a revolution to rethink healthcare systems with an enabling point of view (focusing on the citizen's health-creation process) framing elements of relieving (such as when the citizen becomes a patient lying on the operating table), rather than the other way around.

Making the customer more productive

Figure 7.2, again borrowed from Normann (1984/2000), specifies some useful questions that a company may ask in considering how to improve the efficiency and effectiveness of the customer (in this case particularly the individuals) as a co-producer. Most of the questions are based on observations of customer behaviour which indicates a desire, perhaps latent or unconscious, and perhaps locked in by lack of time or skills or imagination, on behalf of the client. By creatively designing a system so

1. Can the timing of demand be influenced?
2. Does the customer have spare time while he is waiting?
3. Do clients and contact personnel meet unnecessarily face to face?
4. Are such contacts used to maximum effect?
5. Are contact personnel doing repetitive work which the customer could do himself, for example, with customer-operated machines?
6. Do the clients sometimes try to 'get past' the contact personnel and do things themselves? Could that interest and knowledge be better utilized?
7. Do the customers show interest in and knowledge about the tasks of the contact personnel?
8. Is there a minority of customers which disturbs the service delivery system and its effectiveness?
9. Do the customers ask for information which is available elsewhere?
10. Can the customers do more work for each other, or use the resources of 'third parties'?
11. Can part of the service delivery process be relocated to decrease, for example, the cost of premises?
12. Can the customer be given an opportunity to choose between service levels?

Figure 7.2 Examples of some questions in client 'management' (Normann, 1984/2000).

that the customer is provided with capabilities, time, or vision the slumbering potential of a customer can be released.

Technology tools, whether ATMs, Internet, or automatic blood analysis devices, are obvious instruments for those who want to make clients more efficient or/and enable them to reach new realms of value creation. So is transfer of knowledge by other means. Indeed, in some fast-growing areas in today's business world (consider mobile phones or Internet portals) competition between providers is probably much less related to the quality of their products and services as such, but rather to their ability to transfer knowledge, skills, understanding of what constitutes effective use, and, not least, *vision to imagine business and value-creating opportunities* related to the products and services.

We can seldom assume that we know what customers want. More importantly, we cannot assume that customers themselves know what they need or want. They cannot be aware of the opportunities that enabling technologies and the imagination of creative business developers bring. As the opportunities for value creation proliferate we are increasingly often faced with the dilemma that Plato evokes in his *Dialogues*, pointing out the constraining over-rational view of one of his pupils:

> You argue that a man cannot enquire either about that which he knows; for if he knows, he has no need to enquire; and if not, he cannot; for he does not know the very subject about which he is to enquire.

The game has, indeed, changed from technology push and asking the customer what he wants to a much more sophisticated mode of interaction and to an enabling philosophy. The most interesting business opportunities for reframers lie under the 'cloud' in Figure 7.3. Reaching – or creatively conceiving – them requires mental processes that we will evoke later.

Seemingly simple things like physical design can have a tremendous impact as enabling tools. The most striking example in my own experience is the original Apple Macintosh computer. To people who thought in terms of technology it was a fairly low-spec machine, and therefore inferior to higher-spec/higher-tech alternatives. But that was not the point, *and the people who designed the machine had a completely different frame of reference*. Their point of departure was that of the client's process of creating value, and the available (but sleeping) skills and blockages in

Figure 7.3 Four typical situations of 'provider' versus 'customer' knowledge.

that process. Thus they designed a device which naturally linked in with the customer's capabilities and mind-set, enabling him within a few exciting minutes to learn the machine and to begin to do things that he could never have done before.

Nicolas Negroponte (1995) certainly has a very strong point when he argues that it is disgraceful of any physical device to require an instruction manual – all devices should present an interface such that they instruct the user automatically. Let us not even discuss instruction manuals – such as the one for my computer software (unfortunately no longer Apple) – which uses up practically all the space to tell the potential user how great the product is and that it can do fantastic things for him, without – and I exaggerate only a little – ever coming to *what* it can do, and *how* it is done. And the instruction manual for the music system of my car is endlessly long – much longer than that for the car itself, although the car happens to be rather special and complex. I have been able to find out how to turn it on and off, however.

COOPERATION: CUSTOMER COMMUNITIES

The previous section has focused on the blurring of boundaries between 'producers' and 'customers', on the trend to reallocate value-creation activities between sellers and buyers, thus breaking up the traditional, simplistic and sequential model of their respective roles. The same driving forces make it possible to break down boundaries and escape common definitions in much broader constellations of economic actors in which activities are reshuffled in an increasingly intertwined web.

Broadly, we can discern two categories of such constellations (which very often are combined), namely *customer communities* for cooperation between customers, and *value constellations* (which roughly stands for cooperation between 'providers') . We start with the former type.

> According to a story the Roman emperor Hadrian spotted an old war veteran during a visit to the 'thermae'. The veteran stood by a pillar, rubbing his back against it. Hadrian, who recognized the veteran as a good warrior, walked up to him, greeted him, and asked him why he did not use a slave to rub his back. The veteran retorted that he could not afford a slave. In a generous gesture, Hadrian gave him the ownership of a slave.
>
> The next day, upon entering the thermae, Hadrian found a great number of old war veterans rubbing their backs against pillars. Hadrian walked up to them, and with the amused smile of a man knowing the secrets of life he ordered the veterans to scrub each others' backs.

The idea of 'customers' organizing themselves for cooperation with each other, or being organized by somebody for such co-operation, is far from new. Many types of business explicitly grew out of such movements. Today's insurance companies are extensions of small, local movements by which neighbours agreed to help each other in case of problems. Banks are institutions which help to match people with positive and negative cash flows over stages of life. Producer and consumer cooperatives organize individuals who are weak on their own but who can get together to bargain, buy, invest, and own together.

Today many cooperatives that still exist have lost position, and many 'mutual' organizations such as mutual insurance companies and savings banks are demutualizing. Many such forms of cooperation have led to large bureaucracies which are simply too slow and cumbersome to respond to the speed of today's world. But, perhaps more important, many of them were originally based on the idea that capital is the critical resource, which may have been true a hundred years ago but which is far from true today (see Normann and Nordfors, 1999). Strength from cooperation today is not from adding together small pieces of capital, but from adding together small pieces of knowledge, competence and bargaining power. Many traditional cooperatives seem to be fighting on the wrong battlefield.

Today's 'customer communities' are based on the exchange and complementarity of far more intricate things than capital. When Weight Watchers bring groups of customers together it is in order for the customers to exchange knowledge and experience, and to reap encouragement from each other. When Kaiser Permanente or other health-delivery institutions create group clinics of customers/patients with the same type or related illnesses it is, again, because those customers have so much to learn from each other that the total benefits of the system increase for each participant, and because providing the same level of benefit with individual relationships between physicians and patients would have implied a totally different level of costs.

The fact that individual customers can exchange *time* and *competence* and *experience* and *contacts* with each other in a kind of 'barter arrangement' accounts for much of the growth today of local, spontaneous cooperatives in areas such as child care, old age care, home services. Internet technology allows such customer communities to be created not only on a local basis but at a distance, unlimited by local boundaries. Internet communities are now a well-known phenomenon. Many such communities will probably be of a 'project' character and have a rather short life, and others will have a longer life but with individuals moving in and out on a rather short-term basis. Some will most likely become highly institutionalized. eBay creates a marketplace where customers globally can get together. Nobody knows yet what paths evolution in this area will take, but they will most likely be highly diverse. In areas such as healthcare the potential is enormous.

VALUE CONSTELLATIONS

One type of co-production based on the complementarity of providers is outsourcing driven. By this I mean that an organization – a 'provider' – finds it rational to take some of its activities and re-allocate them to subcontractors with a higher level of specialization, probably leading to higher quality as well as lower cost. This trend is well known in business.

A more radical and interesting type of value constellations are those which identify economic actors and link them together in new patterns which allow the creation of new business that did not exist previously, or which more or less radically change the way certain types of value are created. Here we are not talking about a simple reallocation of existing activities between a set of actors, but of constructing a new, coordinated set of activities resulting in a new kind of output – not just a more efficiently produced traditional output. To investigate the mechanisms behind such constellations, look at the example of EF Education.

> In 1998 EF Education probably received most of its public attention from sponsoring and organizing the boat that won the Whitbread Race. But the story started much earlier than that – in the university city of Lund, in southern Sweden, in the 1960s.
>
> Media had started to make the world more global, and English had seriously become the international language. Language was learnt at school, and there was an old tradition of well-off families to send their children to foreign countries to learn new languages. What Bertil Hult, the founder of EF, invented was a new formula for fulfilling the desire to learn languages (first English, later other languages) by re-inventing and thereby 'democratizing' the old idea of sending young people abroad.
>
> EF did so by recombining resources which had hitherto not been linked to each other. The following were the key actors and a summary of their rationale to participate:

The children:	Need to learn
	Long vacation time available from school during summer
	Wish for new experiences
The teachers:	Need to practise
	Long vacation time in summer
	Wish for good study results for the students
The schools in England:	Empty classrooms in summer
The English family:	Wish for experiences, and for communicating their culture
	Available rooms
	Company for their children in the summer
The parents:	Wish for good development of their children
	(Wish for free time without children during summer?!)

By organizing the relationships between these actors, all with complementary resources and desires, a new system was created. A number of resources – whether an empty classroom, an under-utilized teacher in the summer, or an available unoccupied bed in an English home – were now given more value by being positioned in a larger system and complementing other such resources.

Another example, referred to earlier, is JC Decaux, now a major player in cities around the world. JC Decaux offers to provide a city with bus stops for free over a twenty-year period, and they maintain them perfectly well. The idea is that perfectly well-maintained bus stops are attractive as advertising space for business companies, and in this way JC Decaux links actors into a Value-creating System which did not exist before: the city administration, public transportation companies, advertisers, and the public. From this JC Decaux, now a very international company, has moved to other related city services.

The logic of value constellations

First, we immediately notice that we are dealing with *innovation*, not just increased efficiency of production as is the case in a subcontracting logic. The actors we are talking about here, such as EF Education and JC Decaux, create something that did not exist previously. They invent new markets and create new customers. It is not just that customers find that they can get whatever was previously available less expensively.

Second, this innovation comes about as a result of innovative linkages between hitherto unrelated resources which are revealed as under-utilized, *seen in the light of a mental vision or scenario of the innovation* as conceived by the innovator. Assets and resources are not inherently complementary; what makes them complementary is *an idea* that links them.

Thus, assets may well contribute to the development of ideas, but it is certainly so that *ideas and knowledge are what create value out of assets.*

Our examples are dramatic illustrations of conceiving assets in terms of their 'positional value', as opposed to 'intrinsic value'. As has already been pointed out, it is a key feature of the new economy that the valuation of assets has to be based on the position of those assets in a Value-creating System rather than on any kind of intrinsic value. This shift of perspective to positional value is the essence, in my view, of the knowledge-based economy.

Information does not create ideas. Ideas create information. (Szasz, 1973/1991)

Third, a striking feature of these systems is the very large element of 'barter' involved in the transactions. By organizing relationships between the various actors with complementary resources and desires a barter market was created by EF Education, as well as by the other actors quoted. In this sense, *the Prime Mover innovator/organizer is a market maker for sleeping assets*. The Prime Mover makes these assets *liquid* and *rebundleable* by conceiving a new context in which they can be made useful. In this sense the Prime Mover literally *makes the actors wealthier* by making non-monetarized assets valuable for others.

To equilibrate the barter equation for the various actors a certain (sometimes considerable) amount of 'netting' is required. Even though a British family may in principle be quite willing to swap a bed and some food in the summer for the opportunity to be ambassadors for their country and to have exotic company for their children, it may still consider the exchange uneven and they may want some money as well. This money then has to be paid by the final customer (the child and ultimately the child's parents) through the organizer of the whole exchange (EF). A remarkable number of such swaps are, however, held to be more or less even. And because so many of the transactions in such value constellations are not moneterized but barter based it is often difficult to get an exact evaluation of the total value exchange taking place in the system.

It would indeed be a great mistake to believe that the formal, monetarized economy is a measure of the value creation going on. It merely records the netting after barter has taken place.

For the organizer – EF Education, JC Decaux, Shahal, etc. – it is necessary to have sufficient monetary currency to compensate for the lack of reciprocity in the values swapped (directly but often indirectly through the organizer) of the other actors. In addition, the organizer has costs for creating the market, and needs to be compensated for its role as a *market maker*, as well as getting a risk premium as an entrepreneur. This means that the price that is in the end charged to the customer is composed of the following elements:

(1) What is required for 'netting' between the various participants in the value constellation after barter has taken place.
(2) A fee for the costs of 'market making' of the various assets represented by the members of the value constellation.

(3) The usual risk premium pertaining to all entrepreneurs, giving the opportunity for profit, and the size of which is based on the surplus value created by the organizer in relationship to what the customer is prepared to pay.

In addition, the 'organizer' may be part of the value constellation in that it contributes essential assets in addition to organizing the assets of others into a web-like pattern. For example, EF Education develops sophisticated pedagogical material. JC Decaux contributes high technology-based bus stops as well as an extremely well-organized service system for maintenance of the bus stops. This creates a fourth element in the price that the customer has to pay:

(4) Costs for specific competences and assets that the focal organization contributes to the value constellation beyond the competences as an organizer, at the same level as other actors in the constellation that it organizes.

Paradoxically, the barter economy is in full swing! A remarkable number of business innovations come about as a result of rendering non-monetary currencies available for co-productive economic transactions.

From working with many regulated systems such as healthcare and education, however, I would dare to hypothesize that systems which prevent the emergence of barter-based transactions and value constellations clearly brake the emergence of effective value creation. The regulated and moneterized formalization of many services such as healthcare, child care, old age care, and others – particularly in what is generally thought of as being primarily in the 'public sector' of welfare services in Europe – has, if I am right in my assumption and analysis, led to unnecessarily high cost, low utilization of potential co-production and valuable barter currencies, and most likely lower quality than potentially possible in those service areas.

SUMMARY: THREE DIMENSIONS OF CO-PRODUCTION

We see a proliferation of co-production in terms of customer participation, customer cooperation, and value constellations. Co-production means waking up and enabling sleeping, under-utilized resources, bringing competences together more effectively in time/space, linking actors in new constellations. It is based on an evaluation of assets based not on intrinsic

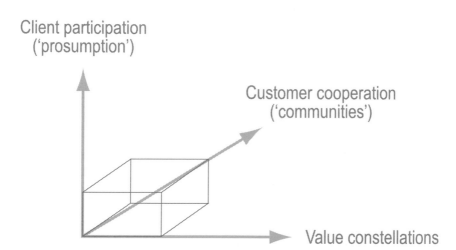

Client participation
('prosumption')

Customer cooperation
('communities')

Value constellations

Figure 7.4 Three dimensions of the co-production opportunity space.

properties but on positional value. The positional value can be discovered only when framed by a concept, an idea.

The discovery of the service logic helped us to better understand one of the key dimensions of co-production, namely *customer participation*. Such participation blurs the interface between providers and customers, and makes the notion of 'consumer' a particularly misleading one in the economy of today.

New information technology, and the increasing art of some companies to be 'market makers' and to link resources with each other in new ways, led to opportunities in the development of *customer communities* as well as *value constellations*.

The three trends are summarized in Figure 7.4. Obviously, there is potential for value creation in all three areas – although tradition and mental blockages tend to make companies stay closer to the lower-left-hand corner than necessary. The upper and deeper right-hand corner, both enabling the customer to be a better participant in co-production and mobilizing (and organizing) customer communities as well as value constellations, is still a largely unexplored area by most companies (and manufacturing companies often fail to see this opportunity at all, rather thinking about the much less sophisticated idea of 'outsourcing' as a way to create a web or a 'virtual corporation'). But here is an opportunity space to invade.

The Offering as a Tool to Organize Co-Production

8

WHAT REALLY HAPPENS IN THE MARKETPLACE?

Economic theory tends to describe the economy as a set of economic actors transacting products and services, all subject to the laws of supply and demand and comparative advantage. But this is not the only way to look at the economy. Rachline, for example, uses a different approach. He sees the economy as a set of 'flows', which are energized by various imbalances. Such a view is not unlike one which I have had described to me by investment bankers – perhaps in relaxed moments of special candour. Huge flows of financial assets are set in motion by randomly occurring imbalances between different parts of the global system, or can in fact be stimulated by actors large enough to create such imbalances; then it is possible for certain players to skim off razor-thin parts of these huge flows for themselves.

Neither of these views is right or wrong. Both are models, metaphors, and both have strengths and weaknesses in describing 'reality' from their respective perspectives. Applying any of these views, or other alternative views again, makes one perceive different opportunities and strategies.

However, for some time I have felt that the established view – that of the economy as a set of actors transacting products and services in exchange for money – is somehow surprisingly poor. As long as we deal with traditional 'hard products' the argument does not at first seem hard to follow. But what about when we come to 'services'? It is much less obvious to understand what a service is. Yet, according to any classification, by far the majority of all transactions in the economy are now about services.

Is the issue resolved if we think about services as 'intangible' or 'immaterial' products? Such a view may have some face validity, but it does not get to the heart of the problem and it is a seriously inadequate metaphor. What services do is to link various elements with each other in new ways. In this way the 'service economy' and the 'knowledge economy' are just different words for the same concept. Positional value, based on system analysis and system design, becomes superordinate to, and frames, intrinsic value. *Services are activities (including the use of hard products) that make new relationships and new configurations of elements possible.*

The previous chapter identified *co-production* as embodied in organized *Value-creating Systems* as the mechanism that enables more density by rebundling actors, assets and activities. Co-production for increased value to actors requires new linkages.

Viewing the economy as a web of activities and actors linked in co-productive value creation gives us another, and I think more creative, view of the nature of 'offerings'. *Offerings are artefacts designed to more effectively enable and organize value co-production.* They are agents created by agents. Innovative offerings can reconfigure co-productive patterns for higher value creation.

Recall the description of the reconfiguration space from Chapter 2. Traditional activity clusters can be 'unbundled' in terms of place (*where* they are performed), time (*when* they are performed), actor (*who* performs them), and actor constellation (*with whom* they are performed). Through the sequence of 'unbundleability–liquidity–rebundleability' it is possible to bring together, for a given time/space/economic actor unit, a much more 'dense' accumulation of assets, human activities, and knowledge, than before, thus heightening the platform upon which value creation can take place in that time/space/economic actor unit.

This chapter will explore and summarize the notion of offerings based on this metaphor of what economic activity is about.

THE OFFERING AS A RECONFIGURATION TOOL

Consider, again, the simple case of IKEA. Some aspects of the reconfiguration are:

- The *place* of the assembly has moved from some factory to the customer's living-room.

- The *time* of assembly has moved (with reference to the time of purchase) from the past to the future.
- The assembly has moved from a factory worker as an *economic actor* to the customer.
- The customer very likely has designed a *value-creating constellation* consisting of friends or family members to do the assembly.

For many (not all) customers, the gains are obvious. The customer uses resources already paid for (his car, his living-room, his time, the 'free' workforce that the family and maybe friends represent). In other words, IKEA frees up barter currencies by organizing assets into an idea-based pattern that enhances their positioned value.

The *offering* of IKEA, then, is far more complex than *the physical product* and its delivery to the customer's home as such. *In fact, the offering is a reconfiguration of a whole process of value creation, so that the process – rather than the physical product – is optimized in terms of relevant actors, asset availability and asset costs.*

It is this reconfiguration of the *process* and of the *Value-creating System*, not the design of the physical *product*, which is the innovative element and comparative advantage of IKEA's offering. To regard this as 'product plus' would be to miss the point entirely.

Compare taking money out of your bank account by visiting the branch or via the Internet. Again, it would be completely out of place to regard the 'service' here as 'getting a hundred pounds out of the bank'. Yes, that is part of it. But the process of getting that money in terms of what the customer has to do, when, and where, is different. We are comparing offerings as *different ways of configuring a process and an actor constellation* which allows liquefication of barter currencies and co-production, not as different 'products' or 'services'.

OFFERINGS ARE FROZEN KNOWLEDGE

Tangible 'products' can be effective instruments into which past activities can be 'frozen' and made available to actors for their present and future value-creating activities. The Industrial Revolution meant that design and production knowledge could be extremely efficiently 'imprinted' on raw materials, which then could act as 'carriers' of this knowledge. The essence of the Industrial Revolution was exactly that mass production technology replaced craft-based production, which made it possible to *share* such design and production knowledge between a large number of users, by reproducing/imprinting it onto so many identical products (economies of scale) and (perhaps less significant then than now) application areas (economies of scope).

As a result of sharing, the raw material cost of the dictaphone the author uses to 'freeze' his or her thoughts is negligible as a share of the price of the dictaphone. It is even more negligible as a share of the price of this book (but it does enter, somewhere!).

Tracing the origins of the dictaphone we can easily imagine it as – literally – the result of activities of many people or economic actors. It was bought in a shop, which may have obtained it from an importer who obtained it from the factory. The shopkeeper has displayed it, put it together with a range of other similar and complementary products, marketed it. The product design comes from generations of research and development, and there is a lot more ergonomic and good industrial design in it compared to an earlier model I had. Production has taken place in a factory, probably with several components supplied from other factories around the world. All these factories have used machinery which, in turn, reflects the accumulated activities and knowledge of endless numbers of researchers, designers, manufacturers, transporters, bankers, ...

So the dictaphone contains a small – infinitesimal, but still – share of the activities and knowledge applied by generations of economic actors. And for its functionality to be meaningful it must be embedded in a system of suppliers of tapes, word processors, educated secretaries... .

A physical product, thus, is a representation – an accumulation – of past knowledge and activities. It is, indeed, 'frozen knowledge'. Its frozen form, its tangibility, makes it – and therefore the accumulated knowledge – accessible and storable for use and perhaps re-use.

We can clearly see how, in this sense, the product is the link between the past and the future. As an inventory, a storage, it gives the user access to the past. Elevated on this platform of the past that is now accessible the user can reach higher. But the quality and amount of value-creating activities that the product will stimulate the user to perform in the future depends very much on the extent to which the product stimulates and enables the user to create value with it.

The product links economic actors of the past with economic actors of the future, but it also links various economic actors in the present and in the future. This is all too obvious in the case of a product such as an Internet-linked personal computer, which allows me practically immediate and worldwide access to endless numbers of other economic actors. But practically all products are designed to create, or result in the creation of, linkages. The dictaphone links me with my secretary in new ways. My climate-control system links me to the electric utility. My sound-reproduction equipment links me to musicians, music magazines, record-producing companies, friends who love to listen and discuss. And to Beethoven.

Physical products are not the only way for freezing and storing past activities. Knowledge is also frozen into people (as a result of education and experience), manuals, systems, language, and culture. Most offerings that bring the possibility of new linkages to a situation are in fact 'multimedia' ones. Physical products are a particularly efficient medium because of their reproducibility and predictability.

THE OFFERING AS A GENETIC CODE FOR LEARNING

Allow me to consider one additional aspect of IKEA. The activity of finding out what furniture to buy is explicitly allocated to the customer (see Chapter 2). This may seem trivial, but in fact in a business related to interior decoration and choice of furniture, which usually requires a great deal of taste and some expertise, it is a very significant statement. Go to the traditional furniture or home-furnishing shop and you will most likely find it filled with people who claim that they are professional experts in interior decoration (while, of course, leaving the final choice to the client), and they will also justify the price levels of their products by claiming to offer highly professional advice.

How, then, is it possible to allocate this activity to a presumably amateurish customer? Surely, IKEA will point out that there are advisors available, but you will hardly notice them, and they will certainly not come and solicit you when you visit the store. *But consider again the offering from IKEA as a process configuration – not as furniture:*

> One day the family finds a new IKEA catalogue in the mailbox. It displays furniture and home-furnishing items, home environments, and, to some extent, lifestyles and life situations of people. In addition, there is a description

of the philosophy of IKEA and how IKEA creates value together with customers.

The family looks at the catalogue and at the house or apartment, and a discussion starts. Scenarios are formed in a conversation which may go on for a long time and which may include neighbours, relatives, and friends (they also have the catalogue). Ideas start to take shape, they are tested, and the conversation goes on.

One day the nearest IKEA store is visited. People do not go alone, they go as families or with friends. The group goes through the maze of the store, looking, trying, reading information. People who can give advice are available but are rarely consulted. No decisions are taken. At the end of the store there is a cafeteria in which the group takes a rest. The cafeteria really serves as a 'decision-making room'; the conversation continues, and it is now that purchasing decisions are taken. The group returns to the store and picks up the items that have been chosen.

Without the customer group being conscious of it, it has been guided through an ingenious and effective learning process. When the customers arrive in the cafeteria this process has come to an end; the customer has now been educated (by way of cleverly designed stimuli and inputs from IKEA for an educational conversation within the customer system) to be a sufficiently good interior decoration expert. Solutions to manifest problems have been found, and the customers have most likely been led to discover new opportunities and see new visions – i.e. they have been enabled. Whether or not all this has originally been consciously and deliberately designed by IKEA can be discussed. In any case, the role of being one's own professional advisor has been explicitly allocated by IKEA to the customer, and therefore IKEA has been forced to design its offering (and itself as a system) in such a way as to educate the customer to fulfil this role.

The inputs given by IKEA judiciously fit into the natural process of the customer, and they build on, and reinforce, the customer's natural process and assets. As with the Apple Macintosh example given earlier, this makes a metaphor of *'business as pedagogics'* highly relevant.

Clearly, there is a great difference between a company which sees itself as distributing 'products' to 'consumers' ('value destroyers'), and one that sees itself as matching and supporting the value-creating processes of 'consummators' ('value creators'). And it is towards the second role that the new business logic pushes us.

However great an inventory of past, frozen activities an offering may be, it would be worthless unless it led to value-creating activities. To be usable it has to find a user, there have to be infrastructures allowing its use, and it must stimulate economic actors to value-creating activities. A useful offering is designed so as to trigger off value-creating activities. In this sense it carries a 'code' (Normann and Ramirez, 1994/1998). *The 'product' cannot be seen isolated from the user.* The design of it must match and extend the capabilities, intentions, context, and processes of the user.

This difference in design between the first Apple Macintosh and other computers at the time, I would say, had less to do with ergonomics than with empathy and pedagogics. It reflected a fundamentally different view of what an offering is: not a physical product, but a way to reconfigure activities and stimulate and enable value creation.

Today's customer offerings, whether packaged as physical 'products' or offered as 'services', 'software', 'portals', 'relationships', or in other shapes, all embedded in a 'brand' concept, tend to be (explicitly or not) designed to evoke and stimulate emotional, intellectual and physical actions within the customer. 'Design' is no longer something *'per se'*, but has the explicit purpose of triggering value-creating activities and put the user in a conscious or unconscious context of creation of 'meaning'. The aesthetic properties of an offering and the extent to which the offering embeds itself and the user and the total context of usage in a realm of meaning and belongingness – socially, and with regard to intent and future direction – constitute a major competitive tool.

Good products are like good toys, such as Lego. They link in with the current, natural processes of the user, stimulating him to do things that he was not able to do previously, but still within the natural operational and evolutionary 'flow' of the user.

The offering thus elevates the user in two ways. First, it *gives the user a platform by providing access to an inventory of past activities in frozen form.* Second, it liberates the user from this platform of past, accumulated knowledge, stimulating the user *by giving him a 'code' for value-creating activities* and stimulating co-production and relationships. The effectiveness of an offering depends both on to what extent it is a good *inventory of past knowledge* and on to what extent it contains a good *genetic code.*

THE 'FREEZING' OF THE CUSTOMER OFFERING: WHO AND WHEN?

The above can be generalized to one of the most fundamental points of today's business world: to be competitive, customer offerings often need to have an element of *learning*. That is, they should be designed with an 'open systems architecture'. Static offerings are much more easy to imitate. If a transaction can lead to a relationship which entails learning and leads to unique, proprietary knowledge in the parties concerned, the offering will improve with age, like a bottle of great wine. It will also become much more difficult for competitors to challenge, since it is both a moving target and something in which all parties have invested.

Naturally, Internet technology offers opportunities for such mutual learning which are unprecedented cost/benefit-wise in history.

In the three strategic paradigms referred to in the first part of the book the perspective on the customer changes from being a 'sink' or receiver with *needs* to be fulfilled at the end of the line, to being a 'source' with whom it is fruitful to build a relationship, and finally to being a 'co-producer' endowed with capabilities and involved in a value-creating *process*. With this evolution the customer's degree of captivity with regard to the provider also tends to change. In a world with practically free information available the customer tends to become more of a 'free agent' and networker. The customer does not have to comply with the rules and offerings provided by local providers or any particular provider. Power has shifted. Although companies develop more and more ingenious methods to create relationships and reward loyalty, the customer no longer accepts to have his or her freedom restricted. Indeed, it has struck me *that the only way to make customers loyal today is to enable them to be disloyal*. Loyalty has to be earned within a context of freedom, it cannot be imposed.

All this has profound implications for how customer offerings are designed. In the industrial era the providing/producing business company investigated customer needs, and then 'froze' the design of an offering that the customer had to accept or (if he had a choice) reject. From the customer's point of view offerings were 'pre-frozen' by the provider. This model no longer is necessary, appropriate, or competitive. Instead of pre-freezing offerings *companies must now enable their customers to co-design offerings in real time*. Of course, the final offering that the customer defines is to a great extent based on pre-frozen elements, but it is nonetheless individualized or 'mass customized' (Davis, 1987). Technology helps. The customer may now draw his own kitchen and have it produced to his own specifications by using a customer-operated CAD-CAM technique. Manufacturers of clothes are moving towards a situation when the customer steps into a machine that measures the body and programs a production process by which 'tailor-made' clothes are produced instantly or shortly after. Financial services software providers enable a customer to more or less constantly tailor-make his or her banking services.

The design of offerings has moved from the past to real time, and from an activity performed by providers to an activity performed by the customer, jointly with the provider.

But an example such as Quicken (a software provider in financial services) or, say, Web MD (which helps employers to tailor-make health-provision systems) also clearly point to another direction. When the offering is frozen this is not only done by the customer, and not only by the customer using the competence of the provider. *Instead assembling the offering involves using elements from a broad range of providers on the conditions of the customer*. Systems such as that of Quicken enable the customer to learn more about the available resources in financial services, thus creating options and a *predisposition* within the customer to be able to rapidly tailor-make an offering *in the future*, and *based on a constellation of providers*, should a situation occur when this is required (Figure 8.1).

In this sense the customer is enabled to be a Prime Mover, organizing a set of economic actors. Not all customers want this job and responsibility, but more and more are discovering it.

OFFERINGS SPECIFY THE RANGE OF EXCHANGE CURRENCIES

The examples of Shahal, EF Education and JC Decaux, among many others, illustrate that what takes place between providers and customers, and in broader value-creating constellations, is far more complex in terms of value transactions than is usually assumed. Economic theory seems to assume that goods and services flow in one direction (from producer to customer) in exchange for money. It is also recognized that transactions in the

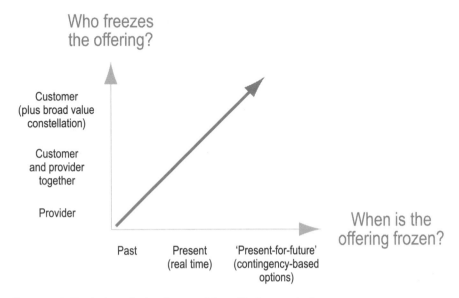

Figure 8.1 Evolution of who 'freezes' the offering, and when.

marketplace are based on, and generate, information, so that in addition to flows of goods and services in one direction and money in the other, information is also exchanged. With today's emphasis on information technology information itself is, of course, a valuable asset, and is therefore the object of economic transactions (i.e. a financial price is often put on information). With sophisticated data warehousing and data-mining techniques providers turn transaction data into valuable information and knowledge about customers, who have therefore not only given money but also information to the provider in exchange for the 'good' or 'service'. Customers as well as public authorities are becoming increasingly aware and sometimes weary about this, arguing that the value exchange has become lopsided and/or that customers are indirectly forced to give away an asset to which the provider has no right.

But the value exchange between providers and customers and within a value-creating constellation consists – as we have seen – of much more than goods/services, money, and information. In so-called 'voluntary organizations' financial transactions are complemented by people giving their *time* and their *involvement*. In some such organizations, such as Médecins sans Frontières (winners of the Nobel Prize for Peace), certain groups also contribute their very specialized *competence* (in this case medical competence).

However, these 'barter currencies' are not at all — as is often assumed — constrained to special 'voluntary' organizations, but are in fact present in practically all value transactions and are therefore an explicit or (more often!) implicit part of all offerings. The list of barter currencies can be made much longer. In the IKEA case the customer not only puts in time and competence (which, as we have seen, is enhanced by the learning or 'enabling' mode of the offering as designed by IKEA!), but also his *infrastructures* (such as his car, his living-room as a factory floor) in exchange for a lower price.

American Express and (in the example quoted in next chapter) Volvo put in their respective *customer bases* and the potential *purchasing power* of these in exchange for fees and/or extra services rendered from shops/restaurants/travel agencies and from oil companies and insurance companies, respectively. The shops etc., on their side, buy *access* to a customer base in exchange for the opportunity to extract economic value from this customer base.

In the traditional, pre-industrial economy a very large part of all transactions took place in the non-monetarized domain and involved barter currencies; nevertheless, transactions and value creation took place. Figures of GNP growth in the economy reflect both that transactions move into the monetarized and therefore registered domain and that more real value creation takes place; it is often difficult to know which of these two effects is the greater. Today's reconfiguration opportunities — that is, opportunities to achieve much more multi-faceted co-production — have created new awareness and new interest in designing value transactions which are formalized and consciously designed but still take place in the non-monetarized domain as barter. It is indeed in highly commercial companies that we tend to find the most astute, conscious use of barter currencies today to achieve new levels of co-production in interactive value constellations.

Often the notion of barter currencies in offerings is so much taken for granted that it is not even perceived. Perception may increase in cases where 'reverse engineering' takes place:

> In 1996 when a municipal housing company in Malmö, Sweden, offered their tenants a lower rent in exhange for their physical participation in

cleaning the staircases, the tax authorities at first reacted by claiming that the decrease in rent should be taxed as income from work. Later the decision was changed. The example clearly illustrates three points. Value-creating activities go far beyond what is registered in the formal, monetarized economy. Second, exchange currencies in transactions can be many things other than money. Third, there seems to be an interesting incompatibility between the logic of tax systems, income distribution systems, and the reconfiguration logic of the new economy...

One result of IKEA's reconfiguration is that certain activities are moved from the realm of 'monetarized activities in the formal economy' to 'non-monetarized activities in the informal/unregistered economy'. Governments will notice this in terms of lower value added taxes as well as fewer income taxes for furniture factory workers. As far as I know, nobody has suggested – so far – that assembling IKEA furniture in the home should be registered with the tax authorities and taxed, since it removes taxable activities from the registered economy. But the 'reverse engineering' case of the Malmö housing company illustrates that the idea may not be all that far-fetched.

OFFERINGS ARE DIFFERENT FROM PRICE CARRIERS

The other day when my mobile telephone had broken down I realized I had to get a new one. In the shop the one I wanted had a very attractive price label, but when I looked more closely I realized that this price was relevant only if I bought the telephone together with a subscription (which I already had). If I bought the telephone 'as such' it was considerably more expensive.

Buying a subscription including a mobile phone and buying a mobile phone as such are, of course, two different things, but the example still illustrates that something may have very different price labels depending on the context. If I buy the subscription with the phone the total offering will consist of several *price carriers*: the phone as such, a fixed fee for the subscription, and a set of variable fees for the use of the phone. It might seem arbitrary what parts of an offering carry a price tag and what parts do not, and how the total price is allocated between the different price carriers, as long as the total price is the same. However, in practice this is not at all the case, and in fact the choice of not only *price level* but *pricing formula* is one of the critical elements of any offering.

The notion of bundling is related to *the pricing formula* of a business, and to how price carriers relate to the totality of the 'customer offering'. To take the example of the pharmacy business, everybody I have met in that business has stressed that pharmacies sell a combination of products, availability of products, and advice (and availability of personnel competent to give advice). These elements together constitute the total *offering* of the pharmacy. However, the price tag almost without exception is on the product only, which therefore becomes the price carrier.

The fact that there is a difference between the price carrier and the total offering, and that the latter is larger than the former, indicates that we are dealing with a case of bundling. Several components are bundled together, but only one of them carries a price. Such pricing tactics are very common in business, but they also become increasingly vulnerable in today's economy.

The formula for bundling and choosing price carriers versus non-price-carrying elements of an offering may be part of a highly astute game between different competitors. A much publicized case not long ago – as this is written – is Microsoft and their decision to include (among other items) an Internet browser 'for free' in their Windows system. Their logic is easy to understand. On the one hand, the marginal cost of adding the browser is extremely low. In addition, they have the opportunity to put a price tag on the basic Windows system, which is more or less a 'must' for users, whereas their main competitor Netscape, which sold a browser 'unbundled', did not have the same opportunity. They had to set a price above average – not marginal – cost, and they had no option to make the browser a loss leader since there wasn't anything else they sold that could subsidize it. In principle, the danger for Microsoft would be if anybody else had a basic system competing with Windows who did not add a browser and who could therefore sell the basic system unbundled at a lower cost than Microsoft. However, because of their dominating position, Microsoft Windows does not have much to fear, at least for the moment, in this respect.

Another classical example of the difference between the offering and the price carrier is the pricing of banking services. Since banks had a regulated monopoly on taking deposits from the public they have such a dominating position in the deposit and lending market that they could use the 'spread' (the difference between interest on lending and interest on deposits) as the price carrier, giving away transactions (checking etc.) to customers 'for free'. With deregulation and increased customer awareness this strategy started to backfire in the 1980s. Large-deposit customers started to realize that they did not get a fair deal, since effectively they subsidized heavy users of 'free' transactions. (In several customer profitability analyses that I did together with colleagues in the 1980s we found that typically 75 per cent of the retail customers in banks generated a negative result for the bank, so that the remaining 25 per cent customers not only had to cover their own costs but also had to heavily subsidize the loss-creating customers.) And with increasing deregulation a number of specialized, limited assortment banks and other financial service institutions started to compete for deposits and for other services on which the banks had put a too high price tag. Not surprisingly there was remarkably little competition about the 'free' services of banks!

Another reason why the pricing formula makes a big difference is that *it influences customer behaviour*. In fact, pricing is as much a pedagogical tool as a way for a provider to recover economic value to cover expenses and profit margin. A classical type of juggling with what parts of the total offering should be price carriers and what parts should not be is the case of 'the free entry ticket'. The 'free' mobile phone that comes with a subscription package, the 'free' product that comes with entering a book club, the 'free' browser that leads to more Internet use, are phenomena we all know.

What has often surprised me, however, is to what a great extent the difference between the offering and the price carrier is poorly understood by companies, particularly in traditional manufacturing industries.

> Recently I had the opportunity to work with a world-renowned chocolate manufacturer. The chocolate box certainly is the price carrier. But in discussions it was obvious that, for example, this fact had made it difficult for the company to see that they were really providing customers with at least two very different offerings: chocolate for personal consumption by the purchaser, and chocolate for gifts. The chocolate box is part of both offerings, but the potential for developing each of the offerings in its entirety was somehow completely mentally overshadowed by the perception of the company that 'the customer buys and pays for chocolate boxes'.
>
> In another case I worked with a large, globally present manufacturer of heavy transportation equipment. The company was organized with manufacturing primarily at the headquarters and a great number of national

importers and dealer networks. It was very clear that the headquarters made their money based on selling the equipment units to importers; that is, the equipment and spare parts were the sole price carriers of the headquarters.

However, in the local markets, and particularly in the most sophisticated ones, managers were becoming increasingly aware that their main competitors were not other direct manufacturers of similar equipment, but large companies who bought such equipment and put it together with a range of services to take over certain functions from industrial customers. They realized that they were no longer in the equipment-selling business but in a service business, and that this involved a strategy much different from just pushing sales of new equipment.

This meant that there was a conflict between the way business was done in the field and the way headquarters made money. To be competitive in the field the range of price carriers and the total pricing formula had to be quite different from production 'units'. The difference in logics of 'making money' led to conflicts and a lack of collaboration about developing a truly competitive offering.

In both these cases the failure to see the distinction between the total offering and the price carrier became a serious mental blockage to innovative offering development.

Sometimes the pricing formula of offerings is very complex and I have seen examples of formulas which were seemingly designed to reward the loyal customer but which, in the end, proved to be highly manipulative. Once I was a customer of Fnac, the French retailer of books, music, equipment, computers, etc.:

One can become a 'member' of Fnac by getting (for a small but not insignificant fee) a special membership card. All purchases are registered, and when the customer has FRF 15 000 of purchases the possibility to be rewarded for being a loyal customer has arrived.

The way this takes place is that the customer can choose one particular day on which he will receive a discount of 10 per cent on all the books, compact discs, etc. that he buys on that day, and 6 per cent on computers, hi-fi equipment, and similar items. The discount is not applicable to items already benefiting from a special price reduction.

If the customer does not use all his discount coupons on the particular day of his choice they expire.

This may sound attractive enough, but the reality is very different. If the customer is a good and loyal customer who, for example, regularly buys the latest compact discs as they appear, he will find that the new ones on that particular day are already being discounted (since Fnac has a policy of discounting new discs for the first month after their appearance, in order to encourage customers to buy them quickly in order to reduce stock). The loyalty 'reward' formula therefore selectively punishes the good customer who buys regularly. Second, the discount is not of much value unless the customer really buys fairly large volumes of undiscounted items on that day. So the system is designed not to reward the loyal customer, but to push the loyal customer to buy even more – and in a way as inconvenient to the customer as possible! I, together with many others, loathe this system, but I am still forced to occasionally use Fnac (though I systematically prefer other alternatives if they occur) since Fnac has skilfully (for the owners) managed to drive out competition in the highly fragmented music retail business in France, severely restricting the customer's alternatives.

Bundling functions as long as the price carrier is more or less an exclusive monopoly of the business in question, or as long as the combination of priced and 'free' components is indispensable for the buyer. But under certain conditions bundling becomes challenged and tends to break down. These are:

(a) When some clients use a lot more of the 'free' (i.e. non-price-carrying) components of the offering than others, in which case we end up with strong cross-subsidies from those customers who use relatively fewer of these free components to those who use relatively more of them.

(b) If the supplier loses the monopoly or near-exclusive right to the price-carrying components.

(c) If, for example, new technologies or other changes make it possible to deliver the 'free' components separately or much less expensively.

SUMMARY

This chapter has opposed the traditional view of the economy as products/services transacted for money to 'offerings' as ways to configure co-productive value-creating processes. Such configurations ideally make use of the potentials for co-production explored in Chapter 7, which lead to higher value density.

We have also exposed a number of myths about offerings and transactions. For example, their design doesn't have to be 'frozen' by providers, but they can be co-designed in real time and even as predispositions for the future. They not only carry knowledge from the past but can be designed with a 'code' that stimulates learning. They involve not only money but also a broad and often complex pattern of barter currencies. The offering is not at all the same as the price carrier.

These insights are crucial for R&D and for business concept innovation design.

Three Trends in Offering Development　　9

Moving away from the established view of products/services as objects (tangible or intangible) transacted between suppliers and customers to a view of offerings as *organizers of co-production in Value-creating Systems* implies a distinct shift of emphasis and opens a number of opportunities to look at properties of offerings and of how they are developed. I do not, of course, imply that products or services are not being transacted – I merely state that such a view can beneficially be framed by a broader, more overriding view which sees the economy as a co-productive web of interrelated actors, with value transactions flowing in all directions and multiple currencies being liquefied so as to become actively used to promote value creation.

One way to summarize this view, and also emphasize some trends in offering characteristics, is to point at three emerging properties that tend to become increasingly prominent in offerings. I will focus particularly on one of these.

SERVICIFICATION

The first of these trends is *'servicification'*. This means that the emphasis, when we look at offerings, is no longer on the production process that historically created them as 'outputs', but in their property as *inputs* in the value-creating process of the customer system. This shift of emphasis from *production* to *use*, from *output* to *input*, from the *past* to the *future*, immediately widens the scope of what an offering is, what kinds of characteristics a company needs to build into its offerings, and what competences are required of the company. It also automatically shifts the emphasis from the transaction to a more long-term *relationship* with the customer.

From the factory to the 'user's' value creation

Offerings define the scope of a relationship or perhaps even several relationships. In a sense it defines the value-creation covenant.

In today's typical manufacturing industry, companies have been forced to look further than to the production and sale of their product (or, in the case of service companies, their service). As analysed by many companies and many researchers, cost structures over the life cycle of a product change. Typically, in relative terms, design and research and development costs go up whereas manufacturing costs go down. Costs of distribution and marketing tend to increase. Cost of use tends to rise, as does the cost of recycling (particularly if recycling comes into the calculation of every particular product instead of being seen as a general overhead cost to society).

According to Giarini and Stahel (1993) costs other than manufacturing now typically tend to be over 60 per cent of the total cost related to the product. In some cases, however, the relationship is much higher. For example, according to a study reported by *The Economist* (January 1997) the purchasing price of a personal computer tends to be about 5 per cent of the total cost related to the use of that computer over its economic life span.

With more demanding customers and competitive pressure forcing companies to look at this larger cost equation beyond manufacturing and sales, it is not strange that business companies tend to shift their focus to the perspective of how their products and services are being utilized, both in terms of how costs to the user can be reduced and how revenue and other value creation can be optimized for the user. This is reinforced by the tendency of 'pure' manufacturing to become commoditized.

For example, a car company may make two calculations: one for the manufacturing of their product, and one for the use of the car. Both are valid, but the second one will clearly show that factors other than the cost of manufacturing are more relevant to the user.

Whether the manufacturing company looks at the manufacturing cost equation or the utilization cost equation (in which manufacturing cost

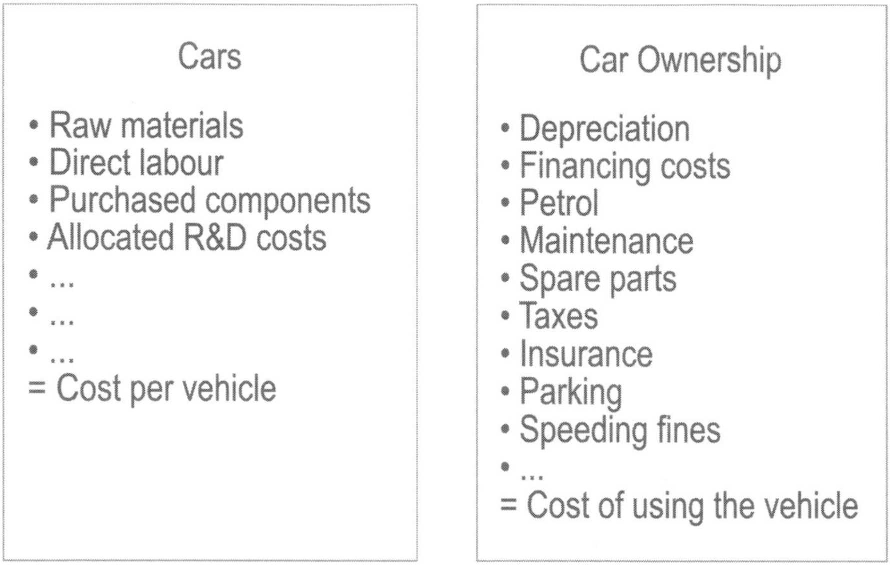

Cars	Car Ownership
• Raw materials • Direct labour • Purchased components • Allocated R&D costs • ... • ... • ... = Cost per vehicle	• Depreciation • Financing costs • Petrol • Maintenance • Spare parts • Taxes • Insurance • Parking • Speeding fines • ... = Cost of using the vehicle

Figure 9.1 Are you in a 'product' or a 'value-creating' business? Two kinds of cost calculation.

and product price are only a limited proportion) will determine its offering design strategy. If it sees itself as selling cars in the traditional industrial mode it will look at the left-hand equation. If it sees itself as selling, for example, 'car ownership economy' (as Volvo, certainly one of the pioneers in this mode of thinking, once put it) its overall offering design strategy will be radically different. For example, Volvo used its high share of the domestic customer base to negotiate deals with an insurance company, an oil company, a rental car company, a credit card company, and others, to ascertain discounts and other services for Volvo customers (in return, Volvo's considerable home market customer base was offered to these particular providers). A number of specific strategies (beyond physical product design) were developed to raise the second-hand value of cars, since depreciation was found to be the largest single cost item for customers. Thus, Volvo mobilized a whole set of economic actors and their assets to leverage the effectiveness of the use of the car – in essence, they designed a Value-creating System which was the real offering to the customer, not the car.

By the same token, offerings serve to 'softwareize' products and services, i.e. making them more effective in the *process of use* by the customers.

The notion of 'softwareization' must be demystified. We are not at all talking about some strange immaterial or intangible properties of the product. Rather, 'softwareization' means *relating assets to each other in such a way that they create more value together*. Thus, softwareization implies re-configuration of assets and actors, making them available for more effective co-production. Offerings link the competences of the provider with the competences and assets of a customer and of other co-producers, so that they together interact in a value-creating process.

In this sense, offerings specify a future process according to certain procedures – a 'liturgy' as one of my Italian clients called it. The genetic code or program depicts a set of steps and interactions between a set of actors working together.

This process may be open-ended. Some offerings lead directly towards a specified goal or end state, but others contain a great deal of discretion or even surprise in their outcome. We go to the movies or to a theme park to be seduced or to be frightened. We enter into a relationship with a bank or an asset manager with the general aim of gaining security. But we do not know exactly what is going to happen and how. The process of future activities is specified only within certain limits. Thus, trust in process is critical.

The offering as a risk management tool

> The revolutionary idea that defines the boundary between modern times and the past is the mastery of risk. (Bernstein, 1996)

The notion of risk and indeed of risk management is implicitly (if not explicitly) *inherent to any offering*. In the industrial economy, producers were typically forced to assume responsibility for the risks related to what had happened in their factories. Products were guaranteed to function as specified and not to break down, as long as customers used them within their design limits.

But in the new economy, with the customer's value-creation process and therefore a longer relationship in focus, the risk picture becomes much more complex. Since it is not really just the product that interests the customer but the whole process of value creation (in which a product plays a part) the provider is expected to take a much longer responsibility and to broaden the scope *from the functioning of the product to the functioning of the Value-creating System.*

> As a part of a consortium the largest Scandinavian construction company, Skanska, got the contract to build an autostrada (motorway) between Helsinki and Lahti in Finland. Of course, they were also held responsible for the road's functioning as a road – that it did not break down, causing excessive repair costs and accidents etc. But, significantly, they are now interested in making the road heavily used, as the compensation from the road authorities is based on traffic volumes, thus promoting initiatives of making the road a generally commercially feasible traffic system.
>
> Users can use the road free of charge. The contract is for 15 years, and it includes the building, financing and maintenance of the road. Finnish National Road Administration will gain the possession of the road in 2012. Until then the contract will bind them to pay based on the use of the road (with an upper limit) to the Skanska-led consortium (other participants are investors, electricity companies, insurance companies).

ABB in Sweden claim that about a third of their business consists of large projects, many of them according to the BOT (Build, Operate, Transfer) formula. Customers do not want a turbine but an energy plant. Or customers do not want an energy plant but energy supply. Or customers do not want energy supply but kilowatt hours delivered to the customers' customers. The difference between building a road and offering a traffic system, or offering a turbine or offering kilowatt hours, is tremendous. Not the smallest of the consequences is that the business company *has to assume responsibility for realms of activities in the future which imply risk and uncertainty*, and which are completely outside the traditional competence area of a product-oriented business organization.

To summarize: As long as offerings were seen as primarily 'outputs' the risk of use was on the side of the customer, whereas the risks normally assumed by the provider were those pertaining to the production process and the technical functioning of the product (for example, product guarantees). With offerings increasingly leading into the future, risks are also related to utilization and value creation in the future. Customers demand (and the competitive game requires) that providers also look to a broader range of risks in the future.

Indeed, many offerings consist more of skills in particular areas of risk management than of anything else. Enron, the energy company which has been appointed 'the most innovative company' by *Fortune* magazine for several years, claims that it has turned electricity and gas distribution into a risk management business. Ryder, the logistics management company, claims that its competitive advantage is its superiority in handling risks related to hardware and to performance when it takes over the logistics function of a client (according to one of their ads: 'If you have downtime you will get missed deliveries and dissatisfied customers'). One of Caterpillar's main competitive arguments has always been that they will be out there in the field very quickly if there is a breakdown (though this example is still generally limited to the functioning of their products, not to the customer's business in a broader sense). General Electric is moving away from selling and charging for aircraft engines to selling functioning engine hours (with a penalty if aircraft are grounded because of engine problems). Companies producing pharmaceutical products, for example insulin, are pushed to provide offerings which are much broader than insulin and which might be termed 'diabetes management'. Thus, LifeChart – a company which focuses on chronic diseases and initially especially asthma – is a joint venture primarily between Nokia and Johnson & Johnson, to reflect the competence mix required for such a business. Car rental companies, and express delivery companies such as DHL, assume the risk that consists of matching the demands of their customer base with the capacity of their fleets on a daily basis. Unless they manage the risk of mismatch they will immediately make losses.

All these and myriads of other companies provide examples of offerings which are based on risk management competences. And the risks that are managed have moved out of the factories and from before the sales transaction and pertaining to the product into the value-creating processes of their customers and into the future.

Traditionally the risks handled by, say, insurance companies were risks caused by 'acts of God'; that is, of factors seen as outside the realm of human control (such as natural catastrophes, illness, lightning, fire, floods). But the risks of today's businesses are highly related to the behaviour of humans and of economic actors – 'acts of people' (Figure 9.2). Illness and its cure, to take one example, is now understood to be to a significant degree a function of life-style and social factors. The consequence of this is that risk assessment and risk management today must be based on other than traditional actuarial competences and on an in-

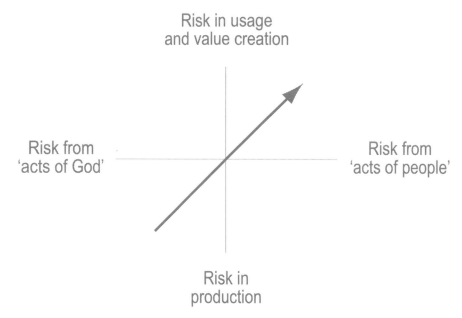

Figure 9.2 The refocusing of risk in the economy.

surance logic. Instead, they must be based on understanding of the functioning of complex systems and of individual and social human behaviour. And the tools for risk management are no longer related only to insurance but also to a logic of _system design_ and of behaviour influencing _pedagogics_ and _incentives_.

The increasing focus on _brands_ is also relevant to risk. In a very noisy world, with many providers, customers evaluate offerings based on many parameters, not least including how much risk they would entail. If the offering is associated with, or identified with, a recognized institutional context or brand this is seen by customers as reducing the perceived risk. It can certainly also reduce the objective risk. In areas where customers themselves run great risks (for example, because they are evaluated by their boards) and where there is great perceived risk or uncertainty, managers tend to choose 'safe' brands: IBM for computers and information systems, McKinsey for number crunching and cost-reduction schemes. Thus the offering

- specifies, explicitly or implicitly, who stands for what risks
- specifies (again, explicitly or implicitly) risk management tools.

E-IFICATION

The second trend could be called *'e-ification'* – with perhaps an opportunistic nod to the popular topic of 'e-commerce' and 'e-business'. I will let that stand as a symbol not only for e-commerce but also for the more general phenomenon that offerings, customer contacts, and interaction, as well as other properties of offerings, can now more than ever be unbundled into various parts and rebundled in new ways. Information can be unbundled from mass. Interaction between a company and its partners and customers can take place by many channels including, of course, the Internet. Companies who do not recognize the opportunities for 'e-ification' in this sense – that is, for the opportunities to change their business models according to the new rules of unbundling and rebundling – will seriously lag in competitiveness. In a great number of purchasing processes customers now use multiple channels including the Internet for gathering information and for fulfilling part of the transaction. When General Electric delivers an aircraft engine or the Xerox Corporation a copying or document-handling machine, those products remain linked to the respective company digitally, and the companies continue to support their effective functioning even if they are physically located in the user system.

The Internet and e-commerce will not lead to a particular sector of the economy doing business over the Internet with another sector not doing so. Instead, the significance of new interactive media is the possibility to analyse all business processes in terms of what parts of them can be performed in the dematerialized information domain and what parts are to be performed in the domain of physical activities. The end result will be major reconfiguration – but not a distinction between two ways of doing business.

EXPERIENCIFICATION

The third trend I will call *'experiencification'*. By this I mean that offerings are now increasingly designed to be linked also into *the mental and symbolic processes of customers* including the meaning and purpose of their value-creating activities. In fact, many offerings which seem like 'products' are simply artefacts which fulfil the function of bringing to the customer a context, a story even, which is somehow meaningful to him. Artefacts link a more general, external 'reality' with an inner, personal, 'reality' into a whole characterized by *the pursuit of meaning and purpose*.

It is claimed that various kinds of 'experience business' are now possibly the largest sector of the economy, if we can talk about such a sector. What I refer to as 'experiencification' is not a sectorial phenomenon but a general and growing *aspect* of practically all or at least most businesses today. For example, cars for most people have long since ceased being simply objects used for functional transportation; they represent symbolic universa, and are therefore supposed to express personality and create meaning for the customer. The car business is an example of a business which, compared to some decades ago, has rapidly become more experiencified, more e-ified, and more servicified.

BUSINESS MODELS, OFFERING PATTERNS, AND RECONFIGURATION

Why is there so much reconfiguration of business today? Earlier we found that an important part of the answer is 'because reconfiguration is possible': because it is now possible to unbundle sets of activities and assets, because it is possible to create liquid global markets for assets and competences and information, and because it is possible to interactively rebundle what has been unbundled into new patterns.

It is possible – therefore it will be done. This is what was referred to as *the vacuum principle*.

When reconfiguration takes place, *'the principle of density'* applies. By identifying (customers') value-creating processes and creating offerings which leverage and match these processes as 'densely' as possible we can begin to formulate principles for effective offerings and for how to combine and link up resources in ways that answer to the criterion of density while simultaneously being internally coherent and consistent with the value-creating processes they match. From this general view of value creation we have come to see offerings as tools to mobilize assets and link them together so that they are brought together to leverage value-creating processes. Offerings are tools for reconfiguration by meeting new patterns of co-production. Three general thrusts of offering design trends have been identified.

'Servicification' means refocusing the offering from the product to the use (or rather value creation) situation. If the context is such that 'servicification' is a good growth strategy (or even a necessary strategy to maintain customer relationships and therefore to leverage existing assets) the set of competences required must change and usually broaden. A company then needs to become the designer of a Value-creating System whose participants can together co-create the new offering. Thus, a pattern of reconfiguration – of new institutional linkages as well as of rebundling at the offering and activity level – will have to take place.

'e-ification' reflects that new technology enables us to separate even more clearly physical activities and various virtual (information and concept based) activities in business processes. To develop offerings according to such new rules of the game new constellations of activities and actors will again most likely be required. Take the example of pharmacy, or healthcare. It is now, for example, possible to sell and inform about drugs and drug use over the Internet, while delivery still must take place physically. It is also possible to further enhance the information content, and to enable further learning on the patient's side through the Internet by not only creating portals and specialized home pages (some companies in the healthcare area create a particular web page for each individual customer, such as Merck-MedCo, a pharmacy benefit manager) but also to enable customers to meet and learn from each other both physically (such as is the case in several experiments in Kaiser Permanente and in other organizations) or over the Internet in chat groups. And physical delivery can be done either over the pharmacy or via a DHL package.

Thus, new technologies lead to many more options in configuring the offering, and therefore in designing the Value-creating Systems and the value constellation that delivers it.

The third trend identified, 'experiencification', enables us to think about more dimensions of the value-creating processing that our offerings match and leverage, leading to more density. Experiencification reflects an enlarged notion of value, beyond the rational and into the realms of aesthetics, ethics, and – generally – mind processes of customers. Here, again, new competences and therefore reconfigured value constellations will be required.

We can also look at the reasons for and patterns of reconfiguration from another angle, namely that of the technical cost structure-related 'business model' used by a company. When technologies change, relative factor availability and factor prices in the economy also change. When information is unbundled from the physical objects the information is about its availability increases and its cost tends to go down – information becomes free. In the information market, marginal cost tends to creep down to zero. Still, average cost may be quite high since the up-front investments and the infrastructure necessary to provide this free information is expensive.

This, then, requires rethinking business models: How can we at the same time claim that the most important battles in the new economy are about information, and yet say that information is free? It is obvious that if we have information but we cannot make money from the information as such we must find other 'price carriers', i.e. a business model which allows us to make money although we may have to give away something for free.

This is the cause, in summary, for *reframing* to achieve *reconfiguration* and *rebundling*. The *vacuum principle*, the *density imperative*, and the *search for new business models* which reflect the shifting values and prices of various assets thus together explain most of the development directions that *offerings* take today. And they therefore also explain why value constellations need to change, and why therefore we see such a very strong *reconfiguration* within and across industry boundaries as well as national boundaries.

To handle this, companies and other organizations must find ways to evolve their mind-sets. This is the area towards which we now turn.

Part IV
The Map-landscape Interaction

INGRESSO ⟶ **PART I**
THE MAP AND
THE LANDSCAPE

Chapter **1**
EVOLUTION OF
STRATEGIC PARADIGMS

Chapter **19**
WHAT LEADERS
NEED TO DO

Chapter **18**
BRINGING EXTERNAL AND
INTERNAL DYNAMICS IN LINE

PART VII
LEADERSHIP FOR
NAVIGATION

Chapter **2**
RECONFIGURING THE
VALUE SPACE

Chapter **16**
FROM GREAT IDEAS
TO GREAT COMPANIES

Chapter **17**
CAPABILITIES FOR ACHIEVING
THE CRITICAL OUTCOMES

Chapter **3**
SOME CONSEQUENCES
OF DEMATERIALIZATION

PART VI
CAPABILITIES
FOR PURPOSEFUL
EMERGENCE

PART II
SHAPERS OF
THE LANDSCAPE

Chapter **4**
CHAINED TO THE
VALUE CHAIN?

Chapter **15**
THE CRANE AT WORK
IN THE DESIGN SPACE

PART III
TOOLS FOR
LANDSCAPING

Chapter **7**
CO-PRODUCTION: TOWARDS
INCREASED DENSITY

Chapter **5**
PRIME MOVERS
AS RECONFIGURERS

Chapter **14**
THE MENTAL SPACE
FOR REFRAMING

Chapter **8**
THE OFFERING AS A TOOL
TO ORGANIZE CO-PRODUCTION

Chapter **6**
PRIME MOVERSHIP
AS ECOGENESIS

Chapter **13**
THE PROCESS CRITERIA
OF THE CRANE

Chapter **12**
ON CRANES AND
SKY-HOOKS

Chapter **9**
THREE TRENDS IN
OFFERING DEVELOPMENT

PART IV
THE
MAP-LANDSCAPE
INTERACTION

PART V
REFRAMING:
TOOLS FOR
MAP MAKING

Chapter **11**
CHANGE AND
CREATION

Chapter **10**
FITTING INTO
THE ENVIRONMENT

Fitting into the Environment   **10**

FITNESS CONTEXT AND MENTAL MODELS

'Fitness context' is a term used in the study of evolution. As we discover, say, the fossil of a curiously configured animal we must assume that this animal has at one time or another been able to survive, and that its configuration – however strange to us – must have had a fit with the context in which it lived. From the study of such fossils we can therefore make inferences about the nature of the environment in which they lived. The same applies to organizations.

Many of today's organizations' business and management models tell stories about old fitness contexts, about the world in which they originated and subsequently evolved.

> Analysing just about any European airline will evoke images of the marriage between military and industrial bureaucracy within a nationalistic context in the pre- or post-Second World War period. 'National' telecom companies (including equipment producers) invariably seem unable to shed basic remnants of their monopolistic and protected situations. Car producers still secretly seem to nourish the nostalgia of the post-war period when customers lined up for years to get one of their products, and are just getting into the 'product plus' stage (or trap) – although some may be on the verge of more profoundly rethinking themselves. European national healthcare systems tell us about an era in which governments benevolently stretched out a hand to people to form a social contract in the post-war period, looking around and finding the industrial model to shape the operational mode of their business; the customer/citizen supposed to be happy with whatever was offered.
>
> Makers of chips and of personal computers had a brief period of glory

until they (or some of them) realized that they were in a price-competitive commodity business; most of them could not change before events had marginalized them.

We can learn two essential lessons from the above. First, every organization must find, as its *raison d'être*, some kind of harmony, fit, consonance, with its environment. This does not necessarily imply a passive adaptation to the environment. The fit may also come from a more proactive stand, in which an organism or organization manages to impose itself and influence or change the environment.

Second, the consonance is not for ever. When the context changes, the organization must change – or again impose itself on the context.

An organization may just find a place to fit in, or it may fulfil an important function in the environment, so that it may in itself be a prerequisite for the state of the total context. In the latter case we may speak about the organism or organization having a 'mission'. The mission is a measure of the extent to which the context would change, or become less efficient, if the focal organization were not there. Some organizations characterized by strong missions have had a decisive influence on the larger context – they have set their footprints on the history of the evolution of business and value creation, in either a global or a more local context. Examples of organizations from the twentieth century who have had, in this sense, a strong mission are Ford, Apple, Microsoft, Nokia – just to restrict ourselves to business organizations. But when the context evolves the institutional scenery changes.

Contextual change is the cradle of new institutions. A very good example is the birth of industrialism. Although it was strongly based on the development of science and of science-based technology the implications for society at large were also deep. The rise of capitalism and of democracy, and of political parties (most of which even today seem to be founded in the conflict between labour and capital which was a characteristic of early industrialism), labour market organizations, financial institutions, society's education system, and healthcare systems – the main institutional structures we see around ourselves can somehow be traced back to the breakthrough of industrialism.

DISTINCTIVE COMPETENCE AND FIT

Nobody has more eloquently described the process by which fit between an institution and the external world comes about than Selznick in his book *Leadership in Administration* (1957). To him, an organization can emerge and exist if it stands for values, mission, or purpose, which are meaningful in a larger context – which give the organization a distinct role in the external world. Thus, the main function of leadership is to express the purpose of the organization in this external context, and the values that allow the organization to pursue its purpose.

However – and still following Selznick's argument – it is not enough with a fit between purpose and values, on the one hand, and the external world, on the other. An institution's purpose and key values must also be 'embodied' in a social structure – what we call an organization. The purpose or mission then becomes *institutionalized*. 'Distinctive competence', as he calls it, is this ability to achieve fit between *the external world*, the *purpose and values*, and *the social organization* that embodies the values and therefore allows the institution to in effect create value that is relevant to the external world. As opposed to more current schools of 'core competence' (notably Prahalad and Hamel, 1990) thinking, Selznick's concept of 'distinctive competence' therefore is a systemic one, expressed as fit between elements rather than any generic element as such.[13] Ramirez and Wallin (2000) get closer to Selznick by distinguishing between business competences and management competences.

Institutionalization or embodiment of purpose, according to Selznick, happens through making *value commitments* which define the *organization's character*, and then building these into the social structure. *Critical decisions* about embodiment such as recruitment, training, systems for representation of group interests, cooperation with other institutions, therefore build the institution. Without such critical decisions an organization is unlikely to be able to fulfil its purpose and achieve distinctive competence. They imply longer-term commitments to structure and values and are therefore character-defining.

The organizational structure therefore is an 'artefact' (Stymne, 2000) that both results from and reinforces the purpose and values of the organization. It is crucial for any institution to defend its values and the structures and artefacts that embody these values, *many of which are precarious* and will be subjected to attacks from external opponents and internal opposition groups, or will simply be likely to peter out unless they are strongly advocated and defended by 'elites' with sufficient autonomy (Selznick, 1957, p. 121). The process of developing the distinctive competence of the organization in this sense is called 'institutional leadership' by Selznick.

The role of artefacts in both maintaining and changing the identity of an institution will be revisited in Chapter 17.

THE 'BUSINESS IDEA' AS AN EXPRESSION OF FIT

Whereas it is futile to find single factors that consistently explain great achievements it seems possible to find certain characteristics of patterns of factors that do so. It is in the co-alignment into a coherent 'Gestalt', where various activities support and reinforce each other, that the secret of at least temporary success can be found.

The subject of my book *Management for Growth* (1975/1977) was this process of achieving consonance (which sometimes requires the creation of tension and use of lack of consonance, as will be illustrated in following chapters). I tried to summarize and operationalize this systemic thinking developed in the SIAR School[14] under the label of 'Business Idea': A unique, historically evolved set of factors related to each other in a pattern. In parallel to the 'business idea' I also introduced the notion of the 'growth idea', which van der Heijden (1996) partly integrated in his evolutionary development of the business idea concept. This notion of fit between elements and activities has also, more recently, been discovered in the American management literature (Porter, 1996).

By the business idea I meant not a banal statement about what business we are in, but the concrete, functioning pattern of factors and their interaction which together determined and explained a company's 'way to make money', to borrow a favourite expression developed by the late Eric Rhenman.

The overall principle therefore is one of *consonance* or *fit*. Every business idea is unique (how boring business would be if this were not the case; and there would hardly be any use for business schools and management consultants!). But it is still possible to discern certain classes of factors which have to be part of a business idea. At the most abstract level one can distinguish between three:

- The external environment, its 'needs' and values and what it is valuing – what is crucial to the larger system in which the organization works and which it can provide.
- The offering (earlier on I used the term 'product' or 'product system') of the company.
- Internal factors such as organization structure, resources, organized knowledge and capabilities, equipment, systems, leadership, values.

To bring all these factors together is no easy task, even though at a superficial level it might seem so. Göran Carstedt, during his period as head of IKEA North America, once told me:

> Everybody sees that we are successful, and many try to copy us. But what they don't understand is the complexity of the system, the infinite number of details which have to be there and the underlying processes that have to function. Our business is the result of a long learning process, and many make the mistake of believing that they can leapfrog that process but so far they have failed.

'The concept of a business idea has a deeper meaning', to quote from my earlier book. It consists of many subtle elements, many of which transcend the domain of the conscious and escape codification.

My studies of service-producing organizations made me more sensitive to certain elements of a business idea related to 'intangibles', such as image and communication strategy, internal value systems, and the capabilities of co-productive customers. The result was the 'service management system' (Normann, 1984/2000); which also builds on Eiglier and Langeard (1987). (see Figure 10.1).

THE CORE PROCESS OF RENEWING THE DOMINATING IDEAS

The core process of a company in the long term is to form new 'dominating ideas' which are in line with the evolution of the external context, and then to ensure that these ideas are expressed in a manifest organizational structure and mode of functioning.

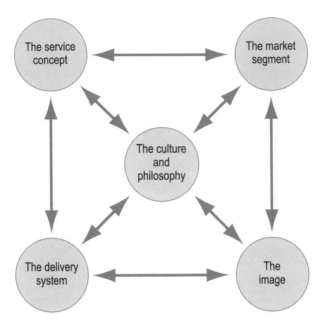

Figure 10.1 'The service management system': A framework for analysis of 'fit' to explain success or lack of success.

No other process in any organization is more fundamental in the long term than this renewal of the dominating ideas, this reappreciation of an organization's identity and way of manifesting it, in the face of environmental change. The process is by no means sequential. Actions that create new linkages, and the invention and use of artefacts that un- and refocus attention will catalyse the evolution of ideas.

When the dominating ideas and the action consequences of them are not in phase with an evolving external contextual logic management has failed in its core process. The appropriate expression for this could be a travesty on Albert Einstein:

> We need a new way of thinking to solve the problems caused by the old way of thinking.

It is not difficult to find striking examples of how the application of a framework – the set of dominating ideas – which was developed for and worked beautifully in one type of situation causes rather than solves problems when applied to a new situation. At the time of writing this I immediately come to think of a number of such examples:

- The French government is trying to cure alarming unemployment levels by shortening work time and making it illegal to work more than 35 hours per week, by making it more difficult for young entrepreneurs to move outside France, by threatening to put special taxes on temporary work, and by making it even more difficult to lay off people. All this might have worked 20 years ago in another world. For reasons obvious from the analysis of the new logic of value creation, all of these measures are certain – other things being equal – to lead to an increase in unemployment and a relative decrease in economic growth in the new situation.

- In a series of articles in the *Los Angeles Times* in 1998, Alvin and Heidi Toffler have made a fascinating analysis of Japan showing how ten golden rules which propelled Japan into the world's second most powerful economy will, if applied today, aggravate Japan's current problems rather than solve them. Typical old truths that need to be reinterpreted and put on their heads, include: men are more important than women; obedience is more important than opposition; large companies are more important than small companies.

CHANGE AS CONTINUITY: THE PARADOX

In his book *The Leopard* the author Giuseppe Tomasi di Lampedusa lets one of his characters from the Sicilian aristocracy utter: 'If we want things to stay as they are, things will have to change.' This phrase is not only filled with human wisdom, it also captures one of the most essential features of systems theory and the theory of complexity. A system cannot be seen, or even defined, in isolation. Its environment is not only the context in which it exists and evolves, but it is actually part of the system. For example, the so called 'Gaia Hypothesis' (Lovelock, 1979) posits that the atmosphere of the earth is not a prerequisite for life but is actually *part* of life. (Perhaps this is what an oil company had in mind when it ran a series of ads for its lubricants stating – perceptively – that 'The oil is a part of the engine'.)

Selznick's idea that distinctive competence and the character of the organization is a systemic concept referring to fit between elements, rather than to any element in itself, is entirely consistent with Gaia and with Lampedusa's statement. An organization that remains stable can lose its identity, whereas an organization that reshapes itself – even dramatically – can retain and reinforce its identity in so doing. The notion of 'sticking to your knitting' may lead a company completely astray, whereas a company that reinvents itself by changing its customer offerings, its organization, and many of its management systems may in fact be perceived as maintaining its ethos.

Illustration: The Swedish consumer cooperative

1999 saw the hundredth birthday of Kooperativa Förbundet, the Swedish consumer cooperative. As birthdays can be, this was a time of reflection, and I was given the opportunity to write a book with a colleague (Normann and Nordfors, 1999), attempting to look ahead from the platform established over a century of existence. We used a Selznick-inspired framework for the analysis as illustrated in Figure 10.2.

When the consumer cooperative was founded in 1899 Sweden was a poor country at the periphery of a European continent which had seen enormous changes in its national boundaries and which experienced deep social tensions. There had been famine and huge emigration to North America. Broad masses of people experienced that society was unfair to

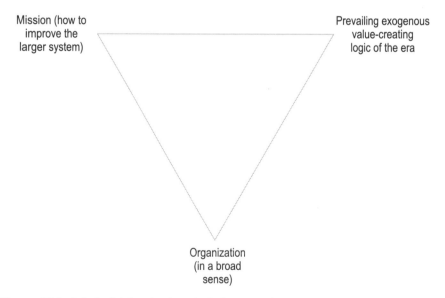

Figure 10.2 A Selznick-inspired analysis framework.

them. Production and also distribution of food was largely in the hands of monopolies or oligopolies and prices were high while supply was scarce. But it was also a period of hope in the developments of science, technology, and industrialist methods of creating wealth and welfare. It was in the tension field between social injustice and the new opportunities enabled by new technology, and between industrialism as a means to create wealth for capital owners and industrialism as a means to create value and welfare for the masses, that the consumer cooperative was born as a highly entrepreneurial act.

Industrialization by then had emerged as a strong force. It had been proven that goods, including food, could be mass produced on a large scale and made available at lower cost than before. So the basic mechanisms to handle the problems indicated in the mission were there; the point was that building factories and distribution systems required capital which was not available.

Industrialism meant that differentiation of tasks along the rational chain of value added activities replaced the traditional agriculture and craft oriented society's local, closed system views of value creation. Scale advantages and mass production took place in huge, rationally planned factories run according to a philosophy of what was later to be thought of as 'Fordism' and 'Taylorism'. Organizations were shaped like pyramids – hierarchical and bureaucratic (note that 'bureaucratic', as described by Weber, was a positive and not a negative concept at that time!). Power came from capital which allowed the creation and ownership of factories.

The organization also realized that for its long-term fulfilment of its mission to create better conditions for broad masses of people not only short-term supply of food and other goods but also supply of knowledge and education was important.

Thus, there was a clear *mission* – something that was really important to the larger system and to a great constituency of people. And the emerging *value-creating logic* of the era was that of industrialism, which held the promise to technically solve the problems and fulfil the mission, and which was accepted and embraced by the cooperative movement. The question was how to get the resources and how to organize. It also accepted the basic hierarchical, 'bureaucratic' organization structure as an efficient means to manage.

The dilemma of the consumer cooperative movement was that it did not have the capital necessary for fully exploiting the new value-creating logic and making the masses benefit from it. So there was a clear idea about the *environment*, about the *mission*, and about the *model of organization*. But the *capital* was lacking. The great innovation was related to the embodiment of the purpose and the means to fulfil it in the *social organization*, namely by changing the role description of the 'consumer', from somebody at the end of the value chain (a term that had probably not been invented at the time but which was certainly a concept alive in the minds of people in the era) to becoming a multiple role holder: that of being also an owner, and to some extent a controller and manager.

Note that the basic idea of the hierarchy was not discarded; the novelty was exactly in allocating more roles to the consumer than was done in other competing organizations.

Thus, letting the customers become owners, and letting the customers reap the benefits that shareholders reaped in other organizations, was a means of transcending the difficulty of mobilizing capital.

In this way there was a balance between conditions in the outside world – the *dissatisfaction* of large groups of people, *the available knowledge and technology* to fulfil this dissatisfaction in the form of industrialist methods, on the one hand; and the *mission and values*, on the other; and finally between the way the purpose and mission and value-creating logic was embodied innovatively in the *social organization* which transcended traditional role definitions. All of this allowed the organization to create more value through cooperative efforts.

This formula enabled the consumer cooperative to make remarkable achievements over a long period of time. Its view of the customer as more than just a buyer of the products also allowed it to be the pioneer in opening self-service shops in Sweden. The built-in involvement and care for the customer's situation also pushed the coop to be a pioneer in customer education and the consumerism movement. However, in the last quarter of the twentieth century it became increasingly clear that the organization was losing market share and that it was also losing its attraction to the majority of the population.

An analysis of the new context, 100 years later in 1999, reveals a number of dilemmas. First, the mission of the organization, namely to help the masses to have access to daily goods materially and inexpensively, is nothing that really engages a lot of people. Anybody can have roughly the same products of the same quality at the same prices from a great number of sources. Nor is KF uniquely equipped to listen to customers any more – other organizations use equally advanced methods to learn about their customers. And, in particular, ownership is hardly important any longer. Huge amounts of capital are available for anybody who has an idea. As we have seen earlier in this book, the critical competences of business companies no longer lie in dominating capital and the factory, but in organizing value creation. More and more organizations see ownership of physical assets more as a burden than a benefit, and instead base themselves on the management of information and knowledge.

What are the consequences for KF? Does it need to scrap itself, does the old formula hold, or does it need to reinvent itself?

Here we stand before a situation in which it is crucial to review what is the true identity of the organization, in terms of fit between the environment, the values, and the embodiment of the values and purpose in a social organization.

In the analysis we made we contrasted two ways of explaining the identity (or, as Selznick would have it, the 'distinctive competence') of KF. The original one had come to be interpreted as the relationship between power and ownership. We suggested a more general one:

The fundamental theme of the cooperative idea is that individuals cooperate to create value for themselves and for each other. The idea is based on our experience that the individual person can get more out of his or her resources if he or she cooperates with others. In cooperation with others value added is created which each individual cannot create on his or her own.

We can generalize 'the triangle' of fit between environment, values and organization for a new era:

- *The environment*: First, today's *'needs'* of households are hardly focused on access to material daily goods. Instead studies clearly show that people are much more concerned with issues such as their health, their long-term education, unemployment, to get a meaningful life. Second, the dominating *value-creating logic* today is not one of industrialism, but one of interactivity and cooperation within a knowledge-based service economy.
- *The purpose and mission and values*: Thus, KF is no longer fulfilling a function that is at the core of people's 'needs' and ambitions in today's world. If the mission is not to give people daily goods but to play a central role in whatever people are mostly concerned about in their lives (as material welfare was a hundred years ago) KF should look at areas other than traditional retailing as its sole activity.
- *The organization and social structure*: The pyramid has given way to net-works, and ownership of physical assets is hardly the critical issue anymore. However, cooperation for creating value with and for each other is a more modern idea than it has probably ever been! But ownership and co-operation are not necessarily closely linked.

What we find, consequently, is that what was a strong and innovative fit between the three elements a hundred years ago can hardly be so any longer, since all the elements have changed so thoroughly. But the key idea of KF a hundred years ago, namely *cooperation* (if seen as something beyond joint ownership), is more modern than ever. There are still very urgent missions out there to be fulfilled for the customers, and many of the established organizations now catering to them are inefficient. And the value-creating logic of organized co-production could be a very strong means of handling the new missions that impose themselves.

Consequently, the organization is at a crossroads. It has lost its identity as a pioneer having a true liberating impact on the masses of people. Re-establishing itself as such a pioneer it would have to reconsider what is the new context, how it could reinterpret its mission (not discard it), and how it could reinterpret its opportunities to fulfil it (by cooperation, but in its modern forms). The opportunities are obvious. The question is whether the institutional and cognitive barriers prohibit such a reinterpretation and its necessary manifestation in new structures.

Might there be a new equation, the possibility to evolve, out of these ingredients, a new fit between the external environment, the fundamental values of fairness and justice, the capability to organize innovatively for co-production around important issues? Could KF prove, definitely, that it was not just a great idea which had had a long life-span, but also a truly great company?

The opportunities for change are there. Change might have radical consequences. Yet, paradoxically, the most fundamental idea of the original identity of the company, if revisited and reinterpreted, would be the obvious thrust of a renewal.

THE CONTINUITY HUB OF REFRAMING: WHAT SHOULD STAY THE SAME?

Change, even radical, in organizations does not mean throwing the baby out with the bathwater. More often than not elements which are relics from an old 'fitness context' remain for too long. But some of the companies I worked with intensely for the last few years had so effectively pruned down their corporate head offices in an effort to demonstrate the need to cut costs (which is often justified, but the question is what and how to cut) that there simply was hardly any structure left to embody the mental processes necessary for renewal beyond slimming down.

What to retain in a change process must be the result of the *mission and of the business idea* that an organization adopts. But whatever is retained –

whatever is the 'continuity' face of change – this something must be re-framed into another systemic context, put into another business idea and management model.

The 'continuity hub' in a change process may be certain existing *physical assets*. In Appendix 1 we describe how the city of Naples found that many of the natural and cultural assets were thoroughly under-utilized. So our recommendation, which was gradually implemented with at least initial success, was to leverage those assets by creating interactive networks among various institutional units in and outside the city and region.

The hub of the reframing may also be *capabilities* (which historically may have been developed based on other assets). Some companies, like 3M, Canon, Olympus, have done this very consciously. By creating organizational structures (such as 'platform organizations', cf. Ciborra, 1996) which continuously nurture crucial capabilities and which institutionalize confrontations and dialogue between people, capabilities, and user situations such companies have been able to continuously manifest themselves in new products and customer offerings.

This notion of organizing around competences or capabilities, introduced by Selznick, was further developed by Emery and Trist (1965). In highly complex situations where it is neither possible to impose oneself on the environment, to forecast and plan, a system may choose to identify with what is clearly a 'leading part' in this turbulent and unpredictable system, and somehow follow and complement that leading part. Another possible choice is to identify capabilities and organize to nurture them. This argument is the essential premise of the 'core competence school' of strategy.

A third hub around which to reframe is the *customers,* who then become elements around which change revolves.

As today's 'dotcom companies' try to find their way this is very often their main (or often last resort) strategy. By developing their website which originally served to acquire customers by offering a certain product (such as books) into a portal they try to leverage the value of the customer contacts. The same logic was behind Sears' attempt in the early 1980s to sell new services to customers visiting their stores ('buy stocks where you buy socks'), or behind bank-insurance mergers. Such reframing strategies thus conform to the second of the strategic logics analysed in Chapter 1. Many of them backfire because they do not reflect the customer's purchasing *process* (though they may reflect the customer's 'needs'), because they blur the company's image, or because they introduce too much operational complexity. My experience is that companies who ask 'What more can we sell?' almost invariably fail. The right question is: 'How can we leverage the customer's value creation?'

DIGRESSION: CUSTOMER BASE ANALYSIS

A particularly strong technique for establishing an organization's point of departure, which my colleagues and I developed in the early 1980s, is customer base analysis. It uses activity-based costing (although we – nor anybody else? – did not know the term at the time) and positions the customer and the customer relationship as the organizing factor of the whole analysis. Essentially, a customer base analysis has four elements:

1   *Customer profitability analysis, CPA*. All the company's customer relationships are analysed from a 'profit per customer' perspective. The revenue side is usually fairly easy, but the cost side is more complicated. What we found in just about any of the fifty or so customer base analyses that we made was that companies had surprisingly little understanding of the various indirect costs (transaction costs, and relationship costs), that were customer dependent (as opposed to, say, product dependent).

2   *Analysis of the customer's value creation logics*. This may entail qualitative analysis such as understanding what business logics various customers have – what value they try to create and how they go about it. This analysis is then combined with the customer profitability analysis. Qualitative methods such as participant observation, in-depth interviews (including with customers' customers), focus groups, and social anthropology, are essential here.

3   *Cluster analysis*. By statistical methods combined with qualitative studies various relevant customer clusters are then identified. The goal is to group together customers who display similar characteristics in terms of why and how the organization succeeds or fails to generate good economic results with and for these customers.

4.   *Identification of key 'battle-fields'*. Typically, each of the clusters displays its own characteristics, requires a particular offering development strategy, and is threatened by various types of external competitors and invaders.

By complementing such analysis with studies and interpretations of the competitive situations (established players versus invaders; see Normann *et al.*, 1989), and by tracking down the key driving forces destabilizing the situation it will be possible to develop a fairly clear idea of where the organization is, what its distinctive competence is, and what sort of changes its situation is undergoing.

In one (typical) example we looked into a bank with 2.1 million individual retail customers. The customer profitability analysis showed that only 400 000 of these generated a profit, whereas each and everyone of 1.7 million generated zero or negative profitability. In fact, the 400 000 customers generated a total result which was four times that of the bottom line of the bank's retail business operations; thus, 75% of the result created by the profitable customers was used to subsidize the rest of the customers while 25% went to management and shareholders.

The next step was to group the customers in a simple matrix of two dimensions (see Figure 10.3): How much revenue they generated in terms of product contribution margin, and in terms of how much (non-product-related) cost they caused the bank. This led to a (quantified) first map of the customer base and indicated a set of first, rough strategies.

The high contribution–low cost customers were obviously very valuable and also highly exposed to attacks by competitors and particularly 'Invader banks' (operating according to principles similar to those of the Oslobanken which was described earlier). Measures to protect and to cement the relationships with these customers were clearly important.

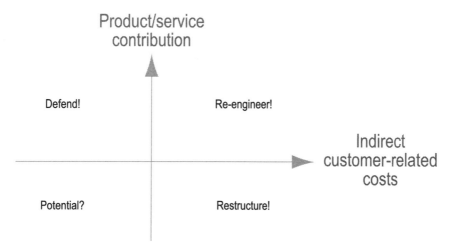

Figure 10.3 Identification of strategic battlefields in the customer base.

The high contribution–high cost group was a large and interesting segment of the customer base which called for action to restructure the customer relationship and particularly to design offerings to induce less costly customer behaviour. New account formulas and pricing systems were developed for this purpose.

The low contribution–low cost segment was considered a lesser priority for the moment, although steps were taken to look more deeply into the potential of these customer relationships.

The low contribution–high cost customers, in contrast, were a high priority. This was a large group, and no distinct patterns could be seen at first. However, in-depth socio-demographic studies, focus groups, and other analyses gradually made it possible to identify a number of very different patterns. For example, some of these customers had a very high potential but had chosen to put the profitable part of their banking business in another bank. Another distinct group consisted of young students who in all likelihood represented a potential for the future, so it was deemed rational to invest even more in this group. Other customers showed in this large but heterogeneous group various kinds of specific behaviour which was highly costly. For example, it was found that about 20 000 customers literally had become world champions in writing cheques ('free' to the customer but costly to the bank). A number of archetype solutions for such customers were developed centrally, and each branch manager was asked to contact the 20 or 30 (on average) such cheque equilibrists personally to suggest an alternative solution to their payment transaction habits. Within a short period, a dramatic increase of profitability in this particular group had resulted.

Since we started this customer base analyses technological innovations in database management have allowed companies to develop CRM (Customer Relationship Management) systems which are often used to differentiate service levels based on customer profitability segmentation. Unfortunately this has often had the consequence that steps (2)–(4) as described above are not carried out. To many companies this has resulted in superficial strategizing, dissatisfied customers, and missed short- and long-term business opportunities.

SUMMARY

Organizations, like organisms, are embedded in external contexts. They not only adapt to the context; they contribute to it, to form an ecosystem of value creation.

Establishing 'fit' with the context is necessary for survival and demands ongoing questioning of the mental framework or dominating ideas, including the mission or *raison d'être*.

But words and thoughts are not enough, they must be manifested in concrete structural arrangements which come about as the result of critical decisions. 'Distinctive competence' and 'Business idea' are notions that stand for a systemic, multidimensional, and dynamic institutionalization of knowledge development.

Contextual change may require radical change within organizations and is therefore the typical cradle of institutional renewal in society. A brief comparison between the top companies in any of the well-known 'Top ...' lists between now and five or ten years ago easily demonstrates the point, and then again such lists do not show how radically different one and the same company is today, should its name happen to appear on both lists.

Yet, no change starts from nothing. The 'old' practically always has elements which can be shown to have a potentially higher *positional value* if put into a new context. *It is such proactive systemic change* – reconfiguration – *in which the value of certain assets is leveraged by fitting the assets into a different system, that we refer to as resulting from reframing.* Such undervalued (because located in an inappropriate systemic context) assets can be identified and serve as the 'hubs' of reframing, i.e. as the points of departure for a redesign.

Change and Creation 11

SUPER-RATIONALITY AND QUASI-INNOVATIVENESS

All activities involve uncertainties. But there is a great difference between uncertainty that stems from variations around some more or less stable 'normal' state, and changes that represent irreversible trends and leaps in the parameters of a system. The former require 'management', applying techniques for optimizing given the more or less predictable risks and uncertainties within a framework, whereas the latter require the questioning and evolution of a framework. Structural change can only be dealt with through structural change. This is the task of leadership.

Can structural change come about as a result of continuous improvement or does it require more dramatic moves in large steps? If the latter approach was favoured by most theories of 'strategic decision-making' of the 1960s and 1970s, continuous improvement has come into favour later on. This is due not least to the success of Japanese companies in the 1970s and 1980s which gradually came to manifest itself in management theory. There was less belief in big decisions from the top, and the notion of 'the learning organization' in which everybody is stimulated not only to operate but also to evolve the system became attractive. In addition, new theories about 'emergence' in complex systems seemed to grant decision makers at the top less power than had been assumed. Thus, 'the rise and fall of strategic planning' (Mintzberg, 1994).

The learning organization which continuously builds new knowledge in small steps and spreads it through the organization is attractive and a necessity, but is it enough? Sometimes it seems to become an alibi for not seriously questioning the overall framework. In addition, the changes in the value-creating context today seem to be of a magnitude that requires extraordinary efforts.

Innovation, and the processes that lead to it, are disturbingly often explained in simplistic terms. The nature of innovation is inherently complex, dialectic, characterized by dilemmas and uncertainty. Innovation, after all, deals with a future state that we cannot really know. Can we 'plan' it? And if not – do we need to abandon any ambition to intervene in it?

All too often we find the archetypal 'rational' organization, operating on the principle of negative (corrective) feedback and steering clear of disturbing and chaotic territories, trying to give the impression that it is in control. Usually, this type of organization tries to pay lip-service to what it is not. It is even quite common for large corporations to keep what can best be described as a 'court jester' who is supposed to scan the environment for the most radical theories and ideas and data and who is regularly heard by top management – but it is always implicitly made clear that nobody is going to take him seriously. Such performances for the gallery represent what Herbert Marcuse (1969) has called 'repressive tolerance' and Donald Schön (1971) 'dynamic conservatism'. In this type of organization the *immune system dominates*.

Lately – in the wake of the recognition that things move so fast! – I have met several organizations who display a seemingly completely different syndrome. They have listened to gurus explaining the 'learning organization', the need for 'chaos', the need for 'freedom and entrepreneurship'. Everybody in the organization is working on at least one exciting breakthrough project. But in the end not very much comes out of it. Activity generates confusion that does not lead to new structure and new frameworks. Nothing seems to be able to rise from the dense web of interrelationships. The conceptual landscape remains flat, horizontal. Something is lacking, something that is related to the quality of a conversation leading from entrepreneurial individualism to useful and conceptually framed intersubjectivity. I have come to think of such organizations as *'hysterically hyperactive'*.

The 'immune system-dominated' versus the 'hysterically hyperactive' organization exemplify a dichotomy where both ends of the spectrum carry grains of truth but which must be transcended by some higher logic to become practical. Stability and control are necessary if a system is not to go up in smoke. So is searching out the uncertain and the unmanageable and the unknown, and acceptance of uncoordinated and redundant behaviour. There must be landmarks for navigation that rise from the horizontal landscape and focus organized action.

As a prelude to our inquiry into structural change and reframing that escapes the dilemmas mentioned here this chapter will look into some sources of inspiration from various theoretical fields.

EMERGING IDEAS ON CHANGE AND CREATION

The simple and the complex

How do systems change? How do they adapt to new environments? How do they develop increased complexity to deal with new 'fitness contexts'? How do they not only adapt but create? Can they not only change themselves but actually invent or 'bring forth' (to borrow an expression from Maturana and Varela) a world, a reality?

Findings and frameworks emerging from various lines of both social and natural science research, which now seem to converge into what is loosely thought of as 'complexity theory', begin to give us fascinating insights into such questions. Neo-Darwinism, cognition theory, economics, brain research, the genome project, research in physics from the cosmos to the smallest particles (if particles they are...) all begin to form a pattern. I have no intention to reiterate or summarize even a small fraction of all this, but in this and the following chapters I will point at certain ideas and phenomena which are particularly relevant to our topic.

One such line of thought concerns the relationship between the simple and the complex. It is a soothing thought (at least for me) that evolution and increased complexity in systems seems to come about not from grand and superhuman designs and blueprints but from simple elements and processes and their interactions.

The theory of 'dissipative structures' advanced by Ilya Prigogine, the Nobel Prize laureate, implies that systems move from one state of complexity to a higher state as a self-induced reaction to moving (or being forced to move) into more complex environments. If the new environment contains new elements, new turbulences, new uncertainties – often fashionably referred to as characteristics of 'chaos' – a system will have to invent new ways of structuring itself to let the new energies flow through it without destroying it. The resulting systemic change is not the result of an *ex ante* grand design but can come about if there is enough resilience and requisite variety to achieve a state of dynamic disequilibrium.

Such theories correspond well with observations on characteristics of learning systems and organisms. For example, Buckley (1967, p. 63) observed that for a social system to be able to undergo structural change the following conditions must be fulfilled:

- Some degree of 'plasticity' and 'sensitivity' or *tension vis-à-vis* its environment such that it carries on a constant interchange with environmental events, acting on and reacting to them;
- Some source or mechanism providing for *variety*, to act as a potential pool of adaptive variability to meet the problem of new or more detailed variety and constraints in a changeable environment;
- A set of *selective* criteria or mechanisms against which the 'variety pool' may be sifted into those variations in the organization or system that more closely match the environment and those that do not;
- An arrangement for *preserving and/or propagating* these 'successful' mappings.

Similarly, Dunn (1971) describes social learning as a process of 'evolutionary experimentation', during which stages of 'adaptive specialization' alternate with stages of 'adaptive generalization'. *Adaptive specialization* implies a refinement and development of the ability to live in and exploit a certain 'niche', while *adaptive generalization* implies that new 'adaptive zones' are made available to the system. This structure-developing process of adaptive generalization appears as a complex interaction between internal attributes of the system and events in the environment. The biological individual is characterized by a set of potential responses and action patterns which are determined by genetic characteristics and the individual's personal history. Most of these possible reaction patterns can, at any one moment, be regarded as latent. But in the individual's interaction with his or her environment, some of these potential characteristics are aroused and reinforced, while others become weaker. Dunn compares the individual and his or her environment to two sets of conditional probabilities which are interrelated and which provide conditions for each other's existence. This also implies that the process of adaptation does not necessarily have to be a one-way road from changes in the outside world to changes in the inside world, but that changes can also conceivably come from the inside and influence the environment.[15]

Simulation models used in complexity theory demonstrate how extremely complex patterns can be formed by utterly simple elements which are combined according to simple algorithms. When such elements, algorithms, and combinations are fed back to themselves at certain points 'fractals' emerge: 'bifurcation points' of instability where the system as a whole may take on new properties that no longer seem related to the original elements or its initial state. At such bifurcation points the system undergoes a 'phase change'. The dramatically increasing interconnectivity in the economy caused by communication technology can vastly accelerate such processes. The phase change is characterized by principles of positive feedback (as opposed to the 'negative feedback' principles characterizing traditional systems research and engineering aiming at producing homeostatic systems).[16]

Such phase changes seem to be a particular characteristic of 'networks', which – when they reach a critical mass – have the ability to dramatically change their character. Phenomena such as faxes, mobile phones, and the Internet are often quoted as having such characteristics (see, for example, Kelly, 1997). As long as there are few faxes my fax is rather worthless; as long as few people are linked to the Internet the usefulness of my connection is limited. But as the network grows the versatility and potential value of each individual piece of equipment or connection grows immensely, and the system has undergone its phase change. This brings us back to a key point in this book, namely that *the relative importance of positional value to intrinsic value rises as a function of increased unbundleability and rebundleability*. This is what expands the reconfiguration space and what makes reframing such an imperative.

In his book *How Hits Happen* Farrell (1998) has investigated a number of social phenomena, from best-selling toys to the *Titanic* film. The common pattern is that the simple actions of individuals accumulate from below, lead to interactions, and at some stage the phase change comes and the 'hit' is there. The hit has been caused not so much by itself as by the actions and ensuing interactions, and the interactions in turn take on a life of their own. Since they need the hit to feed on as a catalyst the hit becomes a result of the interactions. It is both cause and effect.

Thus, complexity and systemic change may well build from below, from the simple to the complex, from the element to the system, from actions to interactions and linkages. There is a logic to the process which makes it possible to understand – if not predict. And although these theories help us get rid of the myths of 'the grand designer', and of control and leadership in the traditional sense, they still clearly provide insights about what kind and timing of interventions might stimulate the process. Neither Pericles nor Goebbels, nor today's masters of 'event management' (such as the Olympic Games) or media moguls have been unaware of such principles.

If the mechanisms and force fields are fairly well understood the *direction* of change may be somewhat predictable, though *timing* may remain extremely difficult to foresee. Geologists believe they have fairly good – certainly not conclusive – ideas of where volcanoes will erupt and earthquakes will happen, but are at a loss to say when. The Internet explosion probably was foreseen by many who knew about the system, but not its timing. In all likelihood cancer will be conquered – but when?

In social systems going through complex change and creation processes – what happens when they arrive at a bifurcation point? This is where the notion of a *selector* mechanism – and leadership – comes in. Margaret Wheatley (1992/1994) believes that some kind of institutionalized purpose and *meaning* is the most effective and fundamental such selector. In this she approaches Selznick (1957).

The discovery of these mechanisms help explain why the evolution of life forms has been much faster than the original Darwinian theories of random mutations and natural selection would have made possible.

Genes and memes

Genes, and gene sets, may change over time, and genes transfer systemic properties to new generations. But in the case of 'higher' living systems a tremendous accelerator has been added to the mechanism: that of language, culture, and institutions in general. Systemic properties are transferred not only by genes but also by the artefacts that we create or that emerge in our interaction.

In his novel *The Lost World* Michael Crichton (1995) – well researched! – makes the point nicely, so why not use it? One of the dinosaur species which was characterized by a highly developed 'social community' life was found to behave in rather predictable ways in most respects. However, their abandoned camp is found to be in a state of lack of order which contrasts sharply with similar camps found by palaeontologists. The conclusion (which in this case was the premise to be illustrated): the *genetically* caused behaviour patterns of these artificially woken up dinosaurs functioned, but their *culturally* transferred behaviour patterns did not.

The other side of this coin is, of course, that culture and language can become very strong *tools* to influence not only individual behaviour but also systemic behaviour. We can create language artefacts, which have popularly become called 'memes' to indicate their similarity with and yet distinguish them from 'genes'. Our civilization is full of such memes. Some of them just seem to emerge while others are consciously and proactively invented and used to influence individual and collective behaviour. They therefore become designed tools to actually change and influence the 'reality' that we live in. Management science and its prescriptive branch – management consulting – has invented memes such as 'total quality management', 'business process re-engineering', 'service management', 'core competences', to name but a few, which have all become catalysts for interaction and which have clearly changed the (individual and social) behaviour of masses of managers, in turn resulting in a changed reality. The world would have been different without these invented concepts. There was nothing that determined, in advance, that exactly these concepts and not others would become particularly important as memes and catalysts to change reality, and there certainly have been competing memes that never came to 'make it' to the same extent. Of course, these memes became successful because they did reflect some emerging 'bottom-up' processes which they reinforced, as well as some level of fit with the context of the era, but there is hardly any doubt that others could have fulfilled similar functions and that the realities we now live in might have been different. There is no determinism at work here.

Social reality and artefacts

One of the books that have influenced me profoundly is *The Social Construction of Reality* by Berger and Luckmann (1967). Although I do not think the notion of complexity theory had been invented as a meme when they wrote the book, they clearly delineate (based on the philosophy of science of phenomenology) the mechanisms by which language emerges in social systems from the interactions and attempts of individuals to cope with their environment; how signs become language and concepts that both emerge from and create collective action; how concepts and idea systems are institutionalized (in buildings, sets of rules, roles, laws, ...); how all this is integrated in terms of 'symbolic universes' such as religion or 'the market economy' and other grand belief systems. All these phenomena are socially constructed, and they have emerged essentially by a bottom-up logic, from the simple to the complex. But, again, this does not happen according to a deterministic process. At any time the process can take many directions.

This process of constructing a social (shared) reality goes through a number of interrelated and, to a great extent, synchronous phases. Subjective experiences and intentions of individuals are *externalized* as signs, sounds, and other actions, and can thus be communicated (recall that 'communicate' comes from the Latin for 'share together') to others. Individual experiences and intents can therefore go from being subjective to being intersubjective, and the signs and language and concepts and other actions that come to symbolize this intersubjectivity become *objectified*. 'Soft objects' (such as words and symbols) as well as 'hard objects' (such as buildings and statues) become *institutionalized*. They are 'artefacts' which serve both as a record of past and common experiences. They are collective knowledge, and serve as a platform for future action. They stand for a specific, intersubjectively shared meaning which makes it possible for individuals to *internalize* the intersubjective world, leading to a process of *socialization* and community building. Institutions transcend the present; they link the past, the present and the future.

Developments in fields such as constructionism, organizational symbolism, the aesthetics of organizations, and neo-institutionalism have provided additional insights into these mechanisms, which are crucial for understanding reframing and reconceptualization (Latour, 1998; Gagliardi, 1990; Czarniawska and Joerges, 1996; Ramirez, 1987).

Cognition theory

Brain research and cognition theory provides us with even deeper insights and many explanations. To me the modern natural science based follow-up to Berger and Luckmann is the 'Santiago theory' developed by Maturana and Varela (1987/1998). It brings together strands from philosophers and physicists such as Leibnitz, Einstein and Heisenberg. It essentially deals with the relationship between systems and the world they live in, and the processes by which systems take on their identity and structure and simultaneously 'enact' and 'bring forth' the reality they live in.

The interrelatedness of the external and the internal 'worlds' is a core theme going through the Santiago theory. The authors do not accept the traditional argument that cognition is the building of an internal model representing, as correctly as possible, the external world. (Their point is totally consistent with that of Berger and Luckmann, but it is arrived at from a different angle.) In contrast, they say, the world outside does not exist independently of the individual. They do not say that the outside world does not exist, and that, for example, physical objects are not there except as a result of our own imagination. But the way we as individuals, and as collectivities, receive and process sensory inputs and identify and define patterns is so dependent on our language, on our physical characteristics, on our constitution, that the world 'out there' is literally structured and shaped by this cognition process. As summarized by Capra:

> According to the Santiago theory, cognition is not a representation of an independent, pregiven world, but rather a bringing forth of a world. What is brought forth by a particular organism in the process of living is not *the* but *a* world, one that is always dependent upon the organism's structure. Since individual organisms within a species have more or less the same structure, they bring forth similar worlds. We humans, moreover, share an abstract world of language and thought through which we bring forth a world together. (Capra, 1996, p. 270)

Maturana and Varela might have said: The business landscape we see out there is not there, but it is also not not there.

These cognitive processes allowing us to 'bring forth a world' are not only accelerated by the existence of memes and language which is such a distinguishing characteristic (at least in degree) of humans and social systems. They can be further accelerated through higher-level processes belonging to the domain of the conscious. Especially interesting is the notion of 'languaging', communication about communication (Maturana and Varela). By engaging in personal and social processes in the language domain *about our symbols* and about the nature of our socially constructed world, about the structure of our language, we are actually able to set the preconditions for changing that world. At one level we coordinate our behaviour through language. At a higher level *by communicating about our language and about our communication we can begin to set the stage for the emergence of new meaning, new reality, and new coordinated behaviour.*

> Language was never invented by anyone only to take in an outside world. Therefore, it cannot be used as a tool to reveal that world. Rather it is by languaging that the act of knowing, in the behavioural co-ordination which is language, brings forth a world. (Maturana and Varela, 1987/1998, p. 234)

Through the process of cognition, the system – whether an organism or an organization – can thus evolve its own structure and its relationship to the external world – and the very structure of the external world. This is the process of 'autopoiesis', 'self-creation'. Because of the great variety pool associated with social systems, and their endless opportunities to link structurally both inside the system and with external systems through networking, and because of the importance of the symbolic, language and meme-related realm, it seems clear to me that social systems should have a capacity for such autopoiesis which far transcends that of the physical individual. But the individual moving between and across institutions may catalyse and catapult this process (like bacteria are believed to accelerate genetic evolution).

The interrelatedness between the socially constructed world and the physical world is evident from these theories. The relationship becomes interdependent, dialectic. Physical structures condition us, trigger and give direction to the mental and social symbolizing processes which give rise to language; but language and the intersubjective social reality also create actions that piggyback on the physical world. Our houses, roads, cities, and wheat fields are all manifestations of our mental world.

Winston Churchill said: 'First we shape our buildings, and then our buildings shape us.' Stewart Brand has written a fascinating book on *How Buildings Learn* (1994). Simon Schama, in his book *Landscape and Memory* (1995) (which I think could have been more pointedly entitled *Landscape as Memory*) vividly shows how virtually any landscape can be read as a map of human history and social process. Novelist Julian Barnes illuminates the dialectic process between Man and Nature manifested in the landscape as artefact:

> I stood on a hill the other day and looked down at an undulating field past a copse towards a river and as I did so a pheasant stirred beneath my feet. You, as a person *passing through*, would no doubt have assumed that Dame Nature was going about her eternal business. I knew better... The hill was an Iron Age burial mound, the undulating field a vestige of Saxon agriculture, the copse was a copse only because a thousand other trees had been cut down, the river was a canal and the pheasant had been hand-reared by a gamekeeper. ... That lake you discern on the horizon is a reservoir, but when it has been established a few years, when fish swim in it and migrating birds make it a port of call, when the tree-line has adjusted itself and little boats ply their picturesque way up and down it, when these things happen it becomes, triumphantly, a lake, don't you see? It becomes *the thing itself*. (Barnes, 1998, pp. 60–61.)

IDENTITY, MANIFESTATION, AND PROCESS

I will profit from borrowing (and in the process stretching and perhaps distorting) another element from the Santiago theory advanced by Maturana and Varela. They describe living systems in terms of three characteristics, complementary and inseparable, all necessary and together sufficient for that overall characterization.

The first of these is what they call the system's *pattern of organization*. This is the list of characteristics and their relationships which is necessary for us to recognize the system as being part of a particular class of systems. The description, if I understand them correctly, can be made entirely in the *conceptual*, abstract domain.

The second characteristic is the *structure* of the system. This is defined as the *physical* embodiment of the pattern of organization, and it is clear that there is not a one-to-one mapping between the organization and the structure. A Ford Fiesta and a Ferrari Maranello both share the pattern characteristics that help us to identify them as members of the class of systems called 'cars', but the ways the *conceptual idea* of 'car' has been *physically embodied* differ completely. Union de Banques à Paris and Deutsche Bank and Citigroup are all clearly identifiable as banks or at least financial institutions, and thus share a number of characteristics that can be described in the abstract, but they are all very different in their structural embodiment.

Are Amazon.com and my local bookstore in La Celle St Cloud part of the same class of systems, i.e. do they share the abstract descriptive elements and their interrelationships which allow us to identify them both as 'bookstores'? To some extent, certainly, yes. On the other hand, it is clear in this case that the way they have embodied the idea of a bookstore in their physical layout, use of technology, use of people, linkages to customers, relationships with suppliers and transporters, and so forth, are so different that we might begin to hesitate. And if we take the analysis one step further – in what directions are they going? Here it appears that the way Amazon.com *has manifested itself structurally* has created a whole new set of relationships with the environment which begins to open up new possibilities for understanding what the system is fundamentally all about. For example, the customer base and the customer database that Amazon.com has evolved through its particular way of concretizing the idea of a bookstore may have the potential to make the company an attractive channel also for many other companies – in other words, we may begin to conceive of Amazon.com no longer as a bookstore but as a generalized access channel, 'portal'. Its original identity has perhaps been transformed and it may now therefore belong to a different category of organizations.

This illustrates an important principle, and one that may explain why social systems may move and change faster than biological organisms and species. Any physical manifestation of a basic organization pattern implies a particular type of *structural coupling* with elements in the environment. When, for some reason, the structure changes this structural coupling also changes, *but this in turn implies new linkages and new relationships which feed back into the system.*[17] And such processes may also lead to a gradual or even sometimes a dramatic and rapid set of consequences for the system's basic identity or 'organization' (to use Maturana–Varela terminology) – *what it is.*

> We do not see what we do not see, and what we do not see does not exist. Only when some interaction dislodges us – such as being suddenly relocated to a different cultural environment – and we reflect upon it, do we bring forth the new constellations of relations that we explain by saying that we were not aware of them, or that we took them for granted. (Maturana and Varela, 1987/1998, p. 242)

The third characteristic of living systems – the first two being identity and structural manifestation – according to the Santiago theory is the *life process*, the way the basic organization pattern manifests and remanifests itself in structure. In living, biological systems such processes take place at the cellular level on a continuous basis. They also occur on an onto-genetic (evolution of the individual) level as the individual goes through its life-cycle, and on a phylogenetic (evolution of the species) level as the species develops over generations. This process will be the fundamental theme of the following chapters.

I will use these three key elements freely, taking the liberty to apply them at least metaphorically to organizations and social systems. I will then think about the basic 'pattern of organization' as the fundamental *mission and capabilities and values* of a company; of the 'structure' as the way this is *manifested in resources, assets, organization, systems, linkages, alliances*; and of 'processes' as not only activities by which the basic identity is structurally manifested but also the *activities through which the basic identity is questioned and evolved*.

SUMMARY

The link between these elements of the Santiago theory and Selznick's framework of 'distinctive competence' and 'character of the organization', and the notion of the development of the 'dominating ideas' and their manifestation in organization and systems is obvious. The set of theories referred to in this chapter allows us, however, to understand more deeply the basic nature of the processes involved in achieving consonance and also in innovating and reframing a system. I have already indicated that social organizations may not be as bad as their reputation as adaptive and innovating systems, compared to most biological organisms. At least we can expect that *their behaviour is guided by a higher proportion of memes to genes than are biological systems*. And at least so far (though who knows what will happen after the genome project and the biotechnological explosion?) we have more options to create memes than genes. By reflecting on the pro-cesses, and by creating tools based on that reflection, we may come closer to a bootstrapping ideal.

These are some inspirational cornerstones laying the foundation for the chapters to come. At the core of change is *the symbolizing activity of the mind*. But the mind is not confined to one person's head. Nor is it only an agglomeration of many heads. It is as much outside ourselves, certainly including in the manifestations of past actions that impinge on our current predicament.

And the mind, by manifesting its activities in artefacts and structural couplings, can create new realms of action space that again feed back to the mind.

Part V
Reframing: Tools for Map Making

INGRESSO

PART I
THE MAP AND
THE LANDSCAPE

Chapter **1**
EVOLUTION OF
STRATEGIC PARADIGMS

Chapter **19**
WHAT LEADERS
NEED TO DO

Chapter **18**
BRINGING EXTERNAL AND
INTERNAL DYNAMICS IN LINE

PART VII
LEADERSHIP FOR
NAVIGATION

Chapter **2**
RECONFIGURING THE
VALUE SPACE

Chapter **16**
FROM GREAT IDEAS
TO GREAT COMPANIES

Chapter **17**
CAPABILITIES FOR ACHIEVING
THE CRITICAL OUTCOMES

Chapter **3**
SOME CONSEQUENCES
OF DEMATERIALIZATION

PART VI
CAPABILITIES
FOR PURPOSEFUL
EMERGENCE

PART II
SHAPERS OF
THE LANDSCAPE

Chapter **15**
THE CRANE AT WORK
IN THE DESIGN SPACE

PART III
TOOLS FOR
LANDSCAPING

Chapter **4**
CHAINED TO THE
VALUE CHAIN?

Chapter **7**
CO-PRODUCTION: TOWARDS
INCREASED DENSITY

Chapter **14**
THE MENTAL SPACE
FOR REFRAMING

Chapter **5**
PRIME MOVERS
AS RECONFIGURERS

Chapter **8**
THE OFFERING AS A TOOL
TO ORGANIZE CO-PRODUCTION

Chapter **13**
THE PROCESS CRITERIA
OF THE CRANE

Chapter **6**
PRIME MOVERSHIP
AS ECOGENESIS

Chapter **12**
ON CRANES AND
SKY-HOOKS

Chapter **9**
THREE TRENDS IN
OFFERING DEVELOPMENT

PART IV
THE
MAP-LANDSCAPE
INTERACTION

PART V
REFRAMING:
TOOLS FOR
MAP MAKING

Chapter **11**
CHANGE AND
CREATION

Chapter **10**
FITTING INTO
THE ENVIRONMENT

On Cranes and Sky-hooks

12

DESIGNING FOR DESIGNING

There is a story (whether it is true is not important for our purposes) about Michelangelo, who after having created his masterly sculpture 'David', was asked how he had gone about the task. He allegedly answered 'I took this big piece of marble, and I took my tools, and then I just took away everything that was not David'. All of us do not have Michelangelo's vision, and the story does not tell anything about what had preceded the making of this sculpture.

Innovative design builds on at least some existing elements, but introduces something new. It corresponds to the basic mechanism of metaphor as force-fitting elements from different realms (Schön, 1963; Koestler, 1969), and the fundamental processes of producing new social reality and hits that were discussed in the previous chapter. It cannot be induced by simple command. But are there any possibilities to understand how innovation comes about and to increase our possibilities of 'leapfrogging' and probability of success? Is there anything that we could use between the rational 'this can be planned and controlled' and the magic 'this just happens and there is no way we can influence it' explanations of innovation (Schön, 1965)?

Evolution may be described as a result of the rational functioning of a Newtonian machine-like mechanism, functioning according to eternal principles and laws of nature. Such an explanation would correspond to the notion of 'because of': the future does not exist *a priori* but is determined by history and by inherent driving forces and mechanisms. Causes from the past create effects now or for the future. This would be the traditional Darwinian explanation. This *deterministic* explanation has fought head to head with another one which attributes evolution to a higher purpose, a goal or an ideal state in the future which exists in some divine mind and which we are gradually approaching – what philosophers of science call a *teleological* explanation. In other words, the explanation of why something happens would lie not in the past but in the future, not in historical driving forces but in purpose – not 'because of' but rather 'in order to'. In this case 'causes' can be seen as acting from the future into the present.

In his book *Darwin's Dangerous Idea* Daniel Dennett (1995) uses an illuminating metaphor. Dennett likens the teleological 'in order to' explanation of evolution to a 'sky-hook', something that comes down from the sky through the clouds, from an incomprehensible realm, to elevate us towards a higher state.

How can we resolve the dilemma between the machine explanation and the sky-hook explanation? According to Albert Einstein:

> Unless one sins against logic, one generally gets nowhere; ... one cannot build a house or construct a bridge without using a scaffold which is really not one of its basic parts.

Can we design a 'scaffold' which then can help us to innovate?

Dennett, in the spirit of Einstein, suggests the metaphor of a 'crane'. Perhaps there are no sky-hooks. And, yes, no doubt, much of what will happen in the future and much of what we can do is conditioned by what history has imposed on us. But it may be possible for us to use existing knowledge to design and build cranes, from which we can then send down a hook to lift us into realms that we could not imagine. This crane, constructed according to known principles, could open up opportunities to move into exploration and construction of the unknown.

Design of a 'new', reframed reality and action strategy would thus take place in two steps. The first step is designing the tool, what we might call the crane, with existing knowledge and technology. The second step is to use the tool for exploring the unknown (but hopefully knowable) and creating unachieved (but hopefully achievable) new business patterns. The creation of that tool, then, is designing for designing.

The following chapters try to outline the design of a crane. Not, certainly, a universal crane, not the only crane. But a crane.

DESIGN CRITERIA FOR PROCESS AND SUBSTANCE

To be effective a crane must be based on principles that we know, and it must stand on ground that is solid. But between this solid ground and the incomprehensible area up there and in the future there is a space which can be filled, and the crane can help us to fill it. The crane helps cover a design space between the known and the unknown. It creates tension between what is and what is not. The crane should recognize that we cannot reframe without increasing our design space and knowledge.

We must map, as thoroughly as possible, the explicit knowledge that exists about the present situation. We must bring out the knowledge that exists and build new knowledge from that base – and we know that this can only be done through interactive social process which must be given a certain space and time to be realized. We must explore areas beyond our present realm of activity. We must create the conditions for surprise, for the appearance of the unknown, and for the uncomfortable and the disturbing.

The crane described here is an artefact, a model which I and colleagues have tried out on several occasions as a tool for consciously and purposefully but open-endedly reinterpreting a business. This means – as has been argued in several of the previous chapters – that it recognizes the validity of certain elements that we have (such as assets, competences, products, services, customer bases, relationships) but tries to put these existing elements into new systems definitions – *reframing* them.

There are two sets of design criteria for the crane. One concerns *process* (what steps the cranes takes us through), the other *substance or content* (what should come out as a result of the crane's workings).

First, we need to derive criteria from a basic understanding of the nature of business today. The first part of this book identified the driving forces reshaping the business landscape, creating opportunities to reconfigure value creation for density. Thus, we expect the crane to produce reconfigured business, using creatively designed offerings that 'densify' value creation as specified in earlier chapters.

Second, with regard to process we do not know exactly how to innovate, but we know a few things about *the logic of innovative processes*. We also, hopefully, know that we don't know everything, but that certain realms of knowledge are available to be explored and used. The crane – the tool – should be constructed in such a way as to *help us to spin a process that maps these fundamental characteristics the mental process of knowledge building* and which does not assume that there is determinism at work.

This second set of design criteria – which are deeply founded in the underpinnings of Part IV of the book – will be further systematized next.

The Process Criteria of the Crane   13

MIND REFRAMING FOR BUSINESS RECONFIGURATION

If the name of the strategic game today is reconfiguration the point of departure of any strategic process should be the *positional* (as opposed to the intrinsic) value of an organization and the various elements of which it consists. The *mental* process that corresponds with reconfiguration is *re-framing*. That is, we must be able to look at ourselves and at our situation from different perspectives; we must bring different realities into it, and we must be able to move into other realities and see ourselves from different vantage points.

This chapter will explore some dimensions of the mental space that is, in principle, available to us in such a reframing process. This overview is certainly not exhaustive, and I might have used other, perhaps even totally different, approaches. In choosing the approach I have tried to satisfy a number of criteria:

- Taking into account some of the most interesting and promising approaches developed in areas such as systems theory, cognition research, the theory of knowledge in organizations.
- Using elements from what is known as 'scientific method', particularly with regard to induction.
- Finding dimensions which appear to have some validity and correspondence with the notion of reconfiguration and 'positional value'; i.e. that introduce shifts of perspective between elements and various systems that elements might be part of.
- Incorporating research results and techniques, such as scenario 'planning', which are not only anchored in theory but which have proved

to be useful (under certain circumstances) in developing organizations and businesses.

I depart from the premise that reconfiguration results from a learning and design process which can be characterized as 'purposeful emergence'. We must assume that we know something, but that we don't know everything, and that we don't know exactly what we don't know, and that recognition of the (at least partly) knowable unknown must be a platform in which we have faith.

Also I have assumed that the 'knowable unknown', which can be thought of both as an under-utilized 'memory' and as a field of exploration, exists in three dimensions.

1   As a potential exploration field and an under-utilized 'memory of the past' as well as 'memory of the future'.
2   Similarly as a 'memory of the individual' and 'memory of the collectivity'.
3   Similarly along the dimension of 'memory of the non-conscious' and 'memory as explicitated, coded knowledge'.

A designed process of mental reframing must help us go through processes (collective and individual) which give us better access to these 'memories'.

KNOWLEDGE: FROM NON-CONSCIOUS TO FORMALIZED

Change and innovation often seem to be just the result of luck or random events, which contrasts sharply with the desire – and belief – that the rational human mind might and should do better than serendipity.

Much of the world we live in is structured by processes and by concepts and symbols that are implicit, tacit, subconscious, or unconscious. Many of our actions are conscious, conditioned by analysis and will, but we also know that a great number of bodily processes take place outside our consciousness and that many of them are guided by our autonomous nervous system. There is no mystery about non-conscious realms and processes – we are physically constructed that way.

Freud, Jung, and many others have explored the influence of the non-conscious on us, and have tried to analyse the relationship between the non-conscious and the conscious. Michael Polanyi (1969) made the point (later developed particularly by Nonaka and Takeuchi, 1995) that much knowledge is 'personal' and tacit rather than explicit and coded. Many management theories have completely neglected the importance of non-conscious knowledge and processes related to such knowledge. Today, however, it would be very hard to disregard the insight that the non-conscious and the tacit represent not only a crucial part of all knowledge but also a huge and very often under-utilized resource.

Such insights may help us understand that serendipity is not necessarily what it seems to be but rather the result of careful preparation and the intuition to understand complex patterns that results from it. Napoleon, when asked how he picked his generals, is said to have answered: 'I pick the ones who have had luck.' The French statesman Talleyrand once appointed a person to an important position as ambassador. When this person came to thank him and said that this was the first time in his life he had really had luck, Talleyrand immediately removed him from the position. My guess is that Napoleon and Talleyrand had insights about the nature of tacit knowledge and how it influences luck and serendipity. Luck comes to the prepared mind. And Jung's concept of 'the collective unconscious' recognizes the simultaneous existence not only of tacit but also inter-subjective knowledge. Such insights surely give us a perspective on understanding and promoting change and renewal.

James Hillman (1995), in a wonderful chapter on leadership, has pointed out that analysis rarely seems to precede action in really effective leaders, but is synchronous and simultaneous with action or even does not seem to exist. We often meet the 'analysis–paralysis' syndrome in organizations. Somebody – I have unfortunately forgotten who – made the observation that performances by the greatest pianists tend to be characterized more by release than by tension. It is like opening a valve in a dam. The great Chilean pianist, Claudio Arrau, who was greatly influenced by Jungian psychology and the notion of the collective unconscious, was very explicit about the need to let go of all kinds of conscious 'control' ambitions and mechanisms in actual performance, since that would come between what had accumulated inside him and the music that he produced. To stay in the world of musicians, Johannes Brahms in a fascinating interview published as late as 1955 states:

> ... I have to be in a semi-trance condition to get such results – a condition when the conscious mind is in temporary abeyance and the sub-

conscious is in control, for it is through the subconscious mind, which is part of Omnipotence, that the inspiration comes. I have to be careful, however, not to lose consciousness, otherwise the ideas fade away. ...

But don't make the mistake, my friend, of thinking that because I attach such importance to inspiration from above, that that is all there is to it, by no means. Structure is just as consequential, for without craftsmanship, inspiration is a 'mere reed shaken in the wind' or 'sounding brass or tinkling cymbals'. (From Abell, 1955/1994)

Ordinary language simply does not capture the essence of change and renewal. We have to learn, with Brahms, to live explicitly in a dialectical mode that takes us between different realms of existence.

Nonaka and Takeuchi, among others, have clearly shown that the types of process necessary for evolving and socializing tacit knowledge are very different from those that are adequate for explicit knowledge. The fascinating studies by Robert Putnam (1993) on Italian regions and their relative development capabilities can certainly be interpreted within a conceptual framework related to the capacity of different kinds of social organization to promote the development and transfer of tacit knowledge. Chris Argyris and Donald Schön (1974) have pointed at the (often very large) difference between the 'espoused theories' and the 'theories-in-use' by actors, and much of this difference can certainly be explained by the fact that 'theories-in-use' necessarily involve the whole realm of the non-conscious, whereas 'espoused theories' rarely do so.

We know that access to tacit knowledge requires social interaction, conversation, and participant observation. If we do not recognize its existence, and if we are not skilful in inventing the processes – personal and social/organizational – by which the non-conscious can be developed into a well of riches for our actions we will be all the poorer for it.

LAYERS OF CONSCIOUSNESS AND REFLECTION

Since we are concerned with designing, we are concerned not only with the process of design and learning but with *our own consciousness of our process of design and learning*. We have looked at some characteristics of systems which are able to learn and develop and even undergo self-creation (autopoiesis).

The simplest form of learning is adaptation and correction within a given framework. This type of learning, which Argyris and Schön have called single-loop learning, is based on the principle of negative feedback – i.e. of corrective action when a misfit between the actual and the intended state of the system occurs. Thomas Kuhn (1962) refers to it as paradigm shifts and (scientific) 'revolutions'.

A second level of learning – very much aligned with the descriptions by Buckley and by Dunn referred to earlier – makes use of positive feedback and questions the very parameters by which the system operates and by which the intended state has been defined. Argyris and Schön call this 'double-loop learning'. This kind of learning is much more dramatic since it implies not only an adjustment within a framework but actually questions the framework itself, i.e. what has become institutionalized in language and structures in a social system. My early studies of innovation (1969, 1971) refer to it as 're-orientation' (as opposed to 'variation', which corresponds to single-loop learning), and demonstrated that it requires changes of cognitive process as well as new power structures.

Single-loop learning is practised by any organism (and by my computer) every day, and double-loop learning also occurs frequently and spontaneously in nature as well as in social systems (but perhaps not always as effectively in organizations as owners and managers and customers would wish). However, when we come to another distinction we probably enter the much more limited realm of human beings and social systems. I am thinking about the distinction between learning (single- and/or double-loop), on the one hand, and *conscious learning how to learn*, on the other.

In his book *Darwin's Dangerous Idea* Daniel Dennett (1995) makes the distinction between three types of 'creatures', representing a more or less advanced reflection on the very process of learning. The first level he calls 'Skinnerians', and they basically develop by trial and error, like Skinner's famous mice. They ask 'What do I do next?' and then they do something, and see whether it works out or not – whether they get positive or negative feedback. A much more advanced form, which Dennett terms 'Popperians', ask 'What should I think about?' before they ask 'What do I do next?'. Here, *reflection on one's activity as a conscious activity in itself* has explicitly entered into the actor's model building of his own learning behaviour.

There is, however, yet another and considerably more advanced 'creature' again, namely 'Gregarians'. Before they ask 'What do I do next?' before which they have asked 'What should I think about?' they have asked another crucial question: *'How should I think better about what to think about next?'*

Thus, we can move between different levels of consciousness *both* with regard *to how we view the world* and in terms of *how we view our own learning-oriented actions*. The crane we are building should fulfil Gregarian criteria for the consciousness of our own process of learning (and that includes consciousness of the non-conscious, and consciousness of the impossibility of being conscious about everything regarding the non-conscious).

GENERATING DIVERSITY VERSUS FOCUSING

A process design characteristic of a crane must be that it reflects the basic dialectic of all creative processes: The one between *generating and reducing diversity*. Every true renewal process takes place in stages (not necessarily sequential but often better described as modes of thinking and acting) characterized by generation of new diversity and information, and then stages of reduction of it and focus on certain types of action. A successful organization must learn to live in both these modes. Earlier we referred to the twin processes of adaptive generalization and adaptive specialization. Perhaps Nørretranders (1998) might call this a process of first generating *in*formation and then a process of generating *ex*formation. We must *open up*, relative to where we are now, but at some stage we also need to *close in and focus* and make choices.

This requires a certain space and calendar time. In fact one of the most common errors – I am tempted to say tragedies – I see in business and other organizations is giving in to the pressure of premature closure, of deciding on a vision or a strategy before a design space has been evolved *so that there is a real choice* between options. In such situations the strategy becomes either rather haphazard or rather deterministically decided; it is not a reflection of a real choice situation which has been attained by the actors. If you have not opened up first there is very little to close in to. If choice has not been preceded by enough generation of diversity to create many options, and with generation of real tension with the present, it is a pseudo-exercise, a ritual of little consequence. We will be faced with an organization which has not realized its opportunities. I am often reminded of Patrick Chéreau's comments on Siegfrid in Wagner's *Ring*, as quoted in the 'Ingresso' to this book.

The crane should not necessarily take us through an entirely comfortable journey. New design rarely comes about without tension or even pain. To reframe our business we need to look at ourselves in a different light. We need to see what we have in a different context. As colleagues of mine have pointed out: we must make the known unknown, and the unknown known. We must make the comfortable uncomfortable, and the uncomfortable comfortable.[18]

One characteristic of the crane, thus, is that it induces an opening-up phase and a closing-in phase. It starts from the ground, it opens up a conceptual space, and it then fills part of this space with new structure. The procedure goes through a series of three questions:

1 'What business *are* we in?'/'What are we?'
2 'What business (or 'businesses') *could* we be in?'/'What could we be?'
3 'What business *should* we be in/do we want to be in?'/'What should we be?'

Pictorially the three questions can be arranged in a sequence of starting from what 'is', opening up and generating diversity, and closing in to focus on a line of action (Figure 13.1). The first of the three questions can be handled rather summarily here. Selznick gives us the rationale:

> A wise leader faces up to the character of his organization, although he may do so only as a prelude to designing a strategy that will alter it. (Selznick, 1957, p. 70)

The tools for analysing it lie in the notions of 'fit' and 'organizational character' as elaborated earlier. Philosophically, it may be argued that it is impossible to establish the point of departure until the larger map has been drawn. Nevertheless experience tells us that it is possible and desirable to make some characterizations of the possible basis for reframing – of the 'hub' (whether in terms of assets, competences, customers, etc.) around which the reframing may take place.

In the case of a business organization the main methodology to be used here is an analysis of where and how the organization is (has been) successful, and by what historical process and critical decisions the organiza-

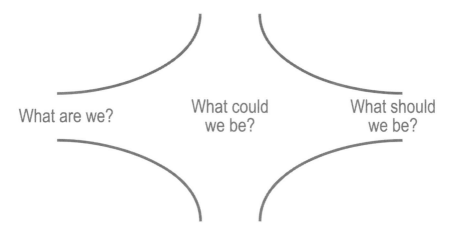

Figure 13.1 Stages of creating diversity versus focusing.

tion has arrived at this position. Traditional product-market matrix studies are often a good starting point, since they indicate something about the 'fit' between internal assets and capabilities, on the one hand, and the external environment and customer base, on the other hand. When strong positions have been identified it may be inferred that there is some kind of good 'fit' (or, in the opposite case, misfit), and this may lead us into investigating the sources of this fit. But it is equally important to understand how the value system, symbols, and the institutional constituency have evolved.

UP- AND DOWNFRAMING

In our thought processes we can move up and down between conceptual levels, or levels of aggregation, as well as between different levels of consciousness. Our language is so constructed that every element or phenomenon, when looked at from a higher level of aggregation, can be seen as belonging to a larger system or as being a specific case belonging to a more general set of phenomena. Language represents the agreed-upon way to structure and exchange experience. Higher-level concepts are accumulations of masses of knowledge which have been agreed upon as representing reality and which therefore contribute to the enactment of that reality. On the other hand, as we move upwards towards higher levels of abstraction we also tend to exclude specific information.

In principle we can move upwards into higher levels of aggregation – 'upframing' – or we can move downwards and focus on more specific phenomena. Upframing allows us to see more structure and pattern, downframing to see more detail. As we upframe from the detail, the detail becomes part of a larger Gestalt; its positional value as opposed to its intrinsic value will stand.

But there is no one single way of upframing. The house in which I write this can be seen as belonging to the more general class of individual homes; or to the general class of row houses; or to the set of 38 houses constituting our little 'village'; or to houses painted in white; or as 'dwellings' together with beehives and birds' nests; or as part of my worklife system, or as part of my children's roots. Likewise, if I want to 'downframe' and focus on a sub-system or specific element of the house I could easily choose between a few thousand possibilities. There is nothing deterministic about upframing or downframing; both can take different paths. Therefore it is essential to design some procedures and rules of thumb for what sort of upframings or downframings can be particularly interesting or fruitful for thinking about reframing your business (see Figure 13.2).

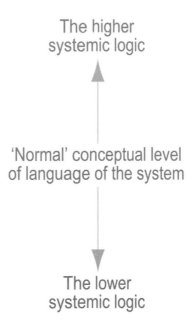

The higher
systemic logic

'Normal' conceptual level
of language of the system

The lower
systemic logic

Figure 13.2 Up- and downframing.

Is there a 'normal' level of abstraction? First, if there is, it is not stable and forever, but dynamic and changing. For example, highly aggregated or theoretical constructs which were originally conceived and understood by few people may gradually (or quickly – consider words like dot-com or e-mail) trickle down and become part of everybody's jargon. This is so in politics, science, and ordinary people's conversations. Other concepts lose their relevance and disappear into oblivion. Second, what is 'normal' is highly individual and can, indeed, only be defined from an existential point of view. Those of my friends who are artists tend to use a language to interact with each other which is fairly different from those of my friends who are particularly fond of 'haute cuisine', and certainly from the language used by myself and others as corporate advisers. So 'normal' depends on what is our peer group and what realm of activity we are involved in, on the relevancy fit between realm of activity, social context, and language. It also has something to do with level of education and perhaps with sheer level of intelligence.

Every organization or social system, as well as every individual or small group, has its particular language which is both structured by and structures the reality that is seen (and enacted) by the members of that collectivity. It does not take advanced socio-anthropological analysis to observe, upon entering an organization, that there is a certain established level of discourse, and a number of specific concepts which are more often used than in other organizations. And certain concepts – say, 'service management' to take an example used earlier – may be practically second nature in a company like ISS (International Service Systems), whereas the same concept may be unknown or seen as new, strange and exotic in a company producing steel.

Whatever our point of reference it is hard to conceive of new knowledge and a different and differently enacted reality without new language, which structures our world differently. Language is a necessary companion of new knowledge and of innovation. Language *is* knowledge. For this reason new language (new memes) is also a potentially strong tool to induce people to see the world differently. More often than not, language is more a master, structuring our world without us even thinking about it, than a slave. But once we become conscious of our use of language, and of the fact that we can move between different frameworks and different levels of abstraction, we can gain some mastery over language, at least to a

much greater extent than if we are unaware of these mechanisms. Memes have us in their grip, but if we know the mechanisms we can make use of memes to alter ourselves and our predicament. New memes can be the attractors and selectors that set a snowball rolling, as complexity theory tells us.

TIME FRAMING

It can be argued that time is always *now* and that there is nothing we can do about that. And that the only thing that happens is that 'the now' is moving (Figure 13.3).

Figure 13.3 How does time flow? The traditional view.

But a characteristic of the human mind is that it is able to transcend, conceptually, the 'now', moving back into the conceptual past as well as moving into the conceptual (hypothesized, imagined, desired, ...) future. Oracles are part of our cultural heritage. But while the official mission of oracles used to be to predict the future, clever statesmen and business executives have always realized that the real reason for mentally moving into the future is to influence the minds and therefore the actions of people living in the present. *The idea behind moving into the conceptual future therefore is to create a different future by influencing action now.*

Brain researchers (Ingvar, 1985) have shown that the human mind continuously creates different mental images of possible futures – what we now think of as scenarios – and that the existence of these can actually be shown physiologically in the brain. Such scenarios are in fact necessary for survival and for being able to structure our present. We use them in a 'what if?' sense. What if the weather will be bad next weekend? What if the car has not yet been repaired? What if mother-in-law comes to visit? What if I don't get the contract? What if I do? By imagining ('living in') and empathizing with alternative possible future states and events we can 'back-cast' to the present, and we can begin to consider what we have to do to handle possible eventualities, prepare ourselves, perhaps influence the course of events. These future scenarios provide us with relevancy structures without which we would have much lower if any possibilities at all to distinguish what is relevant to us or not – we would be drowned by signals and information.[19]

In earlier work I described a logic of 'planning' which I called 'the process view', and which involved a continuous dialectic process between moving 'visions' (which I would now think of as rather more like scenarios with a normative 'would-like-to-achieve' element) and actions here-and-now:

> Visions are not goals. They are intuitive ideas of reasonable (although in relation to the present state, sometimes highly deviating) future states of the system, which sometimes only exist as subjective ideas nursed by a few discerning and possibly significant actors in the present system. To have a vision does not mean committing oneself to any special future state, or even to any one of the future states that appear at present to be possible; it means rather that the vision can be used as an aid in choosing the parts of the present system that should be regarded as a source of inspiration and perhaps even as a challenge. (Normann, 1970, p. 39)
>
> What, then, is the distinguishing mark of a vision and what does it look like? Above all we would like to emphasize the vision's character of being a whole, a system in the shape of a potential business idea. ...
>
> ... the vision is a tool in the learning process, but at the same time it is also subjected to learning; for this reason it will change as learning proceeds. ...
>
> Thus the flexible vision plays an important part in the growth process. It *steers learning*; at the same time changes in the vision also constitute a *yardstick of learning*. Moreover, the terms 'vision' and 'visionary' contain an element of progressiveness and invention, which can indirectly provide a driving force by arousing commitment in the company. (Normann, 1975/1977, p. 98)

This is not the same as saying that ordinary human beings use scenarios in the same way as 'futurists' tend to use them. What I am arguing for here is that it is part of the nature of the human mind to move conceptually and more or less freely between the conceptual past, the here-and-now, and the conceptual future. In fact, the more and the richer experiences we can dig out and bring into the future from the past, the richer the present. Therefore we should try to be *'exiles from the past'*. And the more we can bring of insightful and rich scenarios from the future into the present – the more we can become *'visitors from the future'* – the richer the present.

I am not sure that time goes from the left to the right, as most diagrams would have us believe. As the Swedish novelist and poet Christina Claesson (1994) has said: 'Time does not pass. It arrives, arrives, arrives ...'

All this suggests another mental image of how time moves (or how we relate to the time domain), as in Figure 13.4.

Figure 13.4 How does time flow? The other view.

I can think of nothing that more dramatically illustrates how we mentally frame in the time domain than music. The perception of sound in the brief here-and-now moment is only noise – possibly noise with harmony, but otherwise without structure. It is only when the mind – or brain – puts that noise in the context of what has gone on *before* that we perceive melody or counterpoint to be unfolding – it is the 'historical' pattern (which is no longer available through sensory perception but which is stored as a memory) that gives the currently experienced noise a *positional value* which creates a Gestalt composed of a combination of memory and sensory perception.

But this is not all. The composer who conceives of music, the improvising artist, the listener, all determine the 'noise' produced here-and-now not just as a final crowning of the evolving past, but also as a transition to the future. The noise is created and experienced not just as an addition to the past but also in view of what is to come. And what is to come is never predetermined. The composer works with several options, and so does the improvising artist. The listener consciously or unconsciously creates mental images and expectations about where the sequence might now turn, and these images and the resolution of them is very much part of the experience. Even for a very well-known composition – say, a Beethoven piano sonata – the same mechanism is at work. The artist as well as the listener at every moment has an image of the general area which is to come, and then as this future unfolds it is in fact the slight deviations from the standard expectation or image that create the experience and give uniqueness and personality to the interpretation.

Thus, music – since as sensory experience it is so utterly abstract, yet

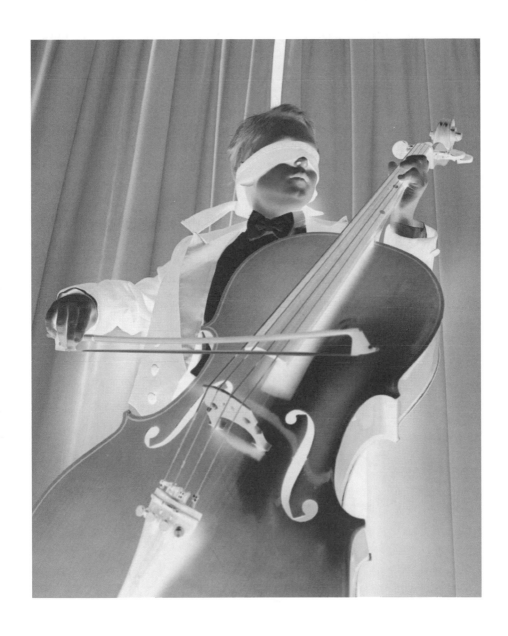

so obviously has a strong impact on the human mind – perfectly illustrates how the present here-and-now is given meaning by the mental process of framing in the time domain – by bringing into the present *simultaneously* both the past and images of the future. Without this merger of the whole spectrum of the conceptual time domain music simply could not exist.

With these two dimensions established – that of conceptual level (resulting from up- and downframing) and that of conceptual time – we can then design a number of exercises and techniques and algorithms which allow us to benefit from conceptual journeys starting in the here-and-now and continuously coming back to the here-and-now to generate action. We have now established the two basic dimensions of the 'scaffold' or 'crane'.

The most interesting part of the scaffold is the upper right-hand corner of Figure 13.5, the one which involves upframing in the conceptual future. This is the area most likely to hold the potential for discoveries of reframing our business to reflect the opportunity and imperative of reconfiguration.

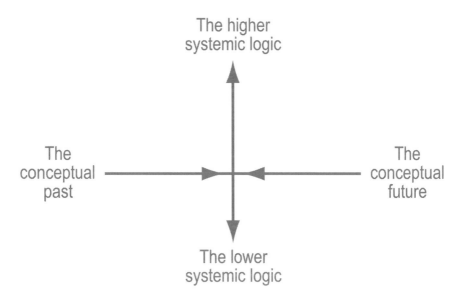

Figure 13.5 Time framing and upframing as the two basic structural dimensions of the crane.

SUMMARY: THE JOURNEY FROM HERE AND NOW TO HERE AND NOW

Exercises such as those mentioned in the previous section help us understand in what general area the construction site of the crane is. Since the purpose of the construction is reframing of the business — renewal by reinterpreting assets in a different context — the crane must allow us to *take stock of what we have, yet distance ourselves from it* and explore new territory. It must be able to bend minds. It must *open up a conceptual space beyond what is known and what can be imagined today, and it must then allow us to fill that conceptual space with new design*. It must *start from where we are* — here-and-now, *take us into unchartered territory, yet allow us to come back* with new insights and start concrete construction work on a reframed business strategy.

The design of a new strategy must start from where we have the feet on the ground, with concrete, actionable first steps.

When we have been on a journey and get back home things are not what they used to be, even though we seemingly are back to where we started. We have seen new worlds. Our knowledge has increased and our perspectives have been influenced. 'Home' is the same but still not the same, *since it is now positioned on a different mental map*. It is now a point of departure for new opportunities.

Thus, the crane is designed to take us on a mental journey from here-and-now to here-and-now, creating new insights and opening new design space during the trip. The crane I want to suggest here helps us move conceptually along two dimensions. They have been chosen based on a great deal of theory and reflection on scientific method as well as theory of creativity; but they have also been chosen based on pragmatic experiences of what works. We will look into them, after a digression, in the following chapters.

The Mental Space for Reframing

14

ACCESSIBLE FIELDS OF EXPERIENCING

We cannot escape our point of departure: here and now, and our established mental map, world view, concepts, model of reality and of ourselves. But to move ahead we need to take advantage of the resources that are available to us. Based on the fundamental, raw 'crane model' with a dimension for framing in the *system aggregation domain* and another dimension for framing in the *time domain*, and slightly rearranging it to take into account the importance of the realm of the non-conscious, we can arrive at a picture of a territory as in Figure 14.1. For visual convenience, I have left out the 'downframing' (going from the level of discourse of everyday world language to the more particular), but this could easily be accommodated. In any case I don't pretend to have a total picture of the mind territory here, but something that is useful and that can then be translated into a practical methodology.

Thus, starting from the knowledge and the world view and the mental map embodied in the language of our *everyday level of discourse* in the (partly) conscious domain, we have at our disposal our personal as well as social, collective, institutionalized *memory of the past*. We also have our ability to move into the conceptual future – indeed, our *memory of the future*. We also have the potential opportunity to consciously conceptualize and theorize ('upframe') into the more *abstract and aggregated domain*.

And, finally, we have potentially available *the realm of the non-conscious*, the unconscious, the subconscious, the tacit.

Using the above as a paradigm we find that the territories available to us can be depicted in the 'map' of Figure 14.1.

Without specifically referring to how business companies and other

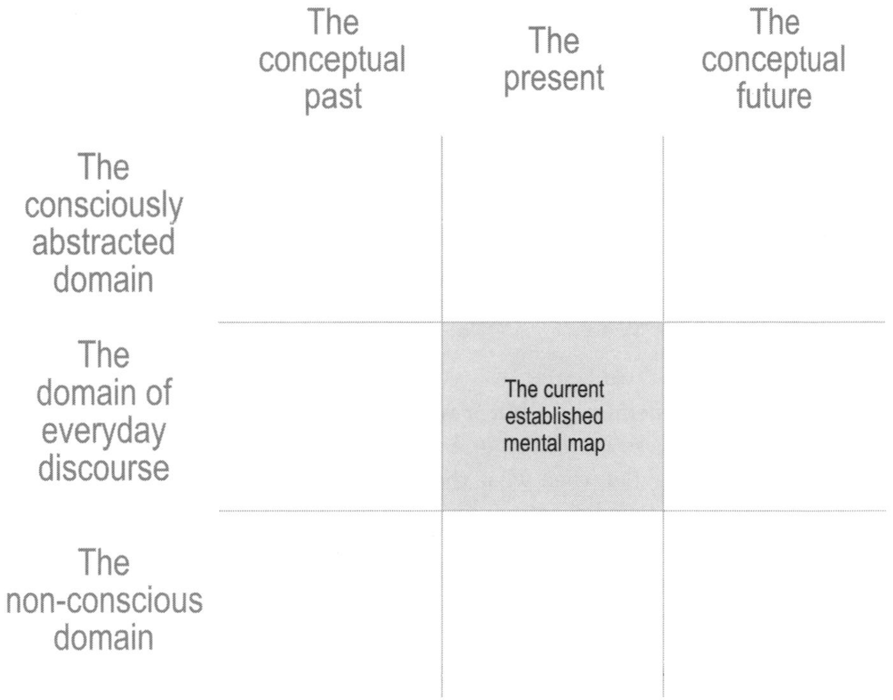

The conceptual past | The present | The conceptual future

The consciously abstracted domain

The domain of everyday discourse

The current established mental map

The non-conscious domain

Figure: 14.1 Accessible fields of experiencing.

organizations reframe I will briefly comment on each of the areas of the map, departing – naturally – from the vantage point of the here-and-now and our place in it. In reframing we do not want to escape totally from the here and now but to remould, to reframe, to preserve some elements of it – the hubs of reframing – while shedding other elements and integrating yet others.

It is by designing *the process and the social context* in which these territorial explorations take place that we can bring in the full potential of the third dimension – that of bringing in the memory of the individual and the collectivity.

OUR HISTORY

The most obvious and objective of the territories we can go into would seem to be our historical past, simply recorded as a sequence of events. We all do this when looking at business companies – we look at track records, critical events, the sequence of historical balance sheets and profit and loss statements. I have, in fact, seen many a top management group becoming greatly surprised by what they found upon looking back – how it helped them understand where they are, what their capabilities as well as their blockages are, why certain values and world views have become established, why certain dilemmas have never been resolved.

We might, of course, question whether there is anything such as an objective track record of the past. In his wonderful book *England, England*, exploring the boundaries between reality and representation of reality, Julian Barnes writes:

> This was a true memory, ... but it wasn't unprocessed.
> ... If a memory wasn't a thing but a memory of a memory of a memory, mirrors set in parallel, then what the brain told you now about what it claimed had happened then would be coloured by what had happened in between. It was like a country remembering its history: The past was never just the past, it was what made the present able to live with itself. (Barnes, 1998, p. 6)

And Esa-Pekka Salonen, the prodigious young Finnish conductor, comments on listening to Bach:

> 'You cannot change the fact that when I listen to Bach, I have heard Haydn', Salonen points out. 'I have heard Beethoven, I have heard Brahms, I have heard Stravinsky, I have heard Jimi Hendrix, I have heard The Beatles, I have heard John Adams.' An authentic performance of old music is possible, an authentic experience of it is not. (Sony Classical, 2000)

These insights illustrate how important it is to understand the events that shaped our mental maps that shaped our interpretations of events that lead to action that lead to new events that ... in a never-ending spiral (Figure 14.2).

For a business company the history at this level would consist of various facts. We developed this technology. We were listed on the New York Stock Exchange. We reorganized. We lost one third of our sales in Italy. But it is highly likely that much of this 'objectivity' disappears over time. Certain events remain in the 'official' memory while others are forgotten and repressed, so there is a selection. And events that were objective become interpreted and embedded in lore and theories, thus migrating to

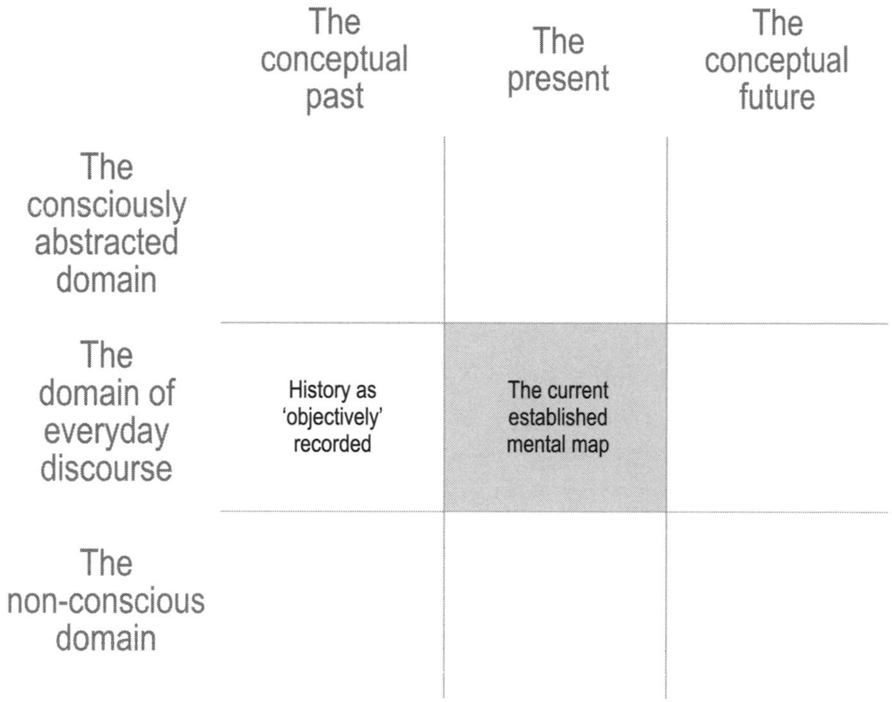

	The conceptual past	The present	The conceptual future
The consciously abstracted domain			
The domain of everyday discourse	History as 'objectively' recorded	The current established mental map	
The non-conscious domain			

Figure 14.2 Getting experiences from the past.

the domains of the non-conscious and the theory domains. (Anyone who has the slightest doubt about this should read and compare how history books in schools in France, the USA, and Sweden describe the Second World War, to take an example.)

PREVIOUSLY CONSTRUCTED THEORIES

The past certainly is exposed to conscious analysis and conceptualization. For example, it is now very difficult to think about the history of General Motors without considering the story as told by Alfred P. Sloan in *My Years With General Motors* where he not only tells 'objectively' what happened, but also discusses and extracts the theories he used to make things happen, and the concepts he synthesized as a result of his story and experiences. These 'theories' shaped the minds of thousands of thinkers and managers, whose actions then influenced business history.

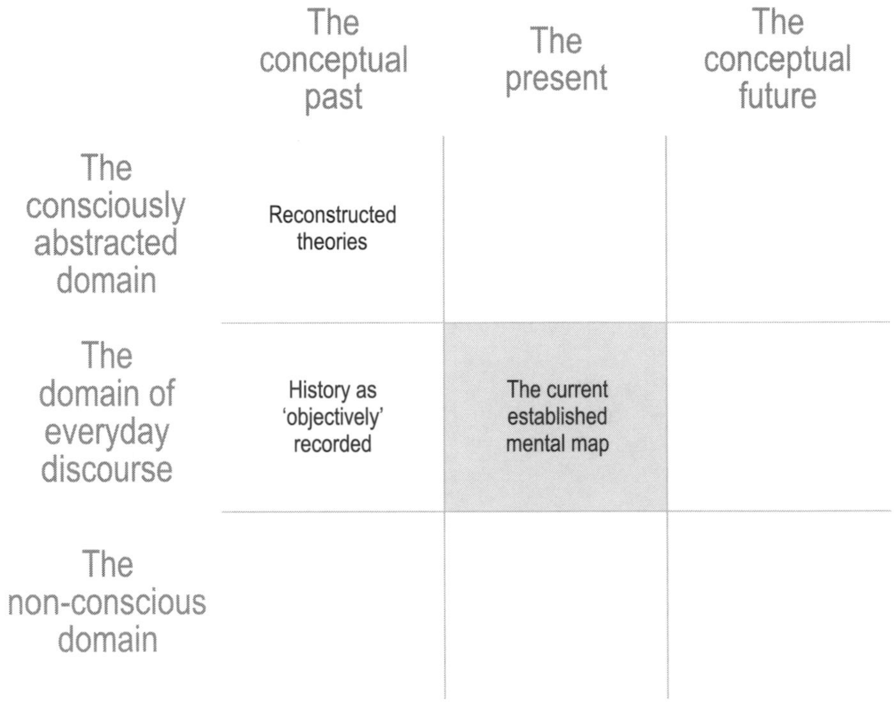

	The conceptual past	The present	The conceptual future
The consciously abstracted domain	Reconstructed theories		
The domain of everyday discourse	History as 'objectively' recorded	The current established mental map	
The non-conscious domain			

Figure 14.3 Searching the theories based on the past.

Like all theories, concepts based on historical events may and hopefully will carry a great deal of truth and be generalizable (Figure 14.3). But they may be more or less good, or they may simply not apply to a situation with new parameters. The French theorized a great deal about what had happened in the First World War, and as a result they built the Maginot Line. A best-selling management book from the early 1980s which generalized principles about long-term success from studies of a certain number of very successful companies found half of those companies floundering seriously very soon after publication. So we must consider whether the old theories were good in the first place, and we certainly cannot be sure that they will apply to a new situation. Yet we can learn from them, especially if we have a chance to consider the historical context in which they were developed, and if we regard them as part of an accumulated and on-going knowledge development and mind-shaping process.

THE NON-CONSCIOUS DOMAIN OF THE PAST

This is the domain of Freud and – since we are interested in organizations – perhaps even more of Jung, with his notion of the collective unconscious. The past, Jung would have claimed, stays with us, but in a form which (to use language that Jung would not have used) can be handled within the bandwidth of our information processing capability but which can bring us access into whole non-conscious universes. The essentials of the past have been synthesized into narratives, archetypes, exemplars, heroes (Campbell, 1949/1973), myths describing fundamental human modes of behaviour and human dilemmas. Ulysses, Shakespeare, Beethoven, Ford, Napoleon – they are all there in our conscious minds as tips of icebergs. Whether we want to go into the depths and look at the predicaments they stand for is our option. Great artists will certainly try to understand the whole cultural context and the archetypes which influenced the writers and composers and painters whose works they try to recreate or learn from. They do so not in order to replicate exactly a performance as it would have been like at the time of, say, composing a work of music (if Beethoven had had access to a modern grand piano he would have embraced it completely without looking back!), but to get to the spirit that helps them co-align their work in today's world with a historical context (see Figure 14.4).

Going into the non-conscious past also helps us understand how the physical context we function in is an embodiment of actions of the past and therefore – very often without our even thinking about it – controls much of our actions. By unveiling these forces from the past we can become more conscious of how we came to what and where we are, of our blockages as well as of our opportunities.

Alfred P. Sloan still is in the walls of General Motors, as is Jan Carlzon of Scandinavian Airlines, and as Jack Welch will be in General Electric.

SENSORY PERCEPTION AND SIMULATION

In his book *The User Illusion* (English language edition, 1998) the Danish scientific journalist Tor Nørretranders tells a fascinating story about perception and cognition, which well complements frameworks like those developed by Berger and Luckmann and Maturana and Varela referred to

	The conceptual past	The present	The conceptual future
The consciously abstracted domain	Reconstructed theories		
The domain of everyday discourse	History as 'objectively' recorded	The current established mental map	
The non-conscious domain	Archetypes Collective unconscious Landscapes		

Figure 14.4 Unveiling the influence of the archetypes of the past.

earlier. What Nørretranders does is to take a number of research results from natural science, notably from Libet (1989), while also applying information theory.

Our bodies are continuously exposed to a startling amount of sensory stimuli (and an organization would be subjective to many more...). The question is how we make sense of these. It appears that an individual receives, or has the capacity to receive, something like 11 million bits of sensory impression per second. However, the bandwidth of consciousness is much smaller than that – something like between 10 and 50 bits. (Nørretranders uses 16 bits in his calculations, but brain researchers I have talked to have sometimes quoted figures as low as half of that.)

It can be shown, according to Libet, that it actually takes about half a second from the reception of the sensory impression until we have made sense of the information. So during half a second 11 million bits have been reduced to, say, 16 bits, serving as a 'map' of the 11 million bits.

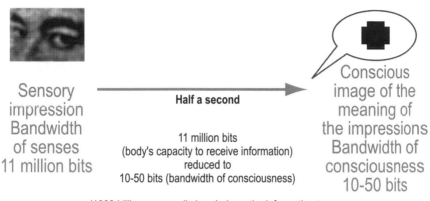

Figure 14.5 The trick of the slow brain.

In this information-processing exercise – which Nørretranders calls a 'simulation' – 1000 billion nerve-cells are involved. The transformation happens outside of our own consciousness, but although it is non-conscious it is controlled by tacit knowledge, models and incentive systems. And these models, though tacit, have not all been genetically transferred to us. Many of them are artefacts which we have more or less consciously acquired and constructed and which have then gradually sunk into the tacit domain (Figure 14.5).

In other words: we continuously receive sensory stimuli of a magnitude that would completely overwhelm us had we not had a more or less automatic mechanism to sort them out and order them into familiar categories. Luckily, our brain reduces this overwhelming complexity to about one millionth. We must, of course, be immensely thankful for the existence of this mechanism!

On the other hand, we may see a lost opportunity here. If there is such an incredible amount of raw material to work with, and if we want to be more innovative than we are – aren't we talking about an enormous waste of resources? And could there be a way to short-circuit the wonderful mechanism, to make it less perfect, to make it more able to surprise us now and then? After all, if part of the simulation mechanism has been constructed by ourselves we might be able to deconstruct and reconstruct it. But the innovative behaviour often produced by such short-circuiting tends to be seen as deviant behaviour which tends to become socially repelled and punished. Researchers in different fields (for example, Foucault, Laing) as well as artists (for example, the Danish film *Idioterna* (*The Idiots*) have mapped and illustrated these phenomena. What is deviant depends on the institutionalized perspective.

The prospect is fascinating, but I have no universal or profound answers. It certainly seems to me that many of the creative people I have met have been 'different' and some would say even deficient in a number of ways. Subjectively I would say that a surprisingly large proportion of them display certain maniac-depressive traits; surprisingly many are left-handed, several of them daydream in one form or another, and it seems that a much larger than average proportion are dyslexic. Perhaps – but here I am on very precarious ground – it is not so much that they are different but rather *that they are able to vary between different existential states and modes of being* to such a great extent that makes them special. Perhaps this makes it possible for them to influence and shut off the internal computer, to temporarily access realms of the unconscious, to perceive differently. The quotation by Johannes Brahms earlier gives a phenomenological description of how somebody who could do it experienced it.

Certainly, most models and techniques of creativity aim at achieving processes that lead to such a state of variability, at *distancing* oneself from a topic and then *closing in*, at walking from the known to the unknown, at exposing oneself to the unexpected and the chaotic which presumably can trouble the perfect functioning of the mechanism and develop new linkages (Figure 14.6).

CREATIVE INDUCTION

Upframing normally implies moving up to a higher conceptual level, generalizing, theorizing, experimenting with placing a phenomenon into different conceptual categories thereby shedding more light on it. It is a process which necessarily has a synthetic, not just an analytic, element to it, and so it is a creative process in itself.

Induction is an integrated aspect of scientific method, though probably the least understood part of it. It involves a leap of faith, an element of bootstrapping, an escape from impeccable logic, that perhaps makes

	The conceptual past	The present	The conceptual future
The consciously abstracted domain	Reconstructed theories		
The domain of everyday discourse	History as 'objectively' recorded	The current established mental map	
The non-conscious domain	Archetypes Collective unconscious Landscapes	Sensory perception Unconscious simulation	

Figure 14.6 Letting the non-conscious out.

subscribers to the mantra of objectivity uncomfortable. It involves the generation of new perspectives and hypotheses which then must be tested for correctness (if we believe we are looking for 'the absolute truth') or relevance and usefulness (if we see ourselves more as architects than truth accountants). The conscious use of metaphors and various rules of thumb to generate alternative frameworks consistent with key observations and assets can help, and such techniques for mental frame-breaking have been developed (Figure 14.7).

INTO THE RATIONAL FUTURE: PROJECTIONS

Our institutionalized, rational selves, of course, deal with the future. We normally do so by forecasting, and by planning. The future then becomes a set of explicit, conscious intents, goals, objectives that we want to move towards and reach. This process is so common (and nowadays – and not without justification – so discredited) that there is no need to dwell on it

	The conceptual past	The present	The conceptual future
The consciously abstracted domain	Reconstructed theories	Upframing and creative induction	
The domain of everyday discourse	History as 'objectively' recorded	The current established mental map	
The non-conscious domain	Archetypes Collective unconscious Landscapes	Sensory perception Unconscious simulation	

Figure 14.7 Stimulating creative induction.

here. In management science it had its heyday in planning and forecasting school of the 1950s and early 1960s.

Nonetheless, a projection can be useful in the sense that it creates a yardstick against which other alternatives can be evaluated, and a measure of deviations as time passes and new events occur. And goals and plans can be set once we have a qualified vision of the future and feel that we master our subject and territory (Figure 14.8).

NON-CONSCIOUS SCENARIOS

The wonderful mechanism that handles sensory perception also, as David Ingvar and others have shown, produces images of the future – we can call them scenarios – on a continuous and unconscious basis. These scenarios probably are not normally very sophisticated. Rather, they seem to be based on assumptions that the models we already hold will continue to be

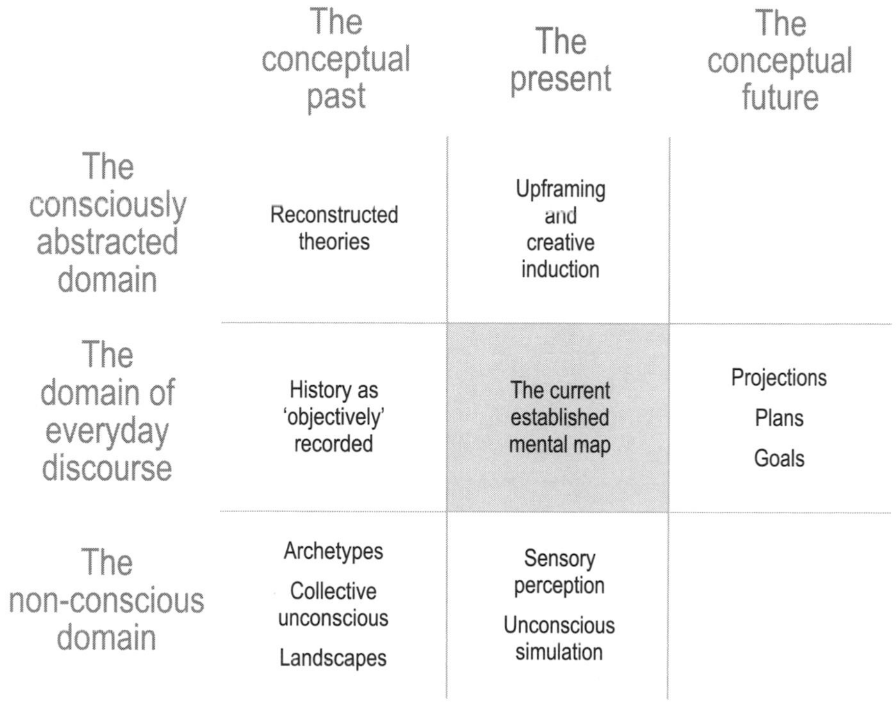

	The conceptual past	The present	The conceptual future
The consciously abstracted domain	Reconstructed theories	Upframing and creative induction	
The domain of everyday discourse	History as 'objectively' recorded	The current established mental map	Projections Plans Goals
The non-conscious domain	Archetypes Collective unconscious Landscapes	Sensory perception Unconscious simulation	

Figure 14.8 Planning – when we master our topic.

valid. They are not, however, projections but mental images of alternative futures mostly within our established frameworks.

Just as our unconscious models serve as selectors and classifiers for our sensory perception, these non-conscious scenarios become selectors and classifiers for events and stimuli – foreseeable and unforeseeable – that come to us over time. As time passes, information is subconsciously sifted against these alternative images of the future, and we basically notice (if that!) only information that indicates towards which of the future states events are bringing us. We then adapt our behaviour according to these signals (Figure 14.9).

ARTEFACT SCENARIOS

We can also move into the conceptual future *with a consciously transcendental, creative intent*. In so doing we try to go beyond the intents, goals and object-

	The conceptual past	The present	The conceptual future
The consciously abstracted domain	Reconstructed theories	Upframing and creative induction	
The domain of everyday discourse	History as 'objectively' recorded	The current established mental map	Projections Plans Goals
The non-conscious domain	Archetypes Collective unconscious Landscapes	Sensory perception Unconscious simulation	Non-conscious scenarios

Figure 14.9 The non-conscious radar signalling into the future.

ives that are normally derived from our established, institutionalized mind-set. We also go beyond the production of non-conscious scenarios automatically undertaken by our subconscious.

Scenarios become stronger as conscious artefacts and as tools for triggering creative action – see the section on visions earlier – if they are based on upframed, creatively synthesized interpretations of the present and the past. The mechanisms by which this happens have already been hinted at, and more examples will be given later (Figure 14.10).

SUMMARY

This chapter has explored mental territories available for the symbolizing processes of the mind along two dimensions: on the one hand, in conceptual time, and, on the other, from the non-conscious to the conscious and conceptually theorized and constructed. A third 'memory' dimension

	The conceptual past	The present	The conceptual future
The consciously abstracted domain	Reconstructed theories	Upframing and creative induction	Artefact scenarios
The domain of everyday discourse	History as 'objectively' recorded	The current established mental map	Projections Plans Goals
The non-conscious domain	Archetypes Collective unconscious Landscapes	Sensory perception Unconscious simulation	Non-conscious scenarios

Figure 14.10 Conscious upframed scenarios as catalysts for reframing.

– that of the individual versus collective – can be taken into account by ascertaining that the processes by which we explore the realms of experience delineated here involve and shape networks and social process.

By being aware of this map of mental territories available for reframing, and by devising ways to explore each of the territories as a resource for innovation, we can hopefully behave more like Gregarians in the sense that Dennett gives this notion.

We now turn to how this can be used in our 'crane tool' for reframing.

The Crane at Work in   15
the Design Space

DESIGNING FOR DESIGNING

The purpose of the tool – here metaphorically called 'the crane' – is to design new, reconfigured business. Thus, we are *designing for designing*.

The business environment today is characterized by the forces that bring about the dematerialization/unbundleability/liquidity/rebundleability/density framework noted in Chapter 2. The result is reconfiguration of business systems into more complex and dense co-production patterns. *Reconfiguration* in the business realm has its counterpart in the mental realm, namely *reframing*. Reframing for reconfiguration is a creative act which does not lend itself to rational control, but this innovative and creative act can be analysed as to its basic properties and logic. A tool-set can then be designed to help simulate 'nature'. Since creative innovation by definition is an open-ended process that takes us into uncharted territories results cannot be predicted or guaranteed. But by designing a tool that takes into account, as much as possible, the logic of the innovative process in a context where the goal is 'reframing for reconfiguration' we can at least hope to provide for the conditions leading to 'emergence'. This is the purpose of the crane tool.

In this chapter I will briefly pull together the threads from the previous chapters to summarize the design criteria for the crane. Then I will briefly reiterate the description of the crane along both its *structural* and its *processual* dimensions. Finally, an illustrative example and an interpretation of it will be introduced. It is not my intent here to go very deeply into either the structural features or the processual features of the crane, but rather to indicate its broad principles.

OVERALL DESIGN CRITERIA FOR THE CRANE

With regard to design criteria for the *content output* of the crane the first parts of this book help us to specify a number of topics that it should be able to handle in order to arrive at reconfigured business concepts: economic value creation, actors in the value-creating scene, co-production, offerings, competences, and so forth. Elements of this general area have been analysed in the first part of this book on 'the business landscape' and the shapers of that landscape.

The second set of criteria – those that regard *process* – have been delineated in Parts IV and V. Here are some of the major characteristics of the process that the crane should be able to spin – again, given that it is mental framing for reconfiguration of value creation that is the *content output* of the whole process.

- The process must depart from the assumption that we are 'Gregarians' (in the sense that Dennett gave it). It must allow us space to reflect on the subject, to reflect on ourselves, and – indeed – to reflect on our reflection. It must assume that we are willing to theorize about our theorizing, to conceptualize and reconceptualize our process of conceptualization. It must allow us to ask questions about the efficiency of the process that we are going through for the purposes that we have stated, and it must also make it possible for us to question those very purposes.

- The essence of the process must be that of 'emergence'. It must transcend the Bermuda Triangle that – first – everything is plannable and can be handled in a rational way; and, second and alternatively, that everything is due to serendipity and chance and that nothing can be planned; and, third, that there is a higher purpose controlling everything. As Capra (1996) has said:

  The current emerging theory of living systems has finally overcome the debate between mechanism and teleology. ... It views living nature as mindful and intelligent without the need to assume overall design or purpose.

- It must combine the rigour of scientific method and the imperative of open-ended imagination (recall again the quotation from Johannes Brahms earlier!). The latter means that it must use the learnings from complexity theory about the emergence of patterns and processes, techniques from fields such as scenario planning, insights from the theory of learning and creation. It must recognize the importance of transitional objects and other artefacts to unite people in interactive play to co-create and co-enact a new reality.

- Given our exploration of the mind space available for reframing, the process must allow and encourage sourcing of information and knowledge from 'memories' in three dimensions: The memory of the *time domain* (past – future – present), the memory of the *individual* and the memory of the *collectivity*; the memory of the *tacit and non-conscious* and the memory of the *encoded, recorded*, as well as of the domain of the *consciously theorized*.

- The process must allow the dialectic between *distancing versus focusing*, opening up and closing, allowing for surprise while maintaining rigour, for movement between existential states (recall the comment on the correlation between creativity and oscillation between 'depressive' and 'maniac' states). This is reflected in the questions 'What are we?' 'What could we be?' 'What should we be?' each representing stages in an iterative and spiralling process which have their own particular logic and rules.

- This also means that the process should allow for sufficient time and disturbance and deviation to short-circuit the mechanism researched by Libet and others and referred to by Nørretranders (and confirmed by brain researchers) – namely that the brain normally, if left alone, will take a dramatic reductionist and compressing view of sensory stimuli, fitting these into previously established boxes.

- The process must be social, participative, interactive, and must include action learning to *socialize*, *encode*, and *create*, tacit knowledge.

I do not claim to have a list of sufficient design criteria here, but all of these certainly are necessary.

The basic crane structure was introduced in Chapter 12. For convenience the visual image of it will be repeated here, with the two basic dimensions of *up- and downframing* at the value-creating systems level and *time framing* (Figure 15.1).

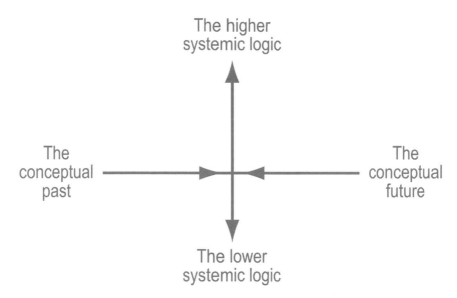

The higher
systemic logic

The
conceptual
past

The
conceptual
future

The lower
systemic logic

Figure 15.1 The basic structural dimensions of the crane.

SPINNING THE PROCESS: MAIN STEPS

The process of reframing in principle takes place in five overall steps, although they may overlap, develop into a spiral with several iterations, or otherwise be modified. In the basic model, the steps are the following:

1 Taking stock: What are we?

Whatever we might want to be or become we cannot afford to disregard the assets we have to start with. Understanding our current predilection involves taking a systemic view much in accordance with Selznick's 'distinctive competence' idea, with special emphasis on the 'business idea' concept (both quoted earlier).

This entails going back in history to track the critical decisions and commitments to values and purpose of the organization, and to how these have been embodied and manifested in various structural arrangements. It means interpreting the successes – and failures – of the organization both in structural terms ('what was so right/wrong about the business idea?') and in process terms ('by what processes did we learn and arrive at taking the decisions and making the commitments that made things go so right/wrong?'). It means identifying the possible 'hubs of reframing' (assets, capabilities, customer relationships and customer bases) that may be reinterpreted in a different/reframed systemic context. It means understanding the competitive structure – not least the invaders who nibble or make indents into our territory and therefore help us understand our weaknesses – as well as mapping the stronger values that may be emerging in our business context.

2 Upframing of business systems

Probably the most commonly used example of upframing used in management theory is about the American railways, who believed (supposedly to their detriment) that they were in the railway business and not in the transportation business. But just to remind us that there is no one and single way of upframing I must relate the experiences I have had with two client companies who both thought of railways as the hub of two quite different kinds of reframing. One thought of them as the basis for a concept of an 'experience business' (and I am sure that the Orient Express would not for a moment consider itself as being in the transportation business!); the other – a very large national railway company – started an extensive process of looking at its railway business as the foundation for a 'city services business' until national party politics stopped the experiment. So 'railways', like anything else, can be upframed in an infinite number of ways.

Upframing (as a phenomenon if not as a word) certainly is not foreign to management thinking. Unfortunately it very often stops as a simplistic or even linguistic exercise of no commitment and no consequence. Oil companies call themselves energy companies (while continuing to produce oil and changing nothing or little), real estate companies call themselves residential services companies (while continuing to do nothing or little for their customers and to make money from buying and selling real estate).

For the ones who really rethink, the consequences may be dramatic and beneficial. Xerox Corporation began to see their copying machines as the hub of a reframing into 'the document company', and took seriously the consequences in terms of exploring what this meant. Coca-Cola went from being a producer of sweetened flavoured water to being the manager of a brand.[20] IKEA may have started as a furniture company but explicitly reframed itself into a company helping ordinary people to create a good home environment for themselves. Enron is trying to redefine itself from being an electricity company to a risk management company in energy business. Tetra Pak had the idea to consider the package as a point of departure to help the dairies and retailers and customers achieve a much more efficient and hygienic milk logistics system. All these companies transformed themselves based on a grounded, thoroughly reflected, visionary upframing concept. The result was more than creative advertising.

Upframing means redefining the boundaries of the system we are in at the moment. Techniques for stimulating creativity are part of the process. However, it is essential that there be solid, relevant, factual inputs into all such processes, so that the upframing is perceived as *grounded*, *legitimate*, and *actionable*. Some procedures which may help in this process are the following (but the list is far from exhaustive):

1   Studies of 'invaders' (one of my clients pointedly calls them 'stealth competitors') who tend to redefine the system boundaries. I always tell my clients: 'Love thy invaders!' They, better than anybody else, have studied the weaknesses of the present system, and they show how it can be broken up. And with the present acceleration of reconfiguration every industry is subject to more or less unexpected invasions.

2   Draw the value stars of the organization's customers (and preferably also of the customers' customers). This means analysing their business, looking at *all* the inputs they receive as part of their value-creating process, and at how they contribute to *their* customers' value creation, and how *their* invaders are competing with their inputs around the customers' customers. The following five questions are useful in this context:

   (a) Of what larger system or process is your offering a part for the customer?

   (b) Who are the actors giving inputs in that system?

   (c) What are your client's key issues in his business
      – operationally?
      – strategically?

   (d) What are the key strategic assets of each of these actors?

   (e) What exchange (barter) currencies do they have, potentially?

3 Design one or several blueprints for alternative co-productive value constellations. This may result in one or several redefinitions of the Value-creating System of which the focal organization is a part. The process probably requires several iterations.

By taking a larger and longer view of the customer situation ideas for upframing may become evident. For example, as briefly noted in connection with the 'servicification' of offerings, a company selling personal computers we worked with was struck by information framed in the following way:

> ... the argument has shifted to the 'lifetime cost of ownership' of computers. Oracle, Sun and IBM quote calculations ... that a PC costs an average company more than $13 000 a year when maintenance, training and time lost by users is included. The cost of buying a PC, amortized over five years, is a mere 5% of that.' (*The Economist*, January 1997)

Should this company continue to strive to bring the 5 per cent down with some decimals, or should it begin to see what might be done about the other 95 per cent, given its capabilities and customer base? Whatever it finally does it will increase its options by mentally reframing its vantage point to that of what we called the 'second level customer relationship', looking at the system far beyond its customers.

3 Travelling in conceptual time: Time framing

My experience indicates that it is useful to start the process of reframing a business with an upframing exercise. This may result in a loose hypothesis – or several hypotheses – about an alternatively framed Value-creating System and about your own organization's – the focal organization's – role, preferably as Prime Mover. The next step, to further increase the conceptual design space, is to move into the conceptual future.

There are two alternative and sometimes complementary ways of doing this. The first, which has been used by Shell and subsequently by other companies, is to make *contextual scenarios*. The methodology for this is to identify the key driving forces and the major 'givens' as well as the major uncertainties of the general context which highly affects the activities of the company. (A major preoccupation of an oil company, for example, would be developing scenarios which unveil factors, actors, and events particularly important to the price of oil.) There are legion techniques for accomplishing this (the reader should turn to van der Heijden (1996) or Schwartz (1991) for thorough descriptions). The result tends to be a set of different narratives, describing mutually exclusive but internally consistent possible contextual futures. Managers can then be asked to go through an exercise in which they are stimulated to inhabit each of these futures as if it were a reality, and then back-cast according to the 'what if?' methodology: If I knew that this was the future x years from now, what would I do today to cope with it as well as possible?

4 Creating strategies scenarios in the opportunity space

But organizations are not only small boats subjected to the vagaries of the big ocean. They can make choices, and they can influence the environment. I often prefer to be more direct and focused on the business of the organization in question at this stage. This implies another type of scenario work, directly aimed at constructing alternative roles or strategic stances for the focal organization. Recall that the upframing exercise probably ended up in one or a few redefinitions of a larger Value-creating System in which some elements of the organization's current business form a part but others are new, and in which value constellations, offerings, and so on, have been redefined. To achieve business design results my experience is that it is useful to focus more on the specific role in this redefined Value-creating System of the focal organization: In what different ways can it play a major role, be a Prime Mover? What specific kinds of value would it create for what categories of customers? What alternative offerings might this imply? What kind of competences and modes of functioning would alternative strategic stances as Prime Mover entail?

The use of stories or narratives can still be retained, even if they are now more about alternative futures for a specific organization than about the contextual environment. Such stories in the form of artefact scenarios greatly help managers to empathize with alternative upframed futures, and help them draw conclusions about what is possible, and what are the action consequences now.

If the result of the upframing and time-framing processes is the unfolding of an opportunity space and perhaps some first strategy scenarios these now have to be made more robust and testable. They may even move as far as going to a process of 'idealized design', a term introduced by Russel Ackoff.

An idealized design assumes that we disregard current artificial and institutional blockages to its realization. It does not, however, allow us to think away any technological restrictions; typically, in an idealized design we have to work with cause–effect relationships that are known to exist and thus with technologies that either exist or can be regarded as certain to develop within a very near future.

One or several scenarios, then, may be developed into an idealized design, or two or more such alternative idealized designs.

It is possible that such an idealized design almost answers the question 'What should we be?' or 'What business should we be in?' But as stated before, we might need some more iterations, and in fact such iterations typically take place in a dialectic process between the established platform ('What are we?') and the emerging answer to the question 'What should we be?' There is a dilemma here which must be handled. On the one hand, the emerging reconfigured business design needs to be tested against the starting platform so that it is not felt to be completely unrealistic, ungrounded, or unactionable. On the other, such testing, if premature and if taking place before the new design has been thoroughly explored and solidified, will easily come to fulfil the function of 'dynamic conservatism' and give people reasons to stop the process or to stay too close to the ground.

5 Back to here and now: Translating a vision into a business idea

In principle the journey appears as in Figure 15.2 opposite, although it may not be as sequential and it may – and probably will – require a few iterations. But if the upframing and artefact scenario-making (time framing) have been thorough and successful, grounded ideas together with action consequences have now started to form in the heads of managers. Actually, very often at this stage a rather clear vision has begun to form, based on one or some syntheses of the strategy scenarios.

Several things remain to be done before we can talk about a new business or an action plan to produce that, however. The vision of the chosen strategy could be tested for solidity against different conceptual

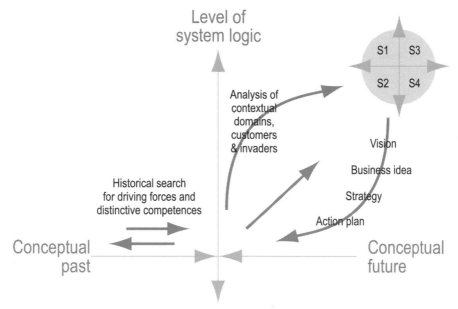

Figure 15.2 The journey from here and now to here and now.

scenarios (which would then constitute a different exercise from that of producing strategy scenarios). A business idea should be blueprinted and then tested – 'windtunnelled', as van der Heijden would put it – to move from the prototype stage. New competences, probably a new organization structure, new alliances – all need to be prepared. And the drama of organizational life that all changes and reframings inevitably create must be handled.

6 Into the planning mode

Finally, the new set-up must be translated into an action plan.

THE CASE OF THE CONSUMER COOPERATIVE: AN EXAMPLE[21]

The crane and the methodology around it can be illustrated briefly with the case of the Swedish consumer cooperative, KF. Originally KF had been founded to help consumers against the monopolistic tendencies of many producers of consumer goods, and the coalition between these producers and existing retailers. By introducing a cooperative structure with ownership by the consumers,[22] with locally organized retail outlets, and with factories producing goods in strategic areas, the monopolistic tendencies were broken and consumers could be supplied with goods of good quality at low prices. In addition they were rewarded if the organization was successful, since they were also owners and profits would go back to owners.

With increasing competition between retailers and producers the original purpose to break the monopolistic tendencies were no longer as relevant as before. And, in fact, as consumers became more choosy KF began to realize that their factories were now millstones around their necks than real assets. So they sold most of the factories, several of which had in any case been loss-generating for some time, and focused on the retailing side. However, other retailers seemed to be closer to their customers, and in the eyes of many the heavy structure of consumer representatives constituted a slow and expensive bureaucracy rather than an asset.

What was to be done? The most frequent recommendation from the business world was to completely abandon the cooperative concept and start to function according to 'sound business principles'. Together with the management group we agreed that this was not necessarily the case, and that this might have meant losing something very precarious and of potentially high value. But, on the other hand, it was clear that renewal was necessary.

A project initially designed in four steps was undertaken. Each step was designated to answer one specific question:

1 *How is the 'value creation' of households in the country changing today?*
  It was found that obtaining access to daily goods was not of great concern for people. Life had become much larger than the supply of necessities. And, in particular, households and people had become much more fragmented in their needs and lifestyles. It was found that many of them had plenty of time which they could spend, but fairly little money, and others had very little time but more money. Research showed that people were generally highly concerned about getting older, about social security, about their health, about housing – and about

having interesting experiences. People also bought a great deal of services, not just household goods. To summarize: their concerns were very different from when KF was started, and they were much more diverse.

2 *What is the current role of the consumer cooperative in the value creation of households?*
As we had expected, it had clearly diminished – not only in terms of market share of providing daily necessities (which was evident), but much more so if we looked at what was recognized to be relevant for people. KF was also felt to be a generally bureaucratic and not very progressive organization, although many people thought that the basic ideas of a cooperative were very attractive and could be further developed. But few had faith in the ability of this particular institution to develop the attractive ideas – there was a gap between the image of the particular *institution* and the image of the cooperative *idea* as such.

3 *Who are the new actors gaining share of value creation of households?*
This turned out to become a study of 'invaders'. Quite a number of such organizations were unveiled, and together with management we started to analyse their businesses and modes of functioning. Not surprisingly, many of them focused on areas outside the supply of daily goods – fields nearer to the new issues closer to the core of people's concerns. They involved areas like education, information, healthcare, services. Many of them tried to use new information technology to create networks. And, surprisingly, many of them helped to link people together in new constellations which were highly co-productive and cooperative in spirit if not by name. In fact we could say with some confidence: the greatest threat to the consumer cooperative is the idea of co-production and not least cooperation!

4 *What possible role could the consumer cooperative play in the value creation of households?*
For this, four basic strategy scenarios – framing in the time domain – were developed. (Note that the upframing had already taken place by defining the general area of exploration as 'the value creation of households' rather than 'the supply of daily goods'.) They were distinguished along two key dimensions. One of these was whether the delivery system was to continue to be fundamentally shops, or whether a multi-channel system – including new technology such as the Internet and

including other partners and existing delivery systems – could be developed. The second dimension was related to whether cooperative (or, more fundamentally, co-productive) ideas involving the mobilization of considerable amounts of barter currencies (such as time, knowledge, involvement in a cause) were essentially to be abandoned (except possibly in name for the sake of image), or whether they should in fact be deepened but reinterpreted for a new era.

From these two dimensions four tentative strategy scenarios emerged. For each of them a narrative was written – what events and critical decisions had led from here-and-now to each of them, and what was the business idea and mode of functioning and values and competences and offerings and customers of the cooperative in each of the four strategy futures depicted by the scenarios.

Some people involved in this exercise observed that the organization was in fact embarking, full speed, on one of these scenarios which in everything but name meant abandoning the cooperative ideas. Although the action consequences of the other strategies were by no means clear to all of top management it was nevertheless decided to make an attempt to look at the consequences of one of them – actually the most radical relative to the current direction but the one most true to the core values – much more deeply. It was found that this road, in fact, meant going back to the competence roots (of cooperation and co-production) and the customer roots but reinterpreted in a modern context.

We will leave the story here since the continuation of it is being played out at the moment, with gradually increasing visibility.

THE CRANE AT WORK IN THE EXAMPLE: SUMMARY

We can discern roughly the following steps in relationship to the crane:

1 Today's situation ('What are we?') was analysed using various kinds of quantitative data, but also in terms of history and how critical events and decisions had shaped the company. There was a well-codified set of theories – 'the company saga' – about what constituted the historical and present formula for success, some of which clearly proved to be out of touch with today's business reality when distinctly articulated and

made discussible. There was also a strong presence of historical arche-types and 'heroes' and symbolic events which everybody in the com-pany knew about. Together with the client we tried to surface these phenomena and make their impact on today's situation and fit with today's reality discussible and conscious.

2 The next step was an upframing process. In this case the upframing took its point of departure in the customers, and regarded the cus-tomers (who were also the owners) as not only buyers and 'consumers' of daily goods but in terms of their much broader concerns and value-creating activities in today's reality. This led to considerable expansion of the mental maps of the possible realm of business development.

   In terms of the concepts introduced earlier it was the shift of per-spective from the value chain of daily goods supply to seeing the customer from a *value star* perspective that proved particularly useful.

3 The client organization's position in this upframed system was then established. It was found that while the organization had – which was serious enough – lost market share in retailing, it had lost much more 'share of customers' total value creation'. While KF had lost market share in terms of what proportion of the population received their supplies of daily goods from KF, and in terms of 'share of wallet', they had lost much more if the whole value star rather than just daily goods was taken as the playing field. This energized the process by further legitimizing the reframing/upframing perspective.

4 The force fields and actors in the upframed system were then analysed. Economic actors who had not previously been seen as competitors (or, for that matter, possible partners) were discovered and entered the mental map, which now consisted of the larger value star. A learning process about what sort of business models and competences were required in this upframed system was initiated.

5 The client organization's assets, competences, customers, values were then analysed as to their fit with this new context and new archetype business models. Not unexpectedly, a number of distinctive gaps were found. It had been known that there were gaps *vis-à-vis* the new com-petitive situation even before the upframing, i.e. in the retail business, but the new analysis displayed other gaps relative to the upframed system.

   But, surprisingly and much to the encouragement of the management group, it was also found that some of the original competences and the espoused (and to a great extent also practised) values of the organization potentially had an excellent fit with the logic of the upframed system.

6 Four strategy scenarios were then developed, none of them contextual but all of them based on tough but realistic *choices* that could be made by the company. These choices were related to the extent to which certain 'soft' values and competences (including the notion of cooperation and the explicit use and market making of barter currencies) would be deployed, and to how 'hard' systems such as shops, Internet solutions, and other logistics and communication tools could be developed.

Some broad alternative strategic roads had now been clarified for the management. The implications of continuing the current road had become more clear, including the long-term impact on the organization's identity.

7 In this situation management chose to explore the most radical strategic scenario track, but also the one that would be most true to the core identity. (This did not exclude continued and simultaneous streamlining of the retail business which confirmed.) But the feasibility of the strategy and its concrete implications still had to be explored and proven. After some consideration a particularly promising and potentially valuable area was picked, namely the healthcare area. A special business area development unit was set up.

8 The overall field that had been chosen gradually became manifested in a number of concrete business development initiatives and were tested through 'windtunnelling' processes. Most of this first went on in a small unit within the organization, but as ideas started to prove themselves there was increased internal networking, and synergies between the new and the old were found in several areas.

At least one journey from here-and-now to here-and-now had been undertaken. More, and more precise and focused, iterations go on and will no doubt follow.

Part VI
Capabilities for Purposeful Emergence

INGRESSO ━━━━━━▶ **PART I**
THE MAP AND
THE LANDSCAPE

Chapter 1
EVOLUTION OF
STRATEGIC PARADIGMS

Chapter 19
WHAT LEADERS
NEED TO DO

Chapter 18
BRINGING EXTERNAL AND
INTERNAL DYNAMICS IN LINE

PART VII
LEADERSHIP FOR
NAVIGATION

Chapter 2
RECONFIGURING THE
VALUE SPACE

Chapter 16
FROM GREAT IDEAS
TO GREAT COMPANIES ▶ **Chapter 17**
CAPABILITIES FOR ACHIEVING
THE CRITICAL OUTCOMES

Chapter 3
SOME CONSEQUENCES
OF DEMATERIALIZATION

PART VI
CAPABILITIES
FOR PURPOSEFUL
EMERGENCE

PART II
SHAPERS OF
THE LANDSCAPE

Chapter 4
CHAINED TO THE
VALUE CHAIN?

PART III
TOOLS FOR
LANDSCAPING

Chapter 15
THE CRANE AT WORK
IN THE DESIGN SPACE

Chapter 7
CO-PRODUCTION: TOWARDS
INCREASED DENSITY

Chapter 5
PRIME MOVERS
AS RECONFIGURERS

Chapter 14
THE MENTAL SPACE
FOR REFRAMING

Chapter 8
THE OFFERING AS A TOOL
TO ORGANIZE CO-PRODUCTION

Chapter 6
PRIME MOVERSHIP
AS ECOGENESIS

Chapter 13
THE PROCESS CRITERIA
OF THE CRANE

Chapter 9
THREE TRENDS IN
OFFERING DEVELOPMENT

Chapter 12
ON CRANES AND
SKY-HOOKS

PART IV
THE
MAP-LANDSCAPE
INTERACTION

PART V
REFRAMING:
TOOLS FOR
MAP MAKING

Chapter 11
CHANGE AND
CREATION

Chapter 10
FITTING INTO
THE ENVIRONMENT

From Great Ideas To Great Companies   **16**

PHOTOGRAPHS AND MOVIES

There is a great difference between a photograph and a movie. Both can be revelatory, but they reveal different things.

These days, when benchmarking is so popular, it is very common to write cases or invite the CEO of a company which has made the headlines, and try to generalize features from that company as drivers of success. I, for one, now and then discuss this year's version of *Business Week*'s 'Top 1000' of market value or the *Fortune* 500, based on sales. But one has to be careful about what conclusions are possible to draw. Most of the time, benchmarking is a sure way to mediocrity.

Managers who tell about their successful companies often tend to quote from a famous guru or consulting company (and knowing the profession I can usually quickly guess which one) rather than from their own unprocessed experience. So what we get to hear is not always what really happened but a reinterpretation of it through current management hype. It is easy to misinterpret the reasons for success, even if the data seem to come from the horse's mouth. What is in the headlines right now, and what is on top of the lists, tends to be like a photo, a frozen picture that does not take into account the movement that it represents, and even less the underlying events and conditions and long historical process that led to this state. For that we need a movie.

Current success and long-term sustainability are not the same thing. From a macro perspective and in the long term this may not make much of a difference. There is no particular reason why, from the perspective of the overall economy, we should be very concerned about the long-term capability of survival and success of particular institutions, as long as the overall system improves and survives. In fact, it is rather easy to conceive of situations in which, say, a national economy would have been better off if this telecom company or that healthcare system had been allowed to stumble and disintegrate. If we are Schumpeterians we should not need to worry about whether companies and other institutions die in the famous process of 'creative destruction', even if they have achieved great things and great fame, as long as there is a macro mechanism – namely the entrepreneur-based market economy – ascertaining that superior companies and institutions take over. But the macro process is shaped and fought out by an infinite number of micro processes, of individual entrepreneurs and small and large and huge companies and institutions trying to survive, to better themselves, to innovate. These individual institutions are the focus of this book. But even if we were only interested in the economy at large we would have to realize that the quality of it is highly related to the quality of all the micro processes that accumulate into the macro process. In today's business world – more than ever – it is probable that macroeconomic growth and the well-being of people is deeply related to the mobilization of entrepreneurship at the micro level and to the quality of institutional renewal. Business institutions, not nation-states, are clearly the Prime Movers of today's value creation and economy. As such their leaders have great responsibility.

But what long-term characteristics should such an organization possess? It is quite clear, for example, that a nation can be quite powerful and successful in the short term under a non-democratic, enlightened government and dictator; yet, few of us believe that such a constitution would be good in the longer term, so we prefer to recommend constitutional democracy as a solution even if that may entail certain short-term sacrifices. Similarly, a planned economy may yield some remarkable short-term results but again few of us would expect an essentially liberal market economy to be less than vastly superior in the longer term.

There is a great market for quick fixes and one-minute solutions. There is nothing wrong with being successful in the short term. But most institutions we are concerned with also want to be successful in the longer term.

WHAT THE PHOTOGRAPH TELLS US

Is Microsoft a great company? IKEA? No doubt, these companies are doing something incredibly right, like many other companies on top of the lists.[23] They demonstrate the power of great ideas, skilfully implemented. Are they great companies? Certainly, for their shareholders, for millions of customers, for a time. But can we draw conclusions about how to be successful from them other than about the beauty and strength of their original or current business ideas? Will they be on the top lists 10 or 20 or 50 years from now? (And is it unfair to ask such a question?) Can we draw the conclusion that one must be at the edge of high-tech business, as Microsoft, to be successful, or what about being in a low-tech business, like IKEA? Is it the stock option plans and high-level rewards to people working in Microsoft that mobilizes people to such a great extent, or is it the parsimonious executive reward system and monkey-class airline tickets of IKEA that does the job?

This and the following chapters deal with the difference between *great ideas* and *great companies* – the latter being defined as those who are able to renew themselves on a more or less continuous or long-term basis.

THE LONGITUDINAL VIEW

So far nobody has found simple push-button solutions for being successful long-term. I can think of no way to avoid crises. There is nothing wrong with having crises. I would expect psychologists to say that people evolve not by avoiding crises but by facing them and struggling through them.

The story of many artists is the story of successfully overcoming crisis. As a lover of classical music, and particularly of great piano playing (unfortunately not part of my own accomplishments) I often notice how young, prodigious, refreshing piano players gradually fade. They may continue to be among the elite, but the immense promises of their youth are all too rarely fulfilled. The exceptions exist, and their life itinerary is often quirky. One such example is the late Chilean pianist Claudio Arrau, already referred to, who was born with all conceivable natural gifts and who had the opportunity to develop them further in his youth. His crisis came early, and he was very conscious of it. That he not only overcame the problems but was able to use them to transcend to incredible new levels of achievement is witnessed by his very latest recordings, made at age 87 and 88 (when, admittedly, his fingers were no longer able to accomplish that ultimate precision of technical execution that they had until nearly age 80). Under the headline of 'The Suffering in the Life of a Musician', Jürgen Kesting (1992) relates 'the last interview' with Arrau made on 11 April 1991, and comments on it (Arrau was born in February 1903):

> At the beginning it had certainly just been a game. That was typical of so-called 'infant prodigies', who, and [Arrau] quoted the psychologist C.G., were 'divine children', beings who were incomprehensible not only to those around them but also to themselves, because they had within them a concentration of abundant vital forces with an unconscious urge for expression. What may have happened to a person at this stage is forgotten, however, as soon as childhood is past – 'when ability is suddenly not a miracle anymore, when the audience is no longer astounded but comes to a concert with great expectations – and when it suddenly comes to your ears that you have not lived up to those expectations.' (Accompanying text to *Claudio Arrau, The Final Sessions, Volume I*, Philips, 1992)

Many attempts have been made to analyse the characteristics of a company capable of maintaining 'consonance' over a long period of time (which inevitably means renewing itself more or less fundamentally). Whereas some of them mainly try to generalize from some existing, rather short-term-based successful companies, others – such as *Built to Last* (Collins and Porras, 1994) and – with *élan* and great personal experience behind it – *The Living Company* by Arie de Geus (1997) – attempt to go further. Peter Senge's work on *The Fifth Discipline* (1990) as well as Nonaka and Takeuchi's book *The Knowledge Creating Company* (1995) are in this tradition, as well. Other notable modern contributions come from Mintzberg (1994), Ghoshal and Bartlett (1997), and Prahalad and Hamel (1990).

De Geus (page 9) uses the biological metaphor of *The Living Company*, clearly – as Peter Senge states in its foreword – referring to the ability of the long-lasting company to *create its own processes* (my italics), 'just as the human body manufactures its own cells, which in turn compose its own organs and bodily systems'. This is in opposition to looking at a company as a machine.

De Geus stresses the company's ability to learn and adapt, its ability to build a community and a *persona* for itself, its ability to build constructive relationships with other entities, within and outside itself, and its ability to govern its own growth and evolution effectively.

Chris Argyris, in his own books and with Donald Schön, has seen what I would consider *the mode of interaction* as the key process by which a company's learning process evolves. If the mode of interaction is governed by macho notions and defensive assumptions of other people's view of the world, and if a number of issues are seen as non-discussible (cf. Latour's discussion on complex arguments locked into 'black boxes' referred to earlier), no or little learning will occur, even if intentions are the very best (Argyris, 1994). Learning will be blocked and – in the language I have used earlier – dominating ideas will not be sufficiently challenged since they will not even be transparent and discussible, with the result that a lack of consonance between the identity of the corporation and the environment will prevail.

Perhaps I am hopelessly nostalgic, but I still consider the study by Burns and Stalker (published 1961) on *The Management of Innovation* to be one of the small handful of best management books ever written. In their study of the electronics industry in Scotland after the Second World War they found that certain organizations were able to change from war conditions to new market and technological conditions, while others were not. The former were characterized by what they called an *organic* structure, with strong horizontal (as opposed to vertical) communication lines, a perception of the whole and of the demands of the total situation by everybody. The second type they called 'mechanistic' organizations (which fulfil the main criteria of early organizational theorists including Weber, Fayol and Taylor: a compartmentalized and usually functionally specialized organization). The *code of conduct* – very close to the mode of interaction that Argyris and Schön focus on – was found to be crucial for the functioning of an organic structure, and this code of conduct was promoted by the example and concrete behaviour of leaders. A key task of leadership also was to handle blockages to change in *the political system* and in *the status system*. These systems tend to defend the status quo by embodying the success formulas of the past and the interests of functionally defined groups.

CRITICAL OUTCOMES

The maintenance of consonance between an organization and its environment is in itself a dynamic process, requiring sensitivity to what happens in the environment and to disturbances both in the environment and in the organizational processes, to achieve corrections and marginal innovations ('continuous improvement'). This is a process of maintaining dynamic equilibrium which we may call 'adaptation and correction'.

At any given time the 'business idea' model, and at an even more profound level the Selznick model of 'distinctive competence', seem to explain satisfactorily why some companies are successful in the short to medium term – the Great Idea consisting of consonance between three major factors: the environment, the values, and the structural manifestations.

In my experience a successful organization has understood three major aspects of *the environment.*

- The *values and the power fields* of that environment. Rhenman (1973) provided an in-depth analysis of the relationship between values inside the organization and the values of the external context. Christensen (1997) has shown how innovation and adoption of new 'disruptive' technologies in a company tend to be blocked or slowed down because of the strong degree of embeddedness of a company's existing technologies in a larger 'value network' (including – particularly – the customers) with its established way of doing things.
- Critical 'dissatisfactions' and assets which are somehow 'unexploited' or 'exploitable', and where action could create a *more efficient larger system.*
- The *value-creating logic* which prevails at any time, depending on the current state of technology and financial and political situation in the environment.

The values are related to *purpose and mission,* which need to be in consonance with the external context, and at best such that the focal organization becomes a crucial or even indispensable element in the functioning of the larger system.

The structural manifestations of the consonance equation deal with how effectively the values have been translated and embodied in social structure and institutionalized into *artefacts* which manifest the mission and the values, and guide individual and collective action both inside the organization and in the larger value constellation.

If these three factors are maintained in consonance through continuous adjustments we have a dynamic equilibrium.

However, situations often occur when a company needs to structurally rethink its business. Electronic commerce, globalization, deregulation, and other current driving forces require it to change its business model and to find a new *type* of consonance between the external environment, the values, and the structural manifestations. This is what we will refer to as a '*frame-breaking* process', where a company reinterprets itself.

At yet another level, a company needs – over the long term – the capability to *not only* adapt within an existing business model and formula, and *not only* the ability to change when circumstances change, but rather it needs a constant process of questioning itself, of developing preparedness so that it can react quickly and structurally rather than with marginal improvements not only once but continuously over time. We may think of this as the ability to achieve *recurrent purposeful emergence* (Figure 16.1).

1. Adaptation and correction	Continuous improvement within a framework.
2. Framebreaking reconfiguration	Structural change of the business to match paradigmatic change in the environment.
3. Recurrent purposeful emergence	Capacity and preparedness to achieve framebreaking reconfiguration when required.

Figure 16.1 Three levels of outcome.

CRITICAL PROCESS

Our organization, then, with its mission and values and its concrete manifestation in structure must be in consonance with the 'fitness context', whether it passively adapts to a given external context or whether its own actions bring about some of that context in an ecogenetic process. *As we move from adaptation and correction to framebreaking reconfiguration and creation of a New Great Idea to the Great Company with recurrent purposeful emergence capability our focus must shift from the consonance of the three factors of the model mentioned above to the processes by which co-alignment between the fitness context, the basic identity of the organization, and its structural manifestation take place.* Recall that *processes* is the third indispensable element for describing any living system, according to Maturana and Varela.

I propose that these processes are, respectively, single-loop learning, double-loop learning, and learning (or knowing?) how to learn (know?).

A first and elementary level of learning and knowledge development process is what Argyris and Schön have called single-loop learning. Such learning does not require change of the basic model that is being applied, only an adjustment of the values of existing parameters. It leads to increased efficiency within a framework.

To achieve frame-breaking reconfiguration a company needs to engage in what Argyris and Schön have called double-loop learning. The outcome is what I refer to as 'reorientation' as opposed to 'variation' (Normann, 1971). In this case we are talking about more than adjustment within a given mind frame. Thomas Kuhn (1962) would have called this a 'revolution', a result of 'extraordinary' problem solving as opposed to 'puzzle laying'. In the history of science this process corresponds to the great changes of world view: from the world as earth centred to the world as sun centred, from the world as a 'clock' mechanism to the world as an 'organism', etc.

But making a reframing does not guarantee that we have the capacity for continuous or *recurrent* emergence. However, there is a higher level of learning again which increases the capacity of an organism or organization to make reframings when necessary or otherwise called for. This is the process of 'learning how to learn', hopefully resulting in 'knowing how to learn' and at least now and then a glimpse of *knowing how to know* and giving us, in Dennett's terminology, 'Gregarian' properties. I will use the expression 'knowing how to know', well aware of its lack of modesty.

Whereas single-loop learning can be fairly well understood, and whereas double-loop learning may be the result of serendipity, hazard, extraordinary leadership and/or the use of our crane such capacity to innovate continuously seems to be fundamentally related to certain capabilities and constitutional properties that lead to the invention and institutionalization of certain processes within an organization. What is it that makes some organisms and systems more likely to adapt to dramatically changing environments than others? What processes are required, on an institutionalized basis, in organizations that want to answer up to this criterion?

As a further underpinning to the argument I will briefly reiterate some characteristics of processes of business renewal from my earlier work (1975/ 1977). Change is unlikely to take place unless the following are in place:

- *Identification and/or creation of driving forces* creating 'space' to explore and enter. Mostly, driving forces for change are there to be utilized unless they are blocked out by myopia or politics. Driving forces may be borrowed *from the external environment* in the form of critical change factors such as new technology, important customers who put new demands, political changes, deregulation creating new opportunities, or new competitors or invaders. They may also emerge *inside the organization* in sway groups, among individuals or in one individual, or in conflicts. Whatever the source or origin of critical driving forces they must somehow be transformed by the internal system of bargaining and politics into the will to change and into power backing it up. This transformation of tension into constructive driving forces is a key task of leadership.

- This brings us into the *political process*. It has two sides to it. One is to *mobilize support* for change aligned to the new driving forces in the external fitness context or among internal entrepreneurs. The other is to *handle blockages* to change inside or outside the organization.

- Third, renewal requires *knowledge development*. This also has two sides to it. We have to distinguish between *innovative knowledge* which implies a change of mind-sets, and *conservative knowledge* which can go very deep but which is categorized in traditional mind-sets. Both are required, but the latter can sometimes become the enemy of the former. In the long term the former is an absolute prerequisite for becoming a great company. There must therefore be a continued process of 'opening up' new areas of knowledge, but without sinking into the 'court jester' or 'repressive tolerance' syndrome – or, for that matter, the 'hysterical hyperactivity' syndrome.

- Fourth, renewal requires *resource development*. There was a time when financial resources were the bottleneck, such as was the case of KF, the Swedish consumer cooperative, a century ago. Today there seems to be capital looking for ideas everywhere. The big problem of knowledge-intensive and fast-growing companies today is not capital but tends to be how to attract talent and how to develop people quickly enough.

But the most essential process for renewal is the one that is often called 'leadership'. To me this process is best interpreted in the context of the frameworks of Selznick and Maturana and Varela (which are, as I have pointed out, remarkably analogous).

CAPABILITIES, PROCESSES, AND OUTCOMES

We have reviewed the anatomy of 'Great Ideas' – for temporary success in the form of fit or consonance. We have looked into the nature of a re-framing process that allows a new consonance configuration to occur. This was done by considering how such processes might spontaneously occur 'in nature' and by attempting to design a tool – a crane. The crane was an effort to consciously simulate 'nature', leapfrogging the limitations of our current framework by creating misfits and opening up new spaces that could lead to consonance at a higher conceptual level, but without falling into the trap of believing that we can invent that higher level within our present cognition process or rationality.

We have recognized, then, that there is a distinction between Great Ideas and Great Companies, and we have assumed this to go beyond even the ability to reframe and to make an innovative reorientation of an organization. In the quest for the identity of the Great Company with capability for recurrent purposeful emergence[24] we are looking to identify underlying structural or even *constitutional* factors nurturing certain pro-cesses – institutionalized and embedded in a social context, since they have to be sustainable and lasting – which can trigger action when the critical or opportune situation occurs. These must be factors and pro-cesses that can lead to reframing, but they must be at a higher logical level again than the reframing process that our crane implies since they are supposed to lead to not one reframing process but to an *underlying ability to reframe* when the situation calls for it.

Thus we are reasoning about three logical levels of *outcome* and corresponding *processes* that lead to them:

1 The first set of processes has adaptation and correction as its outcome.

2 The second set of processes leads to reconfiguration requiring a learning process which implies mental reframing – a new mental framework and road map, new structure, new power relationships, new offerings, new alliances and other structural couplings – but still with elements – 'hubs' – of continuity, now framed as parts of enlarged or changed systems definitions.

The processes at these two levels are analogous to what Argyris and Schön (1974) call single- versus double-loop learning. In single-loop learning the 'master program' and the governing values remain although new action strategies are invented within that framework. Double-loop learning leads to 'a new framework for learning and to new routines' (Argyris, 1993, p. x).

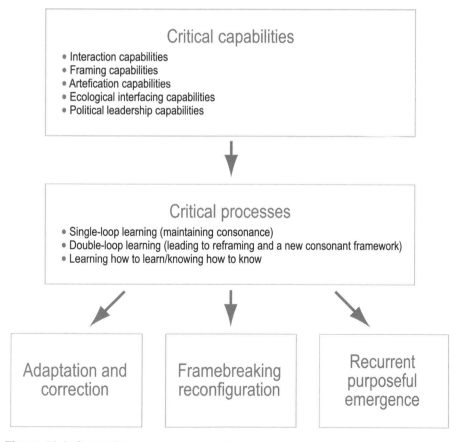

Figure 16.2 Capabilities, process and outcomes.

3 Third, we are looking for processes of autopoiesis – self-creation capability, for the organization that is 'Gregarian' in spirit. We want to understand what are the preconditions for that elusive phenomenon of *recurrent purposeful emergence*. We then have to search for processes at a higher level of consciousness – we want to identify the conditions for learning how to learn, or 'knowing how to know' and even learning how to know how to know.

The following chapter is an attempt – certainly not conclusive – to systematize my own thoughts and experiences. It builds on an article that I published in 1985 (Pennings & Associates, 1985), though the scheme has been much developed in light of later experiences and further reflection.[25] The next chapter therefore deals with *critical capabilities* to achieve the *critical process* that evolve three *types of outcome*, according to Figure 16.2.

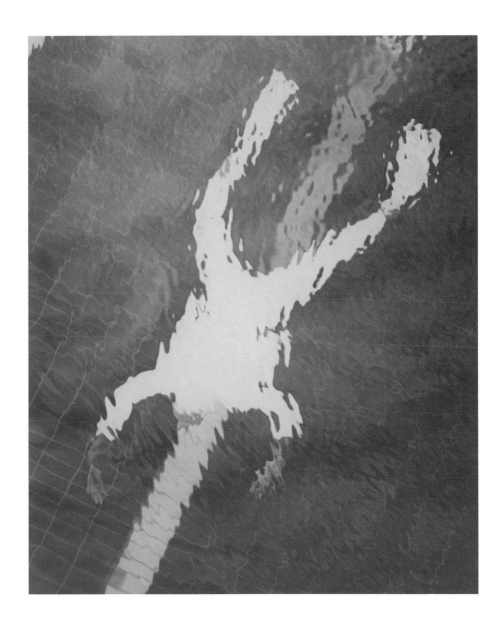

Capabilities for Achieving the Critical Outcomes

17

FIVE DOMAINS OF CAPABILITIES

I will divide the capabilities into five rough categories. The first is related to *the style of interaction*, or code of conduct as practised, not as espoused, within an organization. This would ensure that relevant information and knowledge will be searched for, that critical issues will be discussible and confronted rather than non-discussible and locked into 'black boxes', and that the progress of the organization rather than internal power games – policy rather than politics – govern behaviour. My main source of inspiration in this domain of capabilities is the work by Argyris and Schön (1974, etc).

The second domain of capability relates to the notions of cognition and world views and mind-frames. We are not likely to 'see' new things without new language. As Martin Ingvar puts it: 'We can only see what we have already seen' (personal communication). So what we are discussing here is the ability to move between conceptual levels and of 'seeing' things from the angles of different paradigms – of *framing*.

The third domain I will call *artefication skills*. If the basic world view and values and mission (as enacted) of the organization constitute its identity – as I prefer to translate Maturana and Varela's 'organizational pattern' into the context of social organizations – the concretization and institutionalization in the form of artefacts that manifest the identity is how I want to use their concept of 'structure' (also see Stymne, 2000). Artefacts can be physical or mental – in the latter case they are memes.

I will retain my original concept of *'ecological interfacing'* (Normann, 1985) capabilities for the fourth category. Humans beings and social organizations have the remarkable option to choose, based on reflection, what part of the environment they will interact with, and thus have at their disposal an incredibly powerful tool to influence themselves. This process of influencing may be both conscious and purposeful, yet – and this is the whole point – partly not controllable. We are talking about the famous position 'at the edge of chaos', where structures with dissipative qualities can take on new and surprising shapes. For the purpose of having to reinvent ourselves to survive we can deliberately put ourselves into situations which we cannot fully control.

Finally – after these *social* capabilities, *cognition* capabilities, *design* capabilities and *spatial location* capabilities – there is a category which I think of as *political leadership* skill. This is related to using power to protect emergent processes (and sometimes give them a run for their money!) as well as to mobilizing power to move ahead.

Using these five domains of *capabilities*, the three types of *process*, and the three types of *outcome*, we obtain the scheme in Figure 17.1 which will now be briefly investigated with regard to differences between the capabilities required for the three levels of outcome.

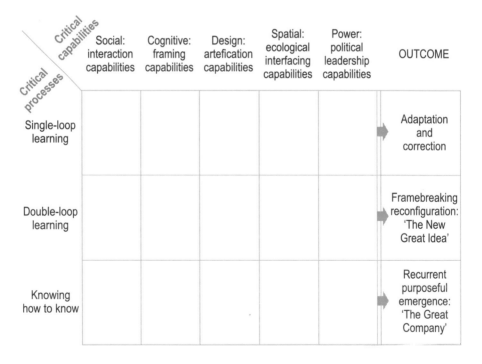

Figure 17.1 A scheme for differentiating capabilities at three levels of renewal.

INTERACTION: THE SOCIAL DOMAIN

At the level of the company which makes continuous marginal corrections within a framework we are generally talking about highly rational interaction, with a framework and with norms of efficiency well understood by everybody. The current emphasis in the business press on 'effective operations' would fall within this category. 'Management by fear', whatever else you think about it, might be quite efficient and functional here. Argyris and Schön call this 'Model I' behaviour:

> Theories-in-use are the master programs that individuals hold in order to be in control. Model I theory-in-use-instructs individuals to seek to be in unilateral control, to win, and not to upset people. It recommends action strategies that are primarily selling and persuading and, when necessary, strategies that save their own and others' face.
>
> In order for a Model I to be implemented effectively, the recipients must be willing to accept being submissive, passive, and dependent.
> (Argyris, 1990)

For framebreaking and to achieve the Great Company other skills are necessary. Argyris and Schön would refer to this as 'Model II' behaviour. They quote the *search for valid information, free and informed choice,* and *internal commitment to action strategies taken* as the three key governing variables. They stress the importance of avoiding 'non-discussibility' of key issues and assumptions (Latour would describe such non- discussibility as the result of having confined complex and precarious arguments in 'black boxes'). They emphasize the necessity to make the basic assumptions on which action is based visible and testable, in order to maintain long-term congruence between 'espoused theory' (what actors say they are doing and why) and 'theory in use' (the actual behaviour as formed by the assumptions they are really holding)[26] to avoid getting into unfruitful, 'self-sealing' processes in which assumptions are hidden and therefore cannot be challenged.

I particularly would like to stress the notion of and importance of 'vulnerability'. If managers are supposed to be invulnerable, never to expose their uncertainties, and if they are never supposed to be wrong, they will lock themselves into 'Model I' behaviour. Black boxes will remain non-transparent. Thus, to invite free and informed discussion one must make oneself vulnerable, i.e. demonstrate that one is prepared to expose uncertainty which is the same as to take the risk of trusting. This implies great courage and also goes against most of the myths of the rational, macho manager so popular in business circles.

Burns and Stalker made much of the notion of 'code of conduct', by which managers at the top set examples about personal behaviour and interaction style. Their characterization of 'mechanistic' versus 'organic' structures is revelatory in this respect. If behaviour at the top follows the traditional command and control pattern, if vertical functional communication has priority over horizontal interfunctional communication, if norms of politics and power (zero-sum games) rather than of furthering the whole organization's performance dominate – then this code of conduct will prevail throughout. Leaders should 'walk their talk'. 'It's your mission to live your vision.'[27]

I deeply believe in the importance of managers holding a basic 'emancipatory interest' (Habermas, 1972) if anything more than streamlined efficiency is to be achieved. They are liberators of what is already potentially there. This does not only imply tolerance of the deviant (advocated by Arie de Geus) but very strong endorsement of people to behave entrepreneurially (cf. Ghoshal and Bartlett, 1997). Margaret Wheatley (1992/1994) goes so far as to want to get rid of norms governing and structuring behaviour, with the exception of norms which state what is unacceptable (for example, unethical or immoral) behaviour.

FRAMING: THE COGNITIVE DOMAIN

A company needs a clear perception of what is *the business idea* or business model as a prerequisite for the consonance that leads to efficiency. The business idea, or what Selznick calls distinctive competence, is a reference point for learning. In this way parameters taking on a value outside the normal can immediately be spotted and reacted to. Sensors and systems which rapidly signal any deviations from standard values in the environment and in internal processes must be in place so that corrections can be implemented with immediate effect.

When we come to the framebreaking level – the development of a new 'Great Idea' – we have seen that the most important skill relates to *upframing* and to *time framing*; the ability to see positional value of the present as part of a higher level, and preferably future context. The use of conscious (or unconscious) techniques for upframing and for time framing (like creating artefact scenarios from which we can back-cast and mould our strategies) is required. Distancing and refocusing, use of metaphor, empathy with 'invaders' and with customers and their 'value stars' help. This implies the recognition – uncomfortable for many – that 'reality' is a relative concept, that things can always be perceived from different angles, that we can make sense of 'factual' observations by applying different thought paradigms; that it is positional value that counts and not inherent value.

At the recurrent emergence level the crucial thing is to maintain, over time, a continuously growing *variety pool* of *business models, possible visions* and *scenarios*. The management of 'the battle of ideas' within the company is of the greatest importance, but without falling into the 'court jester' and 'repressive tolerance' trap, i.e. treating this battle as a ritualistic comfortable routine matter.

How can we know that we don't fall into these traps of confusing routine and lip service with the genuine thing? The best answer I can find is that we probably have to feel that it hurts (or perhaps that we are thrilled, to use a more positive view). We must feel that we are not continuously in the comfort zone, that we lead part of our lives in the zone of discomfort, or that we are literally shattered in our basic assumptions. Otherwise we should become suspicious of ourselves.

The capability concept that best seems to grasp the essence of the framing capability at the Great Company/recurrent emergence level seems to me to be that of *'languaging'*, communication about communication, developing language about language – and about our process to develop language. If we communicate about communication – which is something Argyris and Schön (1974) would certainly advocate – and do so openly within a framework of their Model II behaviour, we probably have the best guarantee, if such a thing exists, for applying framing capability that can maintain us as a Great Company. The essence of languaging is that our present *mode* of communication, and our present world view represented by our language and concepts, will never be left unchallenged.

ARTEFICATION: THE DESIGN DOMAIN

Artefacts are humanly designed objectivations of subjective and social (intersubjective) processes. They serve both as a 'record' of such processes and as a means to transform subjectivity into intersubjectivity. They help to create a social reality and therefore to provoke action – mental and physical. Artefacts represent a man-made 'code' different from but complementary to the 'genetic' code.

Organization structures and systems are artefacts. They express knowledge about strategy and processes that has accumulated, and they express the way we expect behaviour to be focused and interaction to take place. For example, the Asea Brown Boveri matrix structure introduced by Percy Barnevik was a way to, on the one hand, put people into small business units which made everybody responsible and entrepreneurial (a radical break with the past both in Asea and in Brown Boveri Corporation), but also to interact in specific ways reflecting both the local and international market structure and certain ways to combine competences. The General Motors decentralization/divisionalization scheme introduced by Alfred P. Sloan is probably the most significant organizational artefact of the twentieth century.

The attribution of managerial and other *roles* within organizations is also a highly significant act of artefication. In Asea Brown Boveri the original matrix structure was well known for forcing many managers to wear several hats at the same time – for example, to be globally responsible for one business sector, and also for one local market with regard to all business sectors. When the Skandia insurance company appointed a 'director of intellectual capital' (Edvinsson and Malone, 1997) this was a very visible sign of insight about intentions and priorities and about a changing world view in the company. On the other hand, roles can be very conserving – compare the Danish consumer cooperation which still today calls the local store managers of the Brugsen retail chain 'uddeler' ('allocators' or 'rationers' would be the closest English translations).

Physical objects such as architecture are also crucial artefacts which can have a very high impact on mental process and other behaviour. The new head office of Scandinavian Airlines System, erected in the 1980s, with its transparent glass walls was supposed to both symbolize and stimulate the new openness and interactiveness introduced by CEO Jan Carlzon as a key feature of the company's culture for competitiveness. The radical office space design of the Danish company Oticon, where people actually did not have a permanent office space, was a means to bring about a mode of functioning in line with the way it was believed that a knowledge-based company ought to work in a modern era. General Electric's centre in Crotonville became a physical symbol which never failed to remind people of Jack Welch's notion of the 'boundaryless' company and other new strategic principles and policies. In working with the graphical industry it became clear that emphasizing the sheer physical quality of print and graphic design would be a key competitive factor against the hoards of digital invaders.

Also, seemingly neutral *technology and tools* can become important value-laden symbols. There is the story – whether true I am not sure, but telling anyway – about the person who, upon entering the company in which he had just been elected as chief executive officer and finding a time clock, and knowing that one of the slogans of the company was that 'We don't buy people's time but their involvement', asked for a sledge-hammer to crush the time clock.

Corporate symbols and signs have become not only tools for recognition, such as Raymond Loewy's Shell symbol, or the 'Solo' symbol developed by Wolff Olins for what is now Nordea (and MeritaNordbanken), often quoted as the world's most advanced bank in using the Internet and other new technology. They can also be highly deliberate and conscious tools to transfer the notion of a culture and mode of behaviour – compare the apple of Apple, Inc., in comparison with the more baroque and industrial symbol of IBM.[28]

But many of the most important artefacts are purely symbolic, with no *a priori* physical manifestation (cf. Morgan, 1986). *Concepts* are incredibly important artefacts. They are memes often resulting from a long 'cultural' process, or they may be expressions of deliberate rhetorical innovation. When Enron describes itself as a risk management company in (and recently also outside) the energy business, when Xerox goes from the copying machine company to 'The Document Company', or when Mercedes-Benz or Ford talk about selling 'mobility' instead of cars, these notions are highly significant as artefacts. When Observer (a very successful Stockholm headquartered company) launches concepts such as 'communications audit' and 'value-creating communications' they create mental catalysts for reframing the company's business, which started as press clippings where they are the world's leader. The power of concepts is further proven by how extremely conserving they can be. When IBM set up a personal computer division and called it the 'entry products division' this, of course, reflected a whole world view out of touch with emerging reality.

It has been an interesting reflection of the craggy road along the strategic paradigms from Chapter 1 to see how organizations refer to their customers. Banks, for a long time, tended to call their customers 'accounts'. They are now trying to change this though not without slips of tongue. I was even told of an electricity producer where a customer was often referred to as a 'resistance'. Disney World has tried to get into the right mind-set by referring to customers as 'guests'.

In a large recent project I worked with my colleagues to redesign the healthcare system of the Skåne region in Southern Sweden (Levin and Normann, 2000). One of the most controversial issues initially proved to be how to view customers. Physicians and most politicians liked to call them 'patients'. We found that this concept prevented discussibility of many key issues. It was a 'black box' which narrowed down the relevant definition of the system and therefore the scope of the necessary change of it. In a conference I had referred to 'customer' as such a concept, and I was attacked for this, on the ground that 'patient' was the appropriate concept and that 'customer' also evoked unwanted commercial connotations. In a published answer to the attack I therefore proposed a different word from 'customer', namely 'Gakk', a word which I had generated through a random process. I summarized the issue thus:

> The patient concept is good but not enough. Why?
> *Firstly*, 'Gakk' as opposed to 'patient', implies that we look upon the relationship beyond a specific acute care episode.
> *Secondly*, the 'patient' concept has often (not always) implied a narrow, diagnosis based perspective of a person. 'Gakk' encompasses a broader perspective, including a more humanistic one.
> *Thirdly*, the 'Gakk' perspective means that we explicitly focus also on the health creating (not only illness treatment) activities of a person.
> *Fourthly*, a 'patient' is rather defenceless (since, by definition, ill) and, in difficult cases, often has few possibilities to make demands on the health care producing system. However, we know that nothing promotes the capacity of innovation in an organization more than the demands from users with freedom of action and with a voice. Thus, to people who work with the development of a health care system, the customer is a development catalyst. Unpleasant for those who do not like innovation. Good for those who think it is needed. (Normann, 1999)

Let us come back to the meaning of artefication for our three 'outcome' levels. Again, within the correction level we only need small adjustments. Artefacts should *remind* us of, *reinforce*, and *focus* what already is. We find lots of organizations with symbols of past achievements, portraits of the Great Individuals who invented the business, and books reminding us of their values and world views and operating principles, lest we should forget. The walls seem to speak to us.

Reframing, on the other hand, cannot take place without – either as an effect or as a cause – structural change that diverts our attention in new ways and moulds co-production efforts into new ensembles. Artefacts that refocus and point in another direction are necessary.

In one of the most important *Harvard Business Review* articles ever, Ari de Geus (1988) has pointed out the importance of 'transitional objects' – be they a consultant, a new theory, or something else – in what we might think of as a midwife role for new ideas and innovation. *Serious Play* by Michael Schrage (2000) also argues in the same vein.

At the recurrent purposeful emergence level we have to look for a higher logic, though transitional objects work here, too. In terms of organization structure and governance the best word I can find for it is 'constitution'. A constitution defines both differentiation and integration (cf. Lawrence and Lorsch, 1967); it ensures tension and conflict which can help us move into the discomfort zone while setting some rules about how conflicts are supposed to be handled. And a constitution might conceivably institutionalize processes that reflect the logic of de Geus's and Schrage's advocacy.

The role of ownership is crucial here. Rolf H. Carlsson (1997) has pointed out that there are certain 'ownership skills' which need to be applied:

> If the learning of the organization fails, it is the owner who must pick up the tab. His capital is at stake. Thus, the role of the owner involves two fundamental value-creating contributions:
> - Taking risks by exposing his capital in a business venture. This makes the venture at all possible at the same time as it leverages the speed and intensity of the venture process by buffering the risks of other financial contributors (banks etc).
> - Managing risks by ensuring that the fundamental risks the venture is exposed to are reduced or, preferably, eliminated.
> - Taking risks and, particularly, actively managing risks require competence. We can distinguish between four types of risk, each corresponding to an important dimension of owner competence:
> 1. Competences to reduce/eliminate business risks. The logic and dynamics of different type of business vary. There are ample opportunities to specialize.

2. Competence to manage organizational risks. Such risks include everything that can jeopardize organizational learning.
3. Competence to manage risks of legitimacy. It is not enough for a company to be concerned about its process of doing business. It must make sure it has a 'license to do business' as well. Indirectly, this is crucial for fundamental value creation.
4. The fourth competence element could even be called meta-competence. This competence is constituted by an idea of ownership and its supporting system of values. 'Meta' because it integrates all the other competence elements. At the same time, this competence corresponds to specific risks, particularly risks of opportunism and special interests.

The owner is at the top of what can be conceptualized as the renewal hierarchy of a company. Practising the principle of meta-management, the owner should not do what subordinated echelons of boards and executive management are supposed to do. However, the owner must see to it that the renewal and learning processes at subordinate levels function properly. Hence, the most important learning skill that the owner must possess belongs to the level of learning how to learn, or knowing how to know, to apply the concepts used in this book.[29]

Designing the executive role constellation for differentiation and integration that leads to *integrated diversity* is also a highly critical artefication skill. In *Management for Growth* I delineated some of the requirements for executive constellations in companies in different situations. For a company in search of (what I would now call) temporary or constant reframing I identified the following six roles (which are not necessarily the equivalent of six persons) in the executive constellation:

- The variety generator
- The selector
- The interpersonal process moderator
- The potential carrier (the person who embodies and champions the concrete implementation of a potential new business idea)
- The visionary
- The politician or shield maker

As long as there is sufficient complementarity and – of course – tension between such roles, and the role takers can find a *modus vivendi*, a company can often be recognized as being truly innovative over a long period.

Similarly, loss of innovativeness can often be attributed to the departure or loss of power of certain role takers, with a more monolithic mode of functioning as a result.

ECOLOGICAL INTERFACING: THE SPATIAL DOMAIN

Since any system has to have 'requisite variety' (Ashby, 1956/1964) to handle the environment in which it functions, and since to some extent this means that the system has to be a 'mapping' of its environment – whether this mapping occurs from the outside-in, from the inside-out, or from a synthesis of the two (what I have called ecogenesis), *it is possible for a social system to influence itself by choosing what part of the environment to interact with.* Possibly, no other insight is more crucial for long-term learning and development capability than this.

Therefore, to become one of the best one has to interact with the most demanding environments. Athletes need to play in the best soccer clubs in Europe or to sprint in California, Texas, or a few other places. It is very difficult to jump very much higher than the bar is placed. Choosing to live in a comfortable (in the sense of non-challenging) environment implies giving up the ambition to be really excellent. Business companies typically move to areas where there are 'clusters' of other similar or complementary companies – think of Silicon Valley for information technology, or think of Sassuolo in Italy for tiles. Unless fashion producers choose to expose themselves and are able to make it either in Milan, London, New York, Paris, or Tokyo they are probably not much to consider.

I have long had a standard question to my customers: 'Tell me who your most successful and most demanding customers are, and I will tell you how good you are.' The better educated, the more demanding the customers are, the more intricate their business issues are, the more this will piggyback on the company or system providing services. I was shocked, recently, when working with the national health service of a European country, to find that the general attitude to the Internet and other developments among the government bodies involved was that 'Well, unfortunately we probably cannot prevent the customers from becoming more and better informed and more demanding'. By having this attitude instead of welcoming more informed customers the system renounced from one of the most important means to improve itself.

Companies should choose its customers based on a number of different

criteria: one of these should be direct economic returns to the business –
such as profitability per customer relationship. But another criterion for
choosing certain customers is that the interaction with them can serve as
a 'learning stage'. As the CEO of one bank I worked with said:

> Of course we are only a fairly marginal player with [famous customer
> company X], and overall we probably may even lose some money from
> doing business with them. But they are the most advanced customer in
> this country for financial services, and, firstly, we learn a lot from work-
> ing with them. Secondly, unless we had this and a few other similar
> customer relationships, we would be much less interesting to the really
> talented people in our business.

There are several parts of the environment which a company can
choose to interact with 'at the edge'. One is *customers*, as mentioned above.
Another is *technological frontiers*, and not least frontiers of new technologies which may have an impact in the future, such as digital technology,
Internet technology and genetic technology or biotech technology.

Invaders are often – as mentioned earlier in this book – indicators of
areas of the environment which are on the move, and therefore show us
where traditional borderlines are breaking down.

But it is also of the utmost importance to interact with *other stakeholders* who have a key impact on the present definition of the business.
Legal and regulatory changes are one such example. For example, we
found that many companies were highly interested in interacting with
and better understanding the goings on of the European Patent Office,
since this was related to issues of intellectual property which are becoming increasingly important. For pharmaceutical companies, interaction
with the Food and Drug Administration in the United States and the
analogous institutions in Europe is crucial.

What differences, then, can we observe between our three outcome
levels? For maintaining a good fit with the environment at the first level
an effective *sensory and signal system* with the established operating business environment is sufficient. At the framebreaking level we must consciously get out of the comfort zone and *interact with unknown parts of the
environment*. We must 'love our invaders' and learn from them, since they
have studied us and they can serve as a mirror image of our own weaknesses. And since we are not only involved in adaptation but also in
Prime Movership strategies we must fulfil the conditions for ecogenesis –

as depicted in Chapter 6. We must find the plus-sum game and mobilize the capabilities of actors with whom we together want to create the new business eco-system, the new game.

At the third level of recurrent purposeful emergence we must navigate at the edge, always searching for the misfit context. We must continuously interact with, and question, the borderlines. In particular *we must ensure that the intellectual realm we deal with is much larger than the operational realm*. We must be involved in eco-search. To a certain degree Andy Grove (1996) is on this track when he stresses the need to be 'paranoid', though my hunch (supported by some experience) is that a positively searching attitude is more fruitful than an *a priori* defensive one.

POLITICAL LEADERSHIP: THE POWER DOMAIN

Every institution has a power structure. The policies and the processes going on within the institution tend to reflect this power structure, as do the outputs – the customer offerings (in Normann, 1971, I concluded my research into cases of innovation by saying that the (new) product of a company can in fact be described as 'a mapping of the company's power system'). The goals and ambitions of an organization must be backed up with a suitable power structure, reflecting and supporting the direction that the organization is supposed to take to the detriment of other directions. The power structure is both the enabler of action and the immune system, focusing action and weeding out what is considered irrelevant.

Power structures may be homogenous and clear, or they may be heterogeneous, multi-dimensional, and even ambiguous. Whether one or the other is good depends on the type of organization, the business logic, and the stage of development and desired outcome of organizational process. The traditional business organization tended to have a fairly simple power structure, whereas, for example, so-called 'professional' organizations (such as hospitals or consulting companies) need to reflect both the administrative hierarchy and the professional one (for example, the medical profession in healthcare). In organizations where the business logic calls for the pulling together of multiple competences on a case-by-case basis the power system may have a networked and sometimes very complex character.

It is the role of political leadership to ensure that the power system reflects the needs of the institution – its particular situation and business logic and stage of development. For the first level of outcome – basically incremental improvement within an essentially stable framework – the type of political leadership that best seems to reflect the situation is what Weber would have called *'rational leadership'*. It is based on an intellectual understanding of the productive processes of the organization, and supports the efficiency and continuous, adaptive improvement of those processes. It is also founded on an analysis of the 'precarious values' (Selznick) that contribute to the organization's performance, and supports these values.

It was, of course, Weber's thesis that the world ought to move towards rational leadership, from traditional leadership based on the attribution of power by other than rational factors such as tradition, ownership, or on charisma. Logic, not emotion and not tradition or inherited position, was to rule.

But such rational leadership is not enough in situations of structural, disruptive change (see, for example, Rhenman, 1973; Johnsen, 1993; Christensen, 1997). The immune system may become too strong for a company to break out of the frames. Reorientation of a company, changing its business idea or business model, requires a realignment of both the cognitive processes and the power system.

At our second level, then, we need political leadership that can *break up old structures*. The role of the leader in such a situation is to extract, create or co-create, and then articulate a vision and direction which breaks the frame and creates a new one. And, in particular, leadership at this level always means *using power to redistribute power* and change the power system.

Leaders who are able to do this must act either as entrepreneurs who stand for their own new vision themselves, or as 'midwives' able to put together fragments already existing within people in and outside the organization into a new coherent direction.

The need for such visionary leadership is very strong in today's structurally changing value-creation landscape. The challenges are essentially two. One is to articulate and propagate the new direction – a task for which we constructed the crane. The other is to manage the transition.

The latter part is particularly devious and difficult today, since reorientations now often tend to imply not just moving from a 'mature' area with a slowly declining future into some other area with higher prospects of growth, but to actually replace an existing business model with another, in the process literally killing or destroying many of the elements of an organization while retaining a certain hub of the reframing. The new is built on the ruins of the old. In the Xerox Corporation the copying machine, around which the whole culture of the organization had been built, was left as only one element in a changed business concept and organizational structure. Bricks and mortar banks who add Internet banking must change their branch networks unless they just want to be left with extra costs. Charles Schwab took radical steps to change their company with an Internet-based business model.

The drama is enhanced because cannibalism of the new *vis-à-vis* the old must take place. Yet, until 'the new' is large enough to carry the weight of the organization, 'the old' must be defended although it is more or less condemned. The rhetoric and charisma required to navigate across such a transformation of a company is formidable. But it is clear that the leader must take a stand, and be an entrepreneur, a fighter for the new and visionary, the creator of a 'deviating' series of events that brings the company into new territory.

Since so many reframing strategies today involve ecogenetic reconfiguration leadership at this level also must be institutional beyond the confines of the individual organization. It must ensure that the 'organization matrix' (Emery and Trist, 1965) of the larger system and value constellation has an infrastructure of common values beyond the individual actors and their short term self-interests. This theme will be further dealt with in the following chapters.

At the third, 'Great Company', or recurrent purposeful emergence, level the leader as such will be less concerned with a particular direction than with innovativeness and renewal and transformation as processes. It has been said that Jack Welch, when asked about his strategy for General Electric, answered that he had no strategy. As we know, this does not mean that he had no ideas. What can clearly be seen from his behaviour is the promotion of certain process concepts and certain standards: 'Workouts' to improve cost efficiency, the notion of 'boundarylessness', the ambition that the company should not be in businesses unless it was either number one or number two, the strong promotion of – to use our terms – 'servicification' and more recently 'e-ification'. The learning centre in Crotonville was created and promoted as a symbol of the learning and ambitions of the company; the notion of 'employability' was advanced.

All this suggests the image of a leader who doesn't necessarily have to be identified with any particular concrete business vision or any specific framebreaking process, but more with the notion of the searching and knowledge-developing organization, continuously creating new options for itself, continuously nurturing processes that contribute to innovativeness.

Leadership at this level ensures that the other capabilities, and the processes that lead to them, of our matrix shown in Figure 17.1 are in place. It encourages languaging and ecological interfacing 'at the edge of chaos', leading to new structural couplings; it provides stewardship for the creation of catalysing symbols and other artefacts. It ensures that there is a constitution which brings out pressures and conflicts into the open and handles them creatively. It ensures the existence of a vigorous executive role constellation. It does not allow the organization to settle. It does not artificially reduce the ambiguity and the tensions of the real world, but recognizes them and makes them discussible and therefore actionable.

We can summarize our reasoning around capabilities, processes and outcome briefly in Figure 17.2.

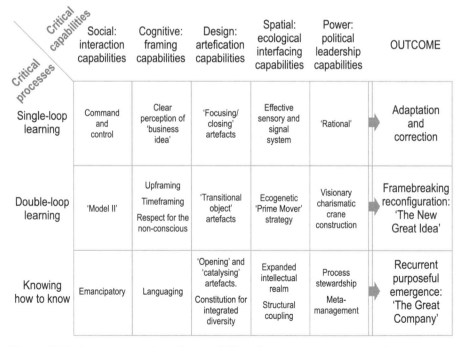

Critical capabilities / Critical processes	Social: interaction capabilities	Cognitive: framing capabilities	Design: artefication capabilities	Spatial: ecological interfacing capabilities	Power: political leadership capabilities	OUTCOME
Single-loop learning	Command and control	Clear perception of 'business idea'	'Focusing/ closing' artefacts	Effective sensory and signal system	'Rational'	Adaptation and correction
Double-loop learning	'Model II'	Upframing Timeframing Respect for the non-conscious	'Transitional object' artefacts	Ecogenetic 'Prime Mover' strategy	Visionary charismatic crane construction	Framebreaking reconfiguration: 'The New Great Idea'
Knowing how to know	Emancipatory	Languaging	'Opening' and 'catalysing' artefacts. Constitution for integrated diversity	Expanded intellectual realm Structural coupling	Process stewardship Meta-management	Recurrent purposeful emergence: 'The Great Company'

Figure 17.2 An attempt to identify capabilities for renewal at three levels.

Part VII
Leadership for Navigation

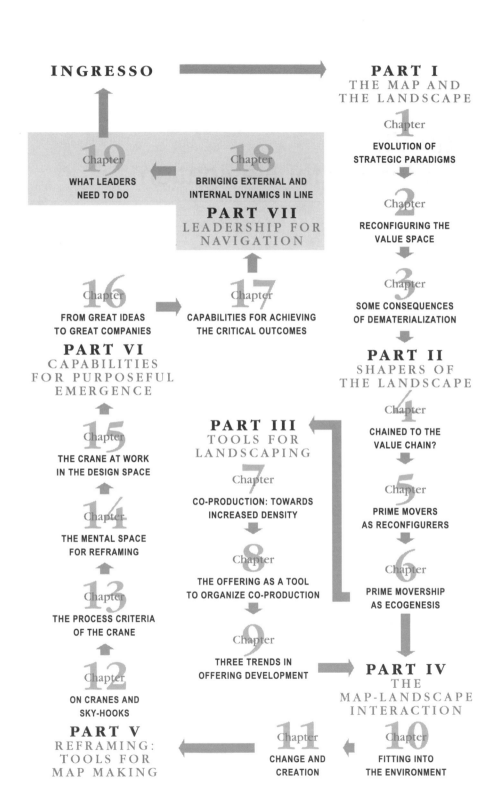

INGRESSO

PART I
THE MAP AND
THE LANDSCAPE

Chapter **1**
EVOLUTION OF
STRATEGIC PARADIGMS

Chapter **2**
RECONFIGURING THE
VALUE SPACE

Chapter **3**
SOME CONSEQUENCES
OF DEMATERIALIZATION

Chapter **19**
WHAT LEADERS
NEED TO DO

Chapter **18**
BRINGING EXTERNAL AND
INTERNAL DYNAMICS IN LINE

PART VII
LEADERSHIP FOR
NAVIGATION

Chapter **16**
FROM GREAT IDEAS
TO GREAT COMPANIES

Chapter **17**
CAPABILITIES FOR ACHIEVING
THE CRITICAL OUTCOMES

PART VI
CAPABILITIES
FOR PURPOSEFUL
EMERGENCE

PART II
SHAPERS OF
THE LANDSCAPE

Chapter **4**
CHAINED TO THE
VALUE CHAIN?

PART III
TOOLS FOR
LANDSCAPING

Chapter **15**
THE CRANE AT WORK
IN THE DESIGN SPACE

Chapter **7**
CO-PRODUCTION: TOWARDS
INCREASED DENSITY

Chapter **5**
PRIME MOVERS
AS RECONFIGURERS

Chapter **14**
THE MENTAL SPACE
FOR REFRAMING

Chapter **8**
THE OFFERING AS A TOOL
TO ORGANIZE CO-PRODUCTION

Chapter **6**
PRIME MOVERSHIP
AS ECOGENESIS

Chapter **13**
THE PROCESS CRITERIA
OF THE CRANE

Chapter **9**
THREE TRENDS IN
OFFERING DEVELOPMENT

Chapter **12**
ON CRANES AND
SKY-HOOKS

PART IV
THE
MAP-LANDSCAPE
INTERACTION

PART V
REFRAMING:
TOOLS FOR
MAP MAKING

Chapter **11**
CHANGE AND
CREATION

Chapter **10**
FITTING INTO
THE ENVIRONMENT

Bringing External and Internal Dynamics in Line

18

EXPLOITING STRUCTURAL CHANGE

If 'management' is the art of achieving efficiency within a more or less defined framework, 'leadership' is the art of navigating an organization through structural change. Structural change may mean adverse conditions.

It is a not uncommonly held idea that management can be learnt while leadership is founded on talent that must be inherited. While there may be more than a grain of truth in this it should not prevent us from analysing and reflecting on leadership. I would much rather go along with the view expressed by Erik Johnsen (1993) that *leadership consists of a set of identifiable behaviours*. There is no denying that most people are not predestined to become neither the world champion of high jumping nor of chess, nor the CEO of a major company. But whatever our genes and other predetermined conditions allow us we can probably increase our capability in either game by reflective analysis and exercise.

Some of the talents and behaviours characterizing good leadership seem to be more or less eternal. This is why it is still possible to benefit from studies of Alexander the Great, Julius Caesar, Mahatma Gandhi, Alfred P. Sloan, Giovanni Agnelli, Marcus Wallenberg or Nelson Mandela. There are also clearly cases in which there has been a specific but possibly time-limited fit between the behaviour of a leader and a particular situation or context – consider Winston Churchill, Charles De Gaulle, John F. Kennedy, Ronald Reagan, Mikhail Gorbachev, and Margaret Thatcher, to take some major political figures from the twentieth century. Percy Barnevik was the perfect person to shatter the comfortable cultures of Asea and Brown Boveri Corporation, Louis Gerstner for realigning a directionless and gloomy IBM, Jorma Ollila for seeing the opportunities created in Nokia and daring to crank it up into top gear. The qualities of leadership required change during the various stages of a business idea or company lifecycle. Different types of leadership are required for stimulating innovation in an organization, for rapid resource growth and market penetration, and for achieving streamlined efficiency. It is even more complex when extremely rapid market penetration and fundamental transformation of the business have to take place simultaneously, such as, for example, in Nokia around the millennium shift.

If leadership is the same as helping an organization navigate through structural change, it must be based on an understanding of both *external* (contextual and business) dynamics and *internal* dynamics.

Our current era sees no lack of change in either. Technology, globalization and deregulation paint a new business landscape. They also deeply influence values, lifestyles and what Michael Maccoby (1988) refers to as 'social character'. The notion that knowledge has become the most crucial production factor (which, as some have pointed out, means that Karl Marx's thesis that 'workers' would ultimately own the production factors may come true in a totally unexpected way) profoundly influences the relationship between people and the organizations they work with (rather than 'in' or 'for'). Complexity has increased radically, and it very rarely is true that 'the boss knows best' – nor that he or she should.

IDENTITY IN A WORLD WITH HAZY BOUNDARIES

Business systems are being reconfigured. No definitions, no boundaries are sacred. Whereas previously we could think of the bricks and mortar, the factories, the physical products, of companies as a reasonable guide to what they 'are', this is no longer the case. Much of what they do goes on in the virtual world. Corporations are described as 'virtual', 'imaginary'. Co-production takes place in networks. 'Workers' are no longer employed but wandering nomads crossing invisible and undefinable boundaries everywhere. Companies invent means to influence what goes on far beyond their legal boundaries. They see customers and other value constellation partners as equally important to manage as 'employees'.

This lack of boundaries, this haze, this lack of definition in the physical world, paradoxically requires us to *think more*, *not less* of boundaries. The paradox that the more boundaryless the world seems to be, the more important it is to think about boundaries has been pointed out by the late Don Michael (1973/1997).

If we are to keep our sense of purpose and identity, we must have an idea of what we are and who we are. *But the more the physical world becomes blurred, the more this sense of identity must come from reflection, from activities performed in the conceptual domain.* Conceptualizing must compensate for the haziness.

I believe we can find the key to resolving this dilemma in the basic model proposed by Maturana and Varela, further developed by Luhmann (1990) for social systems. As organizations are forced to continuously reshape themselves they need to search for identity more in values, capabilities and principles, *more in the abstract domain than in the physical domain.* Thus, as iterated earlier, we need increasingly to distinguish between our *identity* and the physical/structural *manifestation* of this identity. This, again, is what is behind the expression by Lampedusa: 'If we want things to stay as they are, things will have to change.' Not that we can necessarily expect to be the same – but since we need to change the way we manifest ourselves at an increasingly rapid pace we must go back to the principles, the capabilities, the mission, the purpose, the values in order to sense some meaningful stability.

Therefore it is so important, in navigating through contextual structural change, to understand what are the hubs of reframing. Are they capabilities? Assets? Customer bases? Is it a certain social order? Is it a code of behaviour? A mission? Fundamental values?

In the face of change many companies now need to go back and in a sense 'unbundle' the genuine identity from the required manifestations of reframing. How else, other than by reinterpreting itself in terms of some higher basic principle, can a company like Drugstore.com or Amazon.com – both of which proclaim the idea that working in the cyberworld was a superior way of doing business than the old bricks and mortar-based ways – justify that they now also go into bricks and mortar? How else, other than by going back to the fundamentals of risk and knowledge (indeed, 'intellectual capital') can a company like Skandia Insurance clarify why it has left some of its strongest old business lines and completely transformed them, and gone into what are seemingly other ways of doing business such as selling savings products through partners? KF had increasingly come to think of itself as a retail business owned by the consumers. But with tough competitive pressures they gradually began to realize that they had come to confuse their manifestation (a set of retail chains) with their true cooperative identity (creating value for households and consumers in areas where these experienced problems and dissatisfaction through involving them in innovative collaborative schemes).

It is a basic task of leadership to ensure that identity and manifestation of identity are not confused, so that both can evolve appropriately. One reason is that this allows people to understand continuity in change, which brings meaning and some order into life. And separating the principles of identity from the structural manifestation of identity may prove to be exceedingly powerful as a source of renewal.

THE PRACTICALITY OF STRONG CONCEPTS

The 'clocktime' of business has changed as so much of the activities have moved from the physical world of steel mills to the virtual world of the Internet. Time for reflection is limited. When success is determined by rapid and proactive action and often on increasing returns on scale and 'lock-in', the Prime Movers are often the first movers. Few systems are safe from invaders and reconfigurers.

One sometimes hears statements to the effect that strategy as a concept is out, that everything now is simply tactics, operations, and here-and-now action. *I do not for a moment believe that this is true* – I have seen too much misguided hyperactivity to share such a view. On the contrary, as already mentioned, this is an era in which qualified conceptualization – indeed, theorizing – is more important than ever. Those who say that they don't theorize and that their actions are not based on conceptual thinking are simply unaware of their own process. But what is certainly true is that we no longer or at least rarely have time for a traditional sequence of crisis awareness, analysis, strategy design, and implementation. *This sequence must merge into a more dense, more compressed process.* Action cannot be based on past analysis of past events when the territory changes so that maps quickly become old.

James Hillman (1995), in a wonderful chapter on leadership, has described it as something 'which unites thought and action in a single gesture' (p. 150). He thinks of this as 'animal intelligence', characterized less by reflection than by reflex, and also refers to Taoism. Many others have observed this process of establishing a *direct link between reflection, analysis and action*, in which the linking doesn't seem to have to go through the realm of the conscious but where the three processes are compressed and unified in the time domain. The Greek used the word 'kairos', and Heidegger talks about 'der Augenblick' in which many circumstances come together. Burns (1961–1962) sees entrepreneurship and leadership intervention as the coming together of experiences that have been held in abeyance and which are released when the opportune occasion arises, when circumstances come together. Jaworski's (1998) concept of 'synchronicity' also belongs here.

But none of these thinkers would just say that leadership intervention strikes as lightning from nowhere. The on-the-spot improvisations of a jazz pianist are based on many long journeys and experiences. The effect is seemingly more subtle but perhaps even more striking when a great classical pianist attacks one of the last Beethoven sonatas: in the really great interpretations the music emerges as improvisational and not programmed. A direct link between the subconscious and the muscles, bypassing consciousness, seems to be at hand; the music seems to come out as a process of release, not from reflection and pressure.

In referring to the playing of Claudio Arrau as 'organic', Joseph Horowitz (1982) describes these aspects of Arrau's playing as '… linked to his principles of piano technique, which rely on *the wisdom of the body*, and to his principles of psychology, which rely on *the wisdom of the subconscious*' (my italics).

Reflection, conceptualization and theorizing are not inherently in opposition to rapid response and on-the-spot action orientation. Exactly the opposite is true. With our Western modes of thinking, which analytically distinguish between thought and action, we tend to think that an orientation towards conceptualization would exclude an orientation towards action, but we now have enough evidence and sufficient 'rational' theories to realize that such a view is incorrect and that it can easily lead to stereotyping leadership styles as leaning in one way or another.

The distinction is illustrated in Figure 18.1. Obviously, lack of both conceptualization and action will lead nowhere. Strong focus on conceptualization but lack of action orientation is often too slow and leads to 'analysis paralysis'. The organization which does not reflect and concep-

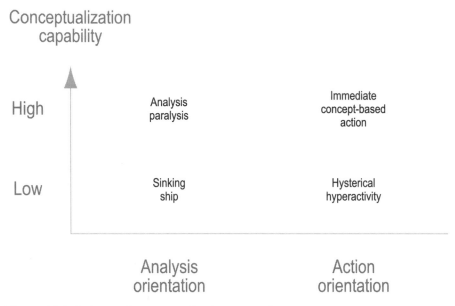

Figure 18.1 Action and conceptualization merged.

tualize what it does but is only geared to encouraging action will become what I think of as 'the hysterically hyperactive' organization, with compartmentalization, politics, and lack of aggregation and structuring of knowledge as a result. Frustration and cynicism will ensue, and leadership will lose its legitimacy.

Simplicity is the essence of profundity – this is how I like to characterize the situation when action is based on pre-reflection and the advanced building of concepts. The task of the leader today is setting the scene for this. Before simplicity can reign, the underpinnings of experience and reflection (conscious or not) must have been gained.

THE LEADERSHIP DILEMMA OF PURPOSEFUL EMERGENCE

Leadership must take into account the 'emergent' nature of change and development, e.g. the idea that it is not entirely plannable, that processes and outcomes are unpredictable and open-ended; yet can be purposeful, grounded and perceived to be legitimate, and – not least important – therefore meaningful for those participating.

This poses a dilemma for leaders. They must, in fact, ensure that they are not in total control – neither with regard to process nor outcomes – while never appearing to be lost. Their Scylla and Charybdis are, on the one hand, the macho style and too much trust in rationality, and, on the other, being seen as lost and drifting along.

The super-rational macho style, often posing as anti-intellectual, in many ways the stereotype of the leader of the past ('the boss'), is a blockage to innovation and reframing. We cannot rule out that there are instances when the all-knowing leader acting in a macho style actually has the groundbreaking new vision and idea, and in those circumstances the style may function. But we cannot take this coincidence of style and content for granted. Normally, this style of leadership is better in situations where pure efficiency in terms of cost and performance within a framework is required, whereas it tends to become counterproductive in situations of reframing.

Displaying some level of vulnerability while maintaining a grounded idea of purpose and direction is instrumental in bringing out the best knowledge and involvement among the people surrounding the leader. Displaying purposefulness and clear 'selectors' as to outcome and also in terms of process and code of conduct; ensuring standards of effectiveness while recognizing intellectual open-endedness and personal vulnerability which engenders trust, seems like the solution to the dilemma.

MISSION AND VISION

Both these concepts are artefacts, invented for specific purposes by specific people in specific situations. They belong to standard business language, but managers, business researchers, and consultants use them in quite different ways. In many companies these concepts are used as a sort of routine leisure activity without any practical consequences except doing lip-service to academia and consultants.

Having said this we must still assume that – since the concepts have become so common and popular, although they mean different things to different people – there may be something universally attractive in them. They may well fit with some underlying logic related to operating and developing companies – or even to the nature of human existence.

I see 'mission' and 'vision' as *artefact concepts which are deliberately used to create purposeful, collective action.* They do so *by making gaps visible.*

The concepts can be understood in the context of our knowledge about how human beings as well as collectivities function. As opposed to other creatures, human beings and collectivities of human beings are able to transcend the present here-and-now, and put this present here-and-now in a larger context; and within a time (past–present–future) framework.

Vision definitely is in the time domain, about the future. It implies a gap between an imagined future state and the present state.

Mission is not related to time in the same manner. Instead, mission is related to what value creating domain we participate in and how, i.e. *what role* we have in *what larger system.*

This definition of mission also means that mission can (but does not necessarily) imply a gap between the present state and some desired state. We might very well be fulfilling our mission right now, today. But we cannot, today, fulfil our vision – we can be on the way to doing it, but we cannot be 'there'; since this would actually imply that we don't have any vision beyond the present state.

So, *mission* is a description of *what difference our existence makes to the context we function in,* whereas *vision* defines a gap between the present and some future state. Vision always implies a gap, mission may imply the existence of a gap but doesn't have to.

We may state the vision in terms of mission. If the vision is stated in terms of mission we say something about *how in the future we would like the larger environment to change or to be affected (presumably: become better) as a result of our own actions.*

But vision does not have to imply mission. Mission always implies reasoning in terms of what effects you have on the external world and its betterment. Vision *may* be about effects on the external world, but it may also be only about the state of our own organization (for example its size, its profitability, its competence, how it makes its shareholders rich, how it gains power). This is summarized in Figure 18.2.

So we have to distinguish between, on the one hand, the present and the future, and, on the other, the effects we are talking about on the external environment as opposed to the effects on our own internal world and organization.

All visions are about the future; all missions are about the effects on

	Present	Future
Effects on external world	Mission	Vision about mission
Effects on the company	–	Vision about company success (shareholder value, size, etc.)

Success defined as:

Figure 18.2 Mission, vision, and how they are related.

the external world. If we talk only about the internal world (the company) and about the present, mission and vision as concepts have no meaning. If we talk about effects on the external world in the present we can describe this as our mission. If we focus on the effects on the company's state in the future we can talk about a vision of the company. If this vision about the future includes the effects we think the company should have on the external world we talk about a vision which is about a mission, a *vision-as-mission*.

You can very well say that a company which measures its success only in terms of shareholder value does not regard itself as having a mission (except to make shareholders wealthy). Whatever effects it has on the external world then is unimportant and purely instrumental. However, if a company truly believes that its *raison d'être* has something to do with how it influences the external world we always have to talk about mission. Then what the company does and stands for is seen as being of value in itself.

Why are vision and mission interesting conceptual artefacts? Because of the inherent importance of 'gaps' and of 'meaning' and 'purpose' to create (individual and collective) action in human beings. As Margaret Wheatley (1992/1994) has stated when trying to apply complexity theory on management: probably the most important 'attractor' equivalent in social systems is 'meaning'. In complexity theory, 'attractor' means some sort of principle or 'magnetic field' which can serve to bring the energy of many seemingly disparate elements and actions to move in some particular direction; when suddenly the system acquires qualities beyond those of its elements. This happens normally when a complex system reaches a 'fracture point' in which it takes on a different logic moving towards a different state of organization and structure.

For example, both mission and vision statements may give various stakeholders, such as customers, investors, potential employees, an opportunity to identify with the company. They therefore may mobilize energy both outside and inside the company. Wally Olins' (personal communication) likes to draw a triangle with the three elements of culture, image and vision, and say: 'It's a matter of whose vision you believe in!'

A vision about a mission may very often be associated with a particular person. In fact, it seems that even if this is not really the case it does help if the vision of the mission is associated with a person; this makes the mission and the vision more tangible, more easy to identify with. Martin Luther King saw as his mission to emancipate blacks and his vision was an integrated society. He died, but he came to personify this mission and this vision, and this has helped many others to pursue it. Henry Ford, Steve Jobs, Ruben Rausing of Tetra Pak are examples of other such visionary leaders who based their visions on missions – on a better and more effective world, not just better and more effective and more profitable companies.

On the other hand, visionary leaders who did not formulate a *vision about a mission* will be much more quickly forgotten. Harold Geneen in ITT had a vision about ITT's growth and bottom line but could convey no sense of mission. Although much admired by bean-counter type of business economists he failed to install the values in his company which really mobilized people for a mission. These examples could be multiplied. *The leaders who are remembered are the ones who had a vision formulated in terms of a mission.* Whether or not there is a mission has a profound influence on whether a business is able to create meaning.

A company can achieve a true identity both for itself and for the external environment by the process of 'ecogenesis'. One way is by having, by serendipity or vision, a particular technology at hand, which can then spread and create a new 'infrastructure'. Microsoft would be such an example. The other is by creating an artefact 'concept', which is usually a vision about a mission, which becomes so much of an 'attractor' that it mobilizes the attention and energy of many players and coordinates their actions in such a way as to make the concept a self-fulfilling prophecy. In such cases the invention of a concept formulated as a vision about a mission can mobilize many people, thus producing action which actually transformed the abstract concept into a concrete, manifested reality.

Note that your vision can be to fulfil the mission formulated by some-body else! This is the case in the Martin Luther King example, and in many companies with great 'vision-as-mission' entrepreneurs.

The emergence of new vision and mission mostly does not come out of rational, preplanned processes. In fact most such visions and missions come from persons who have lived rather special lives and who are, as a result, different – some would say 'a little crazy' – in one way or another. In *Management for Growth* I made the observation that there often seems to be a fit between some misfit in the external environment, on the one hand, and some other misfit inside a person, on the other – so a fit between two misfits! Manfred Kets de Vries (1989) has expressed this notion perhaps better than anybody else: 'Making virtue out of vice'.

VISION, MISSION, AND THE CRANE

My best bet to leapfrog these natural but unplannable and stochastic pro-cesses to develop new identity and vision-as-mission have been iterated in the sections about our 'crane' for business concept innovation.

The process of *upframing* generates a number of ideas about *the game we are part of*, and a number of possible and alternative definitions of who are the other players and what is our role and what could be our role.

Based on the understanding of what upframed system or systems we might be playing in we may now go to the *time framing* dimension, using artefact scenario and 'idealized design' techniques. Such scenarios of upframed system definitions can be used to create visions-as-missions.

Going to a number of alternative scenarios of the upframed system and our role in it (preferably as a Prime Mover) is the equivalent of *testing the fit* between a number of preliminary mission statements resulting from the upframing process and a number of vision-as-mission statements given different possible future states. Once we have made a number of different scenarios of the upframed system, and/or of our role in the upframed system, we may end up with a statement of vision-as-mission.

In order for us to really have a grounded vision-as-mission we also need to think about how it is to be implemented. This is equivalent to testing various ways of manifesting the vision-as-mission in the organization's structure and systems, according to the Selznick and Maturana–Varela models referred to earlier. The vision-as-mission is validated and legitimized, and therefore becomes much more powerful as an attractor influencing people's collective behaviour, *if it can be shown to be actionable and translatable into concrete structural manifestations.* Therefore we need to make the loop from the 'upframed conceptual future' (where we now have a preliminary vision-as-mission statement) back to the present. This part of the trip can be seen as a kind of 'engineering test'. How would we model the organization's structure? What sort of relationship would we have with various external partners and stakeholders? What information technology solutions and systems?

And since the vision-as-mission is rather meaningless unless it can be concretely manifested and translatable into functioning arrangements, this could feed back to the vision-as-mission as such. *So to some extent working out the abstract and working out its concrete consequences are two aspects of the same process,* two sides of the same coin. We can separate them analytically, though perhaps not time-wise. One is based on an implicit or explicit hypothesis of the other.

If we look at interesting examples of how vision and mission have emerged in large companies, we can clearly see that there is a process at work in which the dialectic between, on the one hand, *insight about opportunities or problems or unsatisfactory states or anxieties in the larger external environment* and actors there is involved, and, on the other hand, *insight about internal or mobilizable assets and capabilities* are involved. Xerox saw that the copying process was part of a much larger upframed process related to documents handling and knowledge management, and they thought that they had or could develop the capabilities to play a role in that larger process and system. Tetra Pak (which was born in the packaging company Åkerlund & Rausing) evolved a transcendental vision of the whole distribution chain and user situation of milk packaging, based on already achieved and emerging technological capabilities as well as intimate contacts with manufacturers, retail chains, and consumers. Louis Gerstner of IBM resisted the advice to shatter the company into lots of small units and instead realized that the customer base consisted of com-

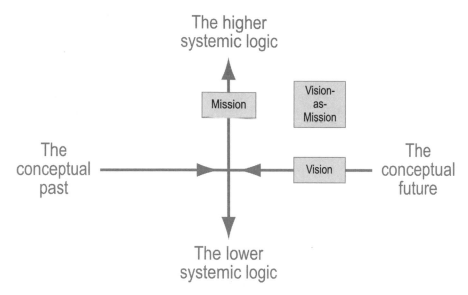

Figure 18.3 Mission and vision plotted into the crane structure.

panies which were all worried about the coming future of some strange thing related to the Internet and electronic commerce, and he knew that IBM was unique in possessing many of the capabilities and experiences – or could develop them – that would enable them to play a role in that game. So in many cases it was somehow *the simultaneous perception* of these inconsistencies or problems or worries in the outside world and present or emerging or possible-to-develop internal capabilities and assets that made the new vision-as-mission come out.

It is the nature of these processes that the design of our crane (with its structural and processual characteristics) attempts to simulate. The perceptive reader will not have missed the identity between the mission–vision illustration in Figure 18.3 and the basic outline of the crane as presented in Figure 8.5.

MEANING AND SOCIAL CHARACTER AS DRIVES

Michael Maccoby (1988) has shown how leadership needs to link in with 'social character'. And social character is something that evolves with the times, as well as varies between national and other cultures. It is highly related to what people consider as meaningful, how they want to enact this meaning, and therefore how they want to participate in collective efforts.

As somebody who crosses borders a great deal and who has lived in four countries I have become highly – certainly not sufficiently – aware of national characters. Leadership is seen as very different in different countries. Replying to the statement 'It is important for a manager to have at hand precise answers to most of the questions that his subordinates may raise about their work' 66 per cent of Italians answer 'yes' but only 10 per cent of the Swedes (Hampden-Turner and Trompenaars, 1993). To some (perhaps significant) extent this may be because the question means different things to them, but I also would guess that there is a real difference in how people view leaders and their role in an organization. Likewise, there are differences between generations. People born in the 1940s (like myself), babyboomers, the X Generation – all have experienced very different realities and are deeply influenced by this. Certainly, the attitudes towards authority and large established organizations, and indeed towards business, have gone through several stages.

So people have different expectations and see life and employment and work in different lights. One of the themes in this book is that we are all value creators. Everything that we engage in is, in one way or another, related to our value-creation activities, to how we see the purpose of our lives, to what kind of value creation we strive for.

Unless leadership is able to link into social character it cannot be effective. An authoritarian leader will have difficulties to bring along people who see personal growth, emancipation, and self-fulfilment as their goal. We can see a clear distinction between those who are willing to engage in any activity creating more wealth as opposed to those who demand that some criteria other than shareholder value and personal wealth must be an integrated part of life.

Industrial society tended to push us into the mould of the 'organization man'. That society was effective when the large structures, rationally designed from top down, functioned efficiently and without disturbances. Since man was seen as a more or less incomplete substitute for yet-to-be invented machines, people working in organizations were expected to be as disciplined and predictable as possible. But this is no longer the case. Not only have the needs of business changed with the advent of the information and knowledge society, but the predominant social character has also done so. There is a trend towards people wanting to be seen as actors, not just order takers, and as performing meaningful activities, not just any activity.

What companies are, and what they produce and create, have become much more abstract. This applies both to those who are outside companies and to those who are inside. It is at least superficially easy for all of us to understand what sort of company Ford – the symbol of the Industrial Revolution – used to be and what they stood for and what they gave us in terms of products. It is very difficult for most people to understand what a company like Microsoft stands for. And – to look at other companies in the very high market valuation league – do we generally realize that General Electric is based on services, and that Coca-Cola, as one of the most valuable companies in the world, really manages a brand?

As already stated, in this world of enormously increasing abstraction and fragmentation, in which dimensions of space and time are shattered, it is necessary to establish identity by conceptual clarity. *Identity is no longer defined primarily by objects but by concepts. These concepts express purpose, meaning, relationships.*

People who carry the knowledge capital or part of it to customers cannot be just automatons, programmed once and for all. Their understanding of the situation and of the concept that they are part of must be much deeper. People are expected to *handle the unexpected* and to adapt to new and unique situations by *inventing the uninvented* – and as we know, only the prepared mind is good at improvising. In addition, improvising and problem-solving require access to 'tacit knowledge' which cannot be acquired quickly through simple instructions but which has to be gained over time by social interaction, learning by doing, and by developing an understanding of cultural and contextual embeddedness. This sense of identity here and now comes from being at the same time an exile from the past and a visitor from the conceptual future. Jung's concept of 'the collective unconscious' comes to mind. Empowerment comes from enacting a vision that has meaning through its relationship with accumulated social history, extending into the future.

Only in this way can the numerous 'Moments of Truth' (Normann, 1984/2000) which individuals in the modern corporation continuously meet be well executed. The question is how a company can ascertain this.

The development of the individual is always at the cross-roads in a force field of three dimensions:

- First, between the experiences of the past and an envisioned, meaningful future.
- Second, between the constrained 'here-and-now' and the image of the larger system in which the here-and-now is embedded.
- Third, between the individual self and the social community of which the individual is a part.

I would like to summarize these developments in a simple scheme. The new demands of business, as well as the development trends for the new social character, imply that we must regard more people not just as order takers and performers of predetermined activities, but as actors who proactively initiate, create, and co-produce. And they will want to see what they create and produce something that has meaning to them, that serves a purpose that they can identify with. In what is, of course, a much-stereotyped form we can thus illustrate the move from previous eras to today's predicament of institutions and business companies in Figure 18.4.

If values favour short-term activity and interests rather than long-term

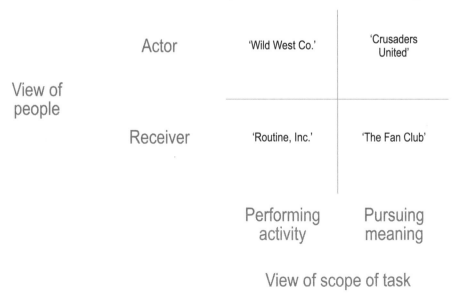

Figure 18.4 Four types of organization culture.

meaning, and if people are basically passivized, they will become order-takers routinely performing what they are being told. Their creativeness and enthusiasm will not be mobilized in the work context. If, on the other hand, people are highly mobilized and entrepreneurial but there is no guiding vision or value system we will have the 'Wild West' situation of highly energized fragmentation – this situation is the one of the 'hysterically hyperactive' organization mentioned earlier.

If values are such that people are essentially more reactive then proactive, but go along with a movement which they see as highly long-term meaningful, we will have 'The Fan Club'. This is a not untypical situation in today's high technology start-up companies, often led by dominating and highly charismatic entrepreneurs whose vision others are eager to join in with. In many ways this may be the most efficient situation for a company in a rapid phase of growth.

For the longer term the situation of 'Crusaders United', in which people are 'actors' rather than 'followers' and 'receivers', but where they are somehow still united by a matrix of overall values and where they are involved in the joint enactment of a meaningful future, should be the most efficient – the one most reminiscent of the criteria for 'recurrent purposeful emergence' and the Great Company. Such an organization benefits both from forces creating diversity and mechanisms of integration.

What Leaders
Need to Do

19

CONSTRUCTION OF ATTENTION AND ATTENTION FOR CONSTRUCTION

Organizations can move when they are able to capitalize on, mobilize and co-align contextual and internal driving forces. This force field is where leadership is exercised.

Esther Dyson (1998) has, perceptively, characterized today's economy as 'the attention economy'. Today's value-creating context means that it is not objects or units but the relationship between them – which gives them positional value – that is crucial. This is reflected in the gigantic process of unbundling assets and activities and then reconfiguring them into new patterns. As Luhmann (1990) has pointed out, this means that communication becomes the most important process of the systems that we call institutions or organizations.

Reality is socially constructed and enacted. This process requires inter-action, and therefore communication. Communication serves to focus attention but is also driven by attention. Reality emerges as the result of a dialectic: mental processes of the mind result in individual and social action which then allows subjective experiences to be objectified and shared. This objectivation and sharing then stimulates more interaction and more mental process. It might be argued that the very art of leader-ship, as we have defined it, is founded in an understanding of this dialectic between mental process and social objectivation which may result in grounded reframing. Leadership means to simultaneously be an *actor* influencing and catalysing this dialectic, and to be an *object* in it. Ideally, leadership should stimulate social process that leads to imagina-tive subjective experiences the energy of which is then also turned outward into joint enactment of the (inter-)subjective images. We have dis-cussed how play and artefacts are process tools in this enactment of a new reality.

VALUE-CREATING COMMUNICATION: CREATING THE LICENSE IN THE CONSTITUENCY

Every organization creates value in a co-productive context, and, as we have seen, such context or value constellations tend to become increasingly rich and complex the more connectivity we have in the economy. The stakeholder model (Barnard, 1938; Rhenman, 1964; Johnsen, 1993) tells us that any organization lives in a tension field in which its freedom of action has to be earned by balancing contributions (monetary but also in other currencies) between the stakeholders.

The 'license to operate' that an organization needs from stakeholders, and the leverage for value creation that skilful mobilization of a value constellation can give, are crucial leadership tasks. The achievement of both depends to a great extent on the mode of communication employed and the skill employed in implementing it.

Communication, in most practical cases, tends to be used for imposing a view, to explain. The word communication comes from 'communicare', which means 'to share'. Of course, sharing can be achieved by imposing, but sharing can also be achieved in an open-ended process in which all participants discover and see things that they did not know before, or that did not even exist before.

Another related but dissimilar aspect of communication is whether the basic world view behind it is that of a zero sum (I win, you lose) or a plus sum (all can win) game. If we combine the two dimensions we get the matrix of Figure 19.1.[30]

While most traditional communication is in the lower left-hand corner of the figure, communication that leads to the growth of knowledge and creative reframing belongs to the north-east corner. What is always important is whether there is symmetry between the views of the actors engaging in value-creating communication. Certainly, I have seen organizations in which the culture has been very much that of the zero sum game and of imposing a view, and where this basic view has guided actual behaviour in spite of official assurances of the opposite. Likewise,

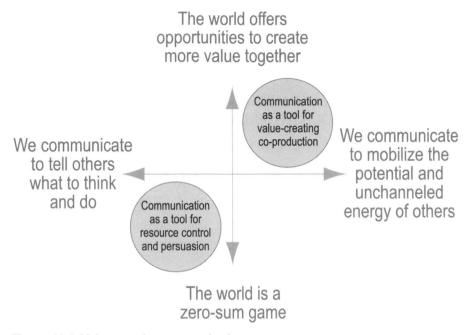

Figure 19.1 Value-creating communication.

when different organizations get together in a value-creating constellation there is the risk of a lack of symmetry in expectations.

> For example, the reactions of many analysts to the cooperation that was announced between Microsoft and Ericsson in late 1999 can be interpreted in this scheme. Nobody doubted that there was the possibility of a genuine plus sum game from a business point of view. All the official statements from the two parties were solidly positioned in the north-east corner of plus sum game and creative open-endedness – in other words, in a mode of co-creation and co-production. There was no doubt about the 'theory espoused'. But many analysts expressed doubt as to whether the 'theory-in-use' of Microsoft was not a different one, namely a competitive win–lose mode of thinking. Perhaps these reactions were mistaken. On the other hand, they had to be understood against the background of Microsoft's way of handling the legal action that had recently been taken against the company.

Personal communicative capabilities of leaders are among the most important determining factors in making the communication process and the resulting co-creation of a newly framed or emerging reality efficient.

The use of rhetoric, inventiveness in identifying emerging Gestalts, the ability to shape these into captivating metaphors and other artefacts that serve as transitional or focusing objects, a sense of timing ('der Augenblick') – such skills characterize great leaders. Such capacity is something of a natural gift, but it can certainly also be consciously learnt and improved.

This capacity together with strong personal powers to imagine can turn the leader into somebody who personally more or less embodies a concept or a direction. Going back to the framework of the mental territories available for reframing this would mean that the leader has a strong personal capacity to perform the mental process of imagining and synthesizing in the domain of the 'upframed conceptual future'. James Hillman (1995) has strongly emphasized the notion that 'leaders are the embodiment of ideas': 'What ultimately gives one the power of leadership is a capacity to embody visionary ideas, to be unafraid of ideals' (p. 155).

This means that Hillman also attaches an ethical or moral dimension, in addition to the more general aesthetics of leadership. This is very much in consonance with Thomas Szasz (1973/1991):

> It is only by trying to resolve his moral uncertainties that man can, *by creating*, discover what he is. Similarly, it is only by attempting to resolve their moral uncertainties that institutions or groups can, *creatively*, discover what they are.

The power to communicate vision-as-mission at this mental and moral level, not only for the individual organization but for the larger constituency of co-producers and stakeholders, is what it takes to create the license to operate, to mobilize the co-producing value constellation. This is how the 'organization matrix' (Emery and Trist, as referred to earlier), the value context, is built.

ARENAS AND ARTEFACTS FOR INTEGRATING DIVERSITY

If the ideal of concept-based action orientation is to be realized, leadership must provide the setting. The demands on such a setting are that all domains of knowledge and insight are effectively being used and shared:

- the tacit and the explicit domains
- the historical domain and the present

- the notion of the organization's identity and its current manifestation
- the contextual environment and boundary breaking-technologies and invaders versus the current definition of the business
- the 'conversation' between capabilities and customers
- the 'conversation' between company-based resources and external network-embedded resources.

The greater the diversity, and the more conversations (within the 'value-creating communication' framework) are going on, the stronger the potential for creative building and integration and synthesis.[31] Again, 'integrated diversity' is a not very well-understood concept since it consists of the unification of two dimensions which are often confused as one (see Figure 19.2).

Homogeneity does not foster creative conversations and tensions which lead to novelty, even if integrated. Diversity without integration leads to balkanization and tribalism. Diversity and integration together provide the foundation for renewal. Lawrence and Lorsch, in their 1960s studies of innovation, empirically showed that organizations which were at one and the same time characterized by 'differentiation' and by 'integration' mechanisms were more successful in achieving innovation than other combinations. Differentiation without strong integration mechanisms, however, was generally more successful than integration without differentiation (Lawrence and Lorsch, 1967).

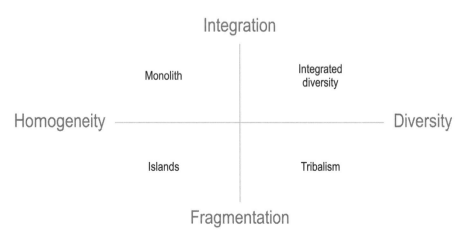

Figure 19.2 Integrated diversity.

Achieving integrated diversity often goes through stages. The traditional hierarchical organization, in which power was concentrated at the top and all units were functionally differentiated but dependent on the chain of command and its exercise of authority typically created a homogenous *dependence* culture. Often, the next step is moving from dependence to *independence* – witness the 'profit center' and 'strategic business unit' and 'divisionalization' movements. But from the situation of diversity created by a culture of independence it is then possible to integrate without losing the identities of the individual units and without going back to dependence – this is the *interdependence* culture, in which (to use terminology from transaction theory) parent–child relationships have been replaced by adult–adult relationships.

What are the arenas and processes that can create integrated diversity? They must allow different actors, and different domains of knowledge – see above – to come together to have conversations. There need to be certain principles and codes of behaviour. A basic infrastructure of trust is required. There must be some presence of 'selectors' and 'attractors' or relevancy systems. Technological infrastructures must be provided.

At best, the procedures of Japanese *keiretsus* (although unfortunately in addition to being arenas for conversation they also tended to function as closed self-protecting systems), conventions, strategic planning processes, scenario exercises, can serve to stimulate the integration of diversity. 'Transitional objects' can, for a time, legitimize and focalize creative conversations. Scenarios sometimes can fulfil the role as such transitional objects. Schrage (2000) relates 'How the world's best companies simulate to innovate', and how, for example, 'prototypes engage the organization's thinking in the explicit. They externalize thought and spark conversation.' (p. 14).

This again brings us to the use of artefacts. They can be designed to trigger and stimulate conversations. They can also become designed during conversations, thus objectifying the joint experiences of those engaged, and serving to further intensify and focus (or unfocus or refocus, if that is required) the conversation. Symbols and new concepts are both a measure and a driver and focuser of process. New language that comes out of a process of integrating diversity can then serve as a selector for the continued process.

Not strange, then, that leadership must be very perceptive to the use of language, and that one of the major functions of leadership is the steward-ship of language (Johnsen, 1993; Normann, 1975/1977).

POLITICS, POLICY AND THE RESOLUTION OF TENSION

Tension is an inherent part of organizational life and of change, and, in-deed, a necessary feature of it. I know of no theories about change which do not somehow include the concept of tension.

Tension in this context I define as a social phenomenon. It exists between actors who have different ideas and therefore envisage different action paths. Behind tension in the social realm there often, probably usually, exists some kind of 'misfit' in the 'objective reality'. Misfit may be between a certain state of affairs and another possible state of affairs, or between the state of an organization and the (changing) state of its en-vironment. Whatever the source, misfit is likely to produce tension in internal organizational life, between individuals and groups. This is natural, since different persons and groups see different parts of reality, or see reality in different ways due to their predispositions, experiences and interests. There are always many different interpretations possible of any phenomenon.

Tension may lead to conflict, and conflict may take different paths. But conflict as such is by no means inherently negative, on the contrary. As long as tension and conflict can be seen as representative of different van-tage points, different interpretations, it is a sign of diversity and therefore an invaluable resource. The leadership process which interprets tension and conflict as data about different reality perceptions and channels them into innovation I have described as 'statesmanship' in an earlier book (Normann, 1975/1977).

Tension and conflict do not, however, necessarily lead to anything posi-tive. There are different modes of conflict resolution, and some of them are clearly counterproductive to renewal. In the ideal case tension and conflict should be channelled into new, higher-level insights and action patterns – indeed, to reframing. When there is true integration of diversity, when there is interdependence and collaboration, this is possible. However, when diversity leads to fragmentation and when tension leads to tribalization and independence, or to excessive dependence, tension has probably resulted in a negative spiral. To describe the difference between these two outcomes the words 'policy' and 'politics' are useful.[32]

One way for an organization to react to tension and 'foreign' elements is simply by *expulsion*, by not recognizing them or taking note of them. I am not saying that this could not be functional – in fact, in many situations when an organization is very efficient in exploiting a streamlined business model it could well be that it would do best by not accepting foreign elements and not questioning itself too much, at least temporarily. It is an important task of leadership to recognize whether an idea should be expelled or whether it should be dealt with in some other way.

Another means of not accepting ideas while seeming or pretending to do so could be called *overlegitimation*. This is the situation where a new idea seems to become highly welcomed and explored. However, in many cases this is a sign of 'repressive tolerance': Part of more or less ritualistic welcoming of new ideas, or participation in prestigious external 'clubs' or projects. 'I have found that we have only become a symbol at which management can point when they are accused of not being change oriented enough, but this is really a way for them to control all sorts of new ideas and make sure that they have put them into a closed box which they can control', as the strategic planner of a well-known company once said to me.

A third way to handle conflict is by *compromise* – a little of this, a little of that, but no real synthesis. A variation of that is *incongruence*, in which certain elements from the new are accepted, but they are never integrated with the old into a holistic concept. The best way to handle tension and conflict is by achieving *synergy*, the same as *integrated diversity*, moulding different and perhaps seemingly inconsistent elements into a higher-level framework.[33]

Good leadership tries to achieve integrated diversity – 'policy', avoiding tribal turf fights – 'politics'. In the policy-formation process energy is dissipated as creative reframing, not into adversarial, communication breaking, zero sum game-oriented fights for position. A policy-oriented culture and code of conduct is desirable. But no organization lives in a vacuum, and also the external environment and the stakeholders outside the organization have their culture and code of conduct, which can be either policy or politics based. The external culture tends to spread to the internal culture, and it is often a strategy of one or the other of possible internal culture bearers to try to feed on and nourish the culture from the environment.

> In a very large European state-owned company in the public transportation area there had been many attempts to turn an internal culture of politics into one of policy. However, since most of the top positions were allocated by the political parties in the country in question the external power fights tended to spread to the internal corporate culture. The new chief executive officer saw this and embarked on a programme to influence the external stakeholders. But his attempts to create a viable 'institutional matrix' and 'license to operate' effectively were never completely successful.
>
> A large and successful service company which had been started by a large group of hospitals and other healthcare organizations who owned it, enjoyed a good and profitable position, fulfilling the wishes of its founder/ owners. However, a new chief executive officer realized that the whole healthcare industry was about to undergo deep structural change, with profound consequences both for his company and for his owners. As he worked hard with his own management group in a 'policy' mode he began to realize that the future would almost inevitably lead to much more diverse strategies and therefore needs for the owners/customer. Some of them would adapt to the changing conditions, while others would become laggards. Some would see 'his' company as a partner in spearheading change, whereas others would prefer the company to remain reactive in fulfilling their perceived needs rather than proactive in breaking new ground together. He could also see potential conflicts emerging between the owners. He realized that it would be increasingly difficult to develop his company in a 'policy' mode if a mode of 'politics' emerged – as there were signs that it might do – among the owners and customers. He began a conscious strategy of reviewing his stakeholder relationships.

The various situations that can emerge out of the distinction between policy and politics in the internal and the external stakeholder world, respectively, are illustrated in Figure 19.3. Leaders must be able to understand how to navigate between these situations, and how to achieve a congruent, policy/policy-based situation. In some cases this is only possible by radical measures such as breaking up a company or changing the stakeholder constellation.

If 'politics' values from the environment are allowed to influence and distort the functioning of an organization, leadership has failed in one of its most important functions: to protect 'precarious values' (Selznick, 1957).

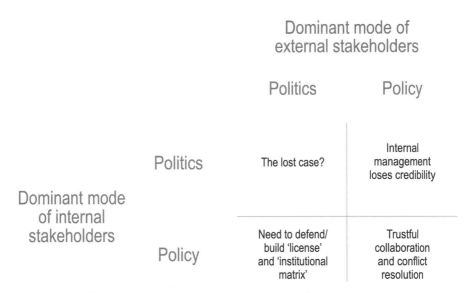

Figure 19.3 What values dominate? Four archetypal situations.

TURNING THE INNER EXISTENTIAL DRAMA INTO EFFECTIVE LEADERSHIP

Leadership, as Erik Johnsen (1993) has pointed out, is a kind of behaviour that can be learnt, and which should at best be exercised by everybody in an organization. Leadership is not for only 'the great man' at the top.

Nevertheless, it is probably correct to say that those who serve as leaders for organizations going through thorough and dramatic transitions (in the face of adversity or great new opportunity) have to exercise these behaviour patterns to an exceptional extent. And, by normal yardsticks, they have to be exceptional people. They also tend to be unusual people. Like great artists or, indeed, exceptional performers in just about any realm of society, they have special characteristics which come from some combination of critical experiences, or simply from accidental coincidences of entering situations which fit their skills and personality traits, and perhaps from genetic heritage.

Such leaders have to solve a number of internal dilemmas, and they are often driven by inner demons (cf. de Vries and Miller, 1987). To be effective they must be rebels while still respectful of others and of the system around them. They may be torn between their desire to serve and their desire to dominate. They must believe in what they are doing and show great conviction, while avoiding to fall into the trap of narcissism and self-deification. They must be able to receive the applause from the crowd for successes without automatically generalizing and believing that they can handle each and every situation. They must steer between the feelings of 'love' which Maccoby (1988) refers to, while tempering their drive to abuse the power they possess. They must be able to function here-and-now while being part of something larger and more extended in the time domain. In his wonderful book *The Courage to Create* Rollo May (1975) says:

> It is the seeming contradiction that *we must be fully committed, but we must also be aware at the same time that we might possibly be wrong.* This dialectic relationship between conviction and doubt is characteristic of the highest types of courage, and gives the lie to the simplistic definitions that identify courage with mere growth. ...
>
> ... Commitment is healthiest when it is not *without* doubt, but *in spite of* doubt. (pp. 12–14)

The desire to conform and live within the social context and to be an opponent or rebel also applies to the relationship of leaders to society at large. Many leaders get their energy from, simultaneously, the vision they have of a 'better world', and their personal experiences of the deficiencies of that world (which may often have been unfair to them in one way or another, or which they may have experienced as being stale, bureaucratic, and in need of change). Thus, the idealized state of the system is their friend, the current state of the system is the enemy – and both drive them.

Appendix 1
A Note on Territorial Actors

UBIQUITY OF BUSINESS

When the virtual, globalized economy becomes as predominant as it is today, business companies are liberated from geographical boundaries to an extent never seen before. In principle they freely move across borders. Policies favouring free trade and free movement of assets and professionals facilitate this. The European Union explicitly emphasizes the right of anybody practising a profession in any of the member countries to do so across the Union. 'Symbol' work – based in the global information and knowledge industry, as opposed to the local physically based mode of value production – is crucial and growing. Scenarios about the future tend to emphasize the predominance of such a more or less nationless category of people unless current trends reverse (Levin and Nordfors, 1999). The other side of the coin is that if companies move more freely across borders they are, of course, also more vulnerable to invaders attacking their previous local dominance.

Strictly, 'companies' as such do not move about. Rather, they tend to unbundle themselves and relocate different activities to various places while being held together by various 'business processes'. They become the very opposites of, say, the traditional Swedish 'bruk' where not only most functions were located at the source of raw materials and the factory but where also the local community was more or less organized as an appendix to the company. But if companies unbundle themselves to become competitive – where do they go?

> Companies looking to relocate don't just want a city. They want a site for at least one of four major business functions: Headquarters, back-

office/operations, research and development, and manufacturing. All
those functions – and what they demand of a city – are in the midst of
transformation. And no matter which operations a company is moving
to a city, it had better be a nice place to live. Top-quality workers
demand a top-quality living environment... (*Fortune Magazine*, 1995)

But if business companies build competitiveness by unbundling and
liberating themselves from geographical restrictions to form new patterns
this must have an impact on geographical – or territorial – units. They
can hardly move about.

Or perhaps they can, in the virtual if not in the physical domain.

THE STATE OF THE NATION-STATE

A look at a map of a part of the world where history has been able to play
out over a long period – such as Europe – will reveal a thing or two about
the nature of borders between nation-states. They tend to follow natural
physical boundaries such as coasts, rivers, or mountain chains. The integrity
and identity of the nation-state has been helped by physical boundaries
that lent themselves to military defence of territory.

Definition and defence of territory by force has been complemented by
policy and regulation. Natural resources, climate, religion and language
have helped to create identity. Infrastructures – whether physical such as
for transportation, or social, such as for education – and societal organization have reinforced national ethos. Such driving forces promoted
cultural homogeneity inside and cultural diversity between nations.

But regulation and physical natural boundaries can do little about
today's business companies and Prime Movers. Control in the old sense
simply no longer function. Not even Stasi, in spite of generous resources,
could control communication in an increasingly mediatized world in the
former German Democratic (sic!) Republic. When in the late 1990s the
Swedish government drastically raised taxes on cigarettes the result was
the rise of a well-organized business of smuggling, more smoking, and less
tax income for the government. They had to go back on their decision.
No wonder that non-democratic dictatorships look at the Internet with
some fear, since it introduces an uncontrollable horizontal, global logic to
communication rather than the vertical control logic of the traditional
state. Even the officially pro-IT French government for years was ex-

tremely ambivalent about it because it brings in non-French culture and language and supposedly threatens traditional French values. France, around the turn of the millennium, experiences significant emigration waves, with young, highly skilled, entrepreneurial people moving out.

But when competitiveness depends on globalization, when companies move their R&D units to Silicon Valley and their legal headquarters to tax havens, and when members of the growing elite of knowledge workers decide where to pay taxes and how much – where do territorial units fit into the value-creation logic of today's economy?

BECOMING A GOOD HOME FOR VALUE CREATION

The conclusion is logical and it is borne out by empirical observations: territorial units are involved in a vociferous race for competitiveness. Competition between areas and cities is not new, although the pace has increased. But the rules of the game are now different. Regulations, protectionism, devaluations no longer fill the bill. Business companies and Prime Movers and knowledge workers can no longer be forced to stay, they have to be seduced to stay or they will relocate at least parts of their activities. With today's web-like structures, relocation can easily take place without formal or publicized decisions.

I would like to formulate the strategic problem of territorial units in the new economy very simply: *How can we become a good home for value-creation activities?* Territorial units must build competitiveness much like business companies and very much based on the same rules.

It is not strange that *Fortune* Magazine, several years ago, began to rank 'the best cities in the world for business' along with its other famous ranking lists such as the *Fortune* 500. There are also numerous lists and audits comparing nation-states to each other. But also cities, or rather metropolitan areas and regions, consciously begin to look at themselves as actors, benchmarking against each other, trying to find the formulas for competitiveness – for how to become a good home for value creation.

Paradoxically, it seems that territorial entities which were very successful in the past may carry the seeds of a potentially precarious situation in the new economy. Manufacturing giants like Germany and Japan, for example, now have obvious difficulties in adapting to an economy which is based more on services and *use* of products than on the production of them.[34] Sweden developed an economy with a unique proportion of truly international companies which typically did 80% or more of their business outside Sweden and had a majority of the people employed abroad. (A long time ago Sao Paolo was the third largest industrial city of Sweden…) This means that a very large proportion of Swedish business people have international experience. This, reinforced by very high taxes and low salaries for knowledge workers, is probably one reason why well-educated Swedes have a uniquely high inclination among highly developed nations not to move back to their country of origin (*The Economist*, 10 July 1999, page 116, sourced from IMD.) Countries with inflexible labour market rules and slow bureaucracy have problems. As a friend of mine pointed out – perhaps not with mathematical accuracy: 'It takes 3 hours to legally start a new company in the US, 3 days in the UK, and 3 months in France. And that is only the beginning.'

We must, however, take care not to interpret permanent or more temporary *diaspora* of knowledge workers as something necessarily negative. If personal or company links with the country of origin remain there may be several positive piggyback effects associated with such movements.

WHY REGIONAL UNITS?

One reason why regions seem to take precedence over the nation-state as economic actors may be that regions can be faster and more coordinated, less dependent on traditional institutions, more close to real-world events, less forced to make compromises with backward and slow-moving areas. The nation-state may have been a natural unit for military defence and for building yesterday's infrastructures. But the large city or metropolitan area and the surrounding region in many ways reflects the requirements of today's economy better. As Törnqvist (1993) says:

> The development of the cities in Europe gives us a corresponding picture of an emerging information society … the cities of Europe are experiencing a renaissance. City functions from before the Industrialism era are again the driving forces behind regional development. Successful cities today function as meeting points, liaison centres and stages of action. Many of them live up to the notion of information cities, with a clear division of their workforces into one part which is oriented towards the outside world, handling information, and with high salaries, and a

locally anchored service part with low salaries. It is the need for proximity when exchanging information that leads to concentration, territorial proximity, and closely linked networks. The big city offers both
of them. (My translation)

Desmond Morris in *The Naked Ape* (1967) advanced the hypothesis
that the big city with its intensity and many sources of stress may not at
all be as anti-human as many want to think. On the contrary, the human
being with its highly developed and complex brain fits very well into the
complexity and rhythm and interactivity that the city represents.

The eminent economic geographer Christian Wichmann Matthiessen
pointed out to me that it is in fact much easier to move a factory than to
move a research department of, say, a pharmaceutical company (personal
communication). The reason is that the knowledge that is such a crucial
part of the research and development in such an industry is embodied in
people and embedded in social networks (and it is probably to a great
extent tacit, which implies that it requires social interaction to be
explicated and transferred; cf. Nonaka and Takeuchi, 1995). So the more
knowledge-intensive and 'personality-intensive' (to borrow an expression
from my book *Service Management*) a business is, the more it thrives by
being part of a context. A territorial actor must strive to get into a
'virtuous circle' in which knowledge attracts knowledge and knowledge
workers attract knowledge workers, and in which knowledge-based
companies attract knowledge-based companies. Conversely, it must avoid
getting into a vicious circle where the opposite happens.

Briefly, regional units are small enough to provide a 'closeness context'
and to allow concerted action, but they are also big enough to contain
many of the factors which contribute to growth of territorial units, such
as those mentioned by Michael Porter (1990) in his analysis of 'clusters',
namely (with some comments and examples of mine included):

- *Factor conditions*, the inputs needed for competition in an industry,
  from physical resources to capital to knowledge.
- *Demand conditions*, i.e. including how early, how large, and how sophisticated domestic demand has been to stimulate the advancement of an
  industry.

The Swedish case is very interesting here. As studies have shown
(Danielsson, 1974) several of the leading Swedish companies – many of

which then became role models for the rest of the country – were born out of an interaction with an ambitious state anxious to build excellent infrastructures, which stimulated innovative domestic infrastructure building companies which then grew internationally based on the excellence they had developed at home. Many of them then became role models for other local companies. Such examples would include AGA, Ericsson, ASEA (now part of ABB).

- *Related and supporting industries*, i.e. the web of competences that are required as a support to the 'core' industry in question.

  It is fascinating to study under what conditions clusters of supporting industries are created by such a core development. Comparative studies between Silicon Valley and the Route 128 phenomenon around Boston, for example, tend to show that the most important firms in those respective areas had distinctly different policies with regard to how open their own boundaries were. The key firms in the Boston area had much more of a 'we do it ourselves' principle than their Silicon Valley colleagues (such as Hewlett-Packard). This policy of unbundling and of open boundaries tends to create a set of highly competitive and diverse 'subcontractors' and businesses which are complementary in different ways. Similar phenomena can be found, for example, in the northern Italian small business clusters (see Figure A1.1).

Figure A1.1 The Italian small business clusters – focus on cooperation, co-production, and the micro-social processes.

> According to several analyses (for example, Normann, 1980, and Carlsson and Hallberg, 1997) the unwillingness of the Swedish state to unbundle large areas of value creation, such as healthcare, in this way has certainly led to a vicious circle of lower quality and lower rate of innovation in the service/business in question, a lack of using it as a driving force for creating entrepreneurial companies, and waste of the potential of huge national investments to create internationally successful businesses. We can refer to this as 'The Swedish Prison' – the imprisoned knowledge capital (Normann, 1984/2000).

- *Firm strategy, structure, and rivalry*, i.e., not least the existence of domestic competition between firms which stimulate their innovativeness and competitiveness.

In addition, Porter stresses the role of government as well as the role of 'chance'. While I do believe in chance I also believe in the old saying that chance favours the prepared mind. As to the latter I would like to point out the importance of international mind-sets and early role models. For example, in the Swedish context the crucial Wallenberg family very early on had a distinctly international outlook, rather viewing names such as Morgan and Rothschild as part of their reference group than other Swedish families and entrepreneurs. Their mind-set was one of international business and growth. Besides, the nation of Sweden was too small a market to support a really major business. This is why it seems that the only companies with a truly international ethos originated in small countries.

REPOSITIONING REGIONAL ACTORS FOR TODAY'S ECONOMY

A region like Silicon Valley was built on the crest of the information technology wave. But most cities and regions have existed for a long time and pose the problem of *repositioning* rather than being built up from scratch. Cities such as Manchester, Birmingham, and many others actually were the symbolic manifestations of the industrial era, and then the problems posed of repositioning are particularly intricate.

Over the past few years I and my colleagues have had the opportunity to study a number of European regions and cities, ranging from Barcelona to Venice, from Stockholm to Naples, and in some cases work with them. Although the contextual factors shape the concrete patterns

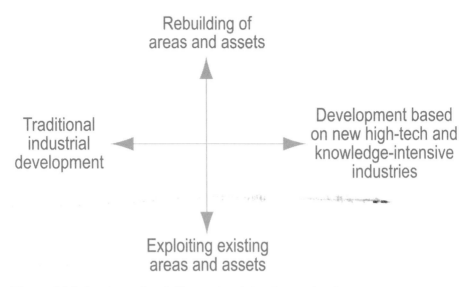

Figure A1.2 A scheme for plotting regional development paths.

of strategic responses of such cities, many of them present similar models of development. Some have attempted to build their future on an industrial logic, others on the industries of the new economy. There are cities which have tried to develop by attracting highly labour intensive factories, becoming efficient manufacturing centres, and presenting as critical success factors the low cost of manpower and capital, logistic efficiency and high quality of hard infrastructure. Others have tried to switch from an industrial logic to businesses typical of the information era economy. All of them have among their critical success factors innovation, the ability to attract highly skilled labour, quality of life, and a good technological infrastructure.

One way to plot the itinerary of such strategic repositioning is described in Figure A1.2.

The case of Hamburg: Recovering from industrial decline [35]

An example of a complex itinerary is the city of Hamburg, which now according to comparative studies enjoys possibly the highest per capita income of major European cities. During the 1970s and 1980s Hamburg experienced a deep economic crisis because of the restructuring and the international recession of its four traditional sectors of economic activity: port, transportation, shipbuilding and oil refining. The city fell from being one of the richest in the European community in 1970 to the average level in 1985. Unemployment rose to 13%. Hamburg's economy fell into a vicious circle, being unable to compensate the reduction of employment in the traditional sectors with the growth of a service sector. During the 1970s the city's political and economic leaders failed to recognize the changing nature of international and economic processes and attempted to promote the setting up of new heavy industries in the Hamburg area. This policy was strongly supported with a large expenditure of public money.

The policy failed for many reasons. In fact, although Hamburg was perceived by many decision makers as one of the most efficient cities in northern Europe, the high cost of labour and of land, as well as the low level of capital incentives, made many manufacturing companies choose other, more remunerative sites.

In the 1980s, when it was almost clear that the economic development strategy pursued was unsuccessful, the city leaders changed their strategy. The city mayor persuaded the different stakeholders within the city – businesses, labour, government and knowledge-based sectors – to participate in the formation of the new economic development strategy.

The new strategy which emerged in the course of the next two years shifted the economic priority from the attraction and retention of labour cost-based companies to high competence- and skills-based companies. Physical urban renewal was planned to improve city retail facilities, housing, tourist attractions, cultural facilities and sports. The new policy shifted the public expenses from the redistribution of wealth to the setting up of the conditions for attracting investment.

To implement the new economic strategy, a public–private non-profit-making company was set up. The partners of the HWF (Hamburg business development corporation) were the city council, the chamber of commerce and ten of the largest banks in the country. The aim of the company was to attract investments in the modern, high-value-added industries, like biotechnology, medical and environmental technologies, aviation, electronics technologies, media, information technology and high-value-added port-oriented services.

The economic growth in Hamburg was fuelled by the rebuilding of new infrastructures that made the location more attractive to high-value-added companies. The city was able to attract investments of 3.7 billion DM primarily in the construction sector. Between 1985 and 1990 HWF attracted 387 new firms, many from overseas, contributing to the creation of 16 000 new jobs.

Technological innovation was supported by the existence of a technical university in Hamburg. During the 1980s many institutional bodies were

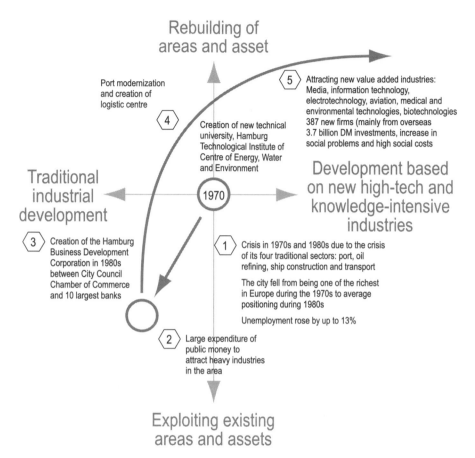

Figure A1.3 The Hamburg case, 1970–1990.

created to boost the innovation processes in different fields. Examples of such bodies are: the Hamburg Technological Institute, the Technological Advisory Centre, the Centre of Energy, Water and Environment.

Meanwhile consistent investments were directed towards the renewal of the port structure, in order to improve the efficiency and the effectiveness of port operations. These investments mainly raised the 'intelligence' in the port services, improving the planning of activities, communications, and logistics in general.

In 15 years the city was able to turn around the deep crisis connected to the crises of its main economic activities. During these years Hamburg was able to renew its port activities, as well as to radically shift the core industries fuelling the generation of wealth in the region. The city economy had been modernized and diversified. The unification of Germany and the opening to the East had improved major commercial and trading opportunities (see Figure A1.3).

MOVING INTO VIRTUOUS CIRCLES

The Hamburg case illustrates both vicious and virtuous circles. It shows that a strategy must be conceived based on an understanding of the true driving forces and genuine opportunities of today's value-creating context. It also illustrates that implementation of (and probably generally also conceiving) such a strategy necessitates certain modes of management and leadership.

It was not until the new coalition was created that a true new strategy could be both conceived and implemented. This corresponds to our observations in a large number of cases. Cities and territorial units now typically try to transform themselves and go through a transition from a very traditional view of city management (seen as *administration and management of various service and infrastructure operations*), via a period when it was realized that cities had to be made attractive and therefore had to *market* themselves, and – now – to a period when the achievement of *genuine strategic management* must be on the agenda.

Such strategic management requires a *coalition of key actors* – in effect a strategic management group, formalized or not – working in the city or regional context to co-align their forces based on a grounded and converging vision of the region's or city's strategic identity and mission. This observation also corresponds well with the observations of Robert Putnam (1993) in his famous studies of Italy, which show that civic traditions promoting a high degree of horizontal relationships locally are highly beneficial to economic and social development.

But unlike business companies, cities and regions rarely have formal boards of management. Actually (worse, some would say) they are supposed to be run by politicians, and other groupings often come to be seen as illegitimate or offensive. However, this does not prevent the existence of formation of a truly strategic management coalition.

Some would – and do – say that the basic and perhaps only task of a 'city' or 'regional' management is to provide the infrastructures and conditions for other actors to grow and thrive. I have nevertheless come to

Figure A1.4 City leadership – four archetypes.

see such management coalitions in terms of four archetypes, depending on whether or not the management sees itself basically in a *support function* or in *a strategic management mode*, and whether it mostly *focuses on infrastructures* or whether it also is actively involved in *developing a distinct strategic profile* for the city/region contentwise (see Figure A1.4).

In cases such as Hamburg or Manchester such strategic management processes and coalitions have come to be installed in view of the prospect of continued decline. In a number of other cases particular *events, new infrastructures*, or the evocation or *'rediscovery' of hidden assets* – always together with local entrepreneurship and emerging leadership – have triggered series of events which have led to such a strategic process. Here are three examples.

Barcelona

Suffering from its long-term rivalry with Madrid, Barcelona was able to use the Olympic Games of 1992 to great advantage. The games became a catalyst for developing the city and the Catalonia region. Large funds became available and were used to create new and better infrastructures, to open up the city to the waterfront, to link transportation infrastructures with each other, to undertake various social development projects, and to create an international image of Barcelona as a highly dynamic city (the ads pointing out that Barcelona was located in the 'country' of Catalonia are famous). Wisely, Barcelona allied itself to the whole region of Catalonia (which now enjoys a high standard of living and dynamic growth) and also with strategic cities in southern France such as Perpignan, Montpellier and Toulouse.

Öresund – bridging Copenhagen and Malmö

In spite of the relative proximity of the two cities studies showed that there was very little business interaction and telephone calls crossing the strait of Öresund. To link Sweden to the Continent and make transportation more efficient a decision was taken – after decades or even a century of agonizing – to build a bridge across Öresund. But a number of local people both in southern Sweden and in the Copenhagen/Zealand region realized that the bridge would not necessarily create anything but more traffic.

As a result of such foresight a number of joint projects were initiated, with the 'Öresund Committee' as the main driving force. Industry clusters, such as food, transportation, and pharmaceuticals were identified and sometimes recognized across the border by institutional initiatives (for example 'Medicon Valley'). Joint research and education was installed. Gradually, the bridge became not just a transportation tool but the symbol of the emergence of a region with new social linkages and visions that stimulated the imagination of actors in both countries, creating interaction between them, which gradually materialized in joint and new economic development projects. Several companies from outside the Nordic region have now set up Nordic headquarters in Copenhagen. The bridge had become a catalyst for the potential emergence of a region with true content, as had the Olympic Games for Barcelona.

Naples

In spite of a long glorious past Naples clearly was a city in decline. But the city got a new mayor, Bassolino, who showed great leadership and began to find ways to turn the city around.

Bassolino did some very unconventional things. He went to Wall Street for financing. And, famously, he sold out a large part of the Naples airport to British Airports Authority which also obtained a management contract, so that flying to Naples finally became more bearable.

I was called to a small think-tank group to reflect on Naples and its strategy. The main results were published in a booklet which was ready for the occasion of the G7 meeting in Naples in 1994, *Naples and Southern Italy: History, Culture, Economics*. Thus, Bassolino also took advantage of an event evoking global attention – the G7 meeting. In one of the contributions to this booklet Franco Modigliani, the Nobel Prize winner in economics, produces evidence of the decline of Naples and the southern region of Italy and reflects on its causes. He points out, for example, how the intervention of the state in favour of the south has led to consumption rather than investment, and how it has relieved the south from the pressure of creating its own management: 'But the price that one pays for this is, precisely, the lack of an integrated and interconnected system that amply produces a true entrepreneurial class and a mechanism of replacement and amplification within it' (Modigliani, 1994, p. 46.)

In my contribution I point out that Naples is full of sleeping resources related to nature, history, culture, scientific research, etc. But all these are more or less neglected and therefore passive and declining, since no or very few social and entrepreneurial processes and horizontal coalitions between various elites of the city context have been built around them. The path ahead, I suggest, is via a combination of resurrection of these sleeping assets together with a rediscovery and reactivation of old civic traditions and the building of horizontal, inter-elite processes and projects. (Normann, 1994, pp. 58–59.) I also propose a scenario-based process involving many of these elites for evolving a shared view of a future 'strategic identity' for the Naples city context. Much of this has actually taken place, and Naples shows signs of coming out of the doldrums.

CITY RECONFIGURABILITY

Many studies have been made about national and, to some extent, also regional and city competitiveness. My hunch is that the prediction value of many of those is limited because they stress the results of past achievement (such as per capita income, quality of infrastructures, etc.) more than the key conditions for living in the new value-creating context.

One factor I would particularly look at today is that of *reconfigurability*. The reconfigurability – or to use an established but not quite as powerful a term, 'flexibility' – of the labour market has recently come to be recognized. But there are many other factors that contribute to reconfigurability. One of them relates to the very core of the European welfare state. When the European Economic Community was created it was first and foremost aimed at establishing peace in Europe, by increased economic interdependence. To achieve the latter it introduced new rules facilitating competitiveness among businesses in Europe.

Paradoxically, however, extremely large portions of the economy are still managed by governments and the public sector and are highly regulated. Half of GNP or more circulate through the state. Service and welfare industries like healthcare, utilities, pension schemes (i.e. savings) are still run by the public sector and are highly protected from competition and from the pressure to innovate.

It is therefore a paradox to find the European Union, on the one hand, promoting competition among business companies, but to see that politicians generally tend to lean towards 'homogenization' and non-competition among what we might call 'societal systems' or 'welfare state models'. It would be very strange, indeed, if the driving forces of the new value-creation economy would not be able to bring about at least as dramatic innovations and productivity and quality improvements in these regulated areas as in all other areas. So one must question whether Europe is not doing its citizens a disfavour by blocking out so many of these potentially favourable change factors. In addition, Europe may well in this way lose out in the development of business in such future-oriented areas as those mentioned.

THE QUALITY OF THE STRATEGIC PROCESS

A second factor I would emphasize much more in looking at competitiveness of territorial units is *the quality of the strategic process*. In preceding sections I have emphasized some characteristics of a good strategic process, such as horizontal interactivity, future-oriented processes to evolve a vision of a strategic identity, the skill and ability to utilize events and various assets and processes to bring people together in creating a new 'social reality' with action implications, etc. These are themes which are treated in other parts of this book.

THE CHANGING FACE OF 'LOCAL EXCELLENCE SERVICES'

The battle for competitiveness between territorial units basically stems from the globalization of the economy and the way it encourages business companies and particularly Prime Movers to escape territorial bonds. Not surprisingly, however, there is also a piggyback from the battle between territorial units to business.

One obvious outcome is that there is now a higher likelihood that business will find better 'homes' for their value-creating activities. But there is also a structural change going on. The example of the airport of

Naples illustrates this. It was realized that efficient transportation in-cluding an efficient and well-managed airport is necessary for a city like Naples. But the management knowledge, the trade unions, the traditions, to run an efficient airport simply did not exist – they had to be found elsewhere. So the sleepy local organization which had been able to exist only because of its protected position was replaced by an international company which reputedly had developed excellence in its area.

When working with the waste management services organization of another very famous Italian city we finally faced the same dilemma. There was strong local support, and certainly from most politicians, to maintain and protect the company that was owned by the municipality performing waste management services. On the other hand, several attempts to re-form that company had failed. The city was extremely dependent on tourism, but studies showed that tourists certainly were not happy with the quality of the cleaning and waste management services which was in evidence everywhere in the streets. So what about bringing in one of the international giants with far greater excellence and experience? A fight was staged between traditional politics, favouring the old solution, and the notion that the city as a whole had to become more competitive.

IN SEARCH OF THE COMPETITIVE REGION: A WISH LIST

The purpose of this appendix has not been to give anything near an ex-haustive overview of the conditions for regional and city development. Several highly skilled and imaginative scholars have done just that including Åke E. Andersson (see, for example, Andersson, 1989) and Christian Wichmann Matthiessen (1998) around issues in the Öresund region. There is a whole science – well grounded in the mathematics of linkages and of complexity theory, and highly related to the notion of infrastructures and their effects – of local and regional development which I have left out almost completely of this brief discourse.

My purpose has been to point out the paradoxical but logical fact that the ubiquity of value creation and of business actors, usually summarized under the theme of 'globalization', has a logical counterpart, and that the other side of the coin is local and regional competitiveness. The fact that territorial actors are in one sense firmly located to the physical ground, yet have to play in the dematerialized realm of the economy to survive, makes these actors at least as interesting as the Prime Mover business companies. To be successful they have to make particularly good use of the global information- and symbol-based economy in order to sway physical processes and actors of flesh and blood to choose their territories as playgrounds.

Some present tendencies within the European Union to try to 'harmonize' (in other words, protect from competition) territories in terms of a number of crucial factors related to 'how to be a good home for value creation' seem particularly inappropriate. The search for local and regional identity and competitiveness must take its point of departure in the recognition of the new logics of value creation, not in the denial of them.

The issue of developing regional competitiveness must not be confused with that of tax havens and other, fairly short-term strategies – here the same rules apply to regional units as to business companies, as developed under the section of imperfection-based strategies in this book.

Finally, let me end with a simple and perhaps not very scientifically rigorous list of what I would expect to find in the competitive region.

- It would be the 'nerve centre', the node, of some international Prime Mover business companies.
- There would be certain clusters of companies of different kinds and sizes around these larger internationally oriented Prime Movers.
- It would be the home of some highly competitive knowledge-intensive service companies, since they – rather than traditional manufacturing – now lead the development of the economy.
- Physical and informational infrastructures would be of a high standard.
- There would be a high quality of life for 'global knowledge entrepreneurs', including areas such as healthcare, culture, ecology, nature.
- There would most likely be a high proportion of people coming from unconventional business circles, like entrepreneurial immigrants, women, becoming involved with business innovation and new start-ups.
- There would be several meeting-places for 'tacit knowledge', both within industry clusters and across various realms of society including between industry, culture, politics.

- I would expect a good portion of 'the bacteria phenomenon', as I have come to think. Bacteria, having much shorter lifecycles than, for example, human beings, can change their genetic codes comparatively very quickly. Perhaps the analogy is dangerous and partly incorrect, but we see a similar phenomenon in places like Silicon Valley. Individuals move about and cross-fertilize between organizations much more quickly than organizations are created and develop and die. So just as bacteria supposedly can change and therefore influence their environment in the most unexpected ways, people who move from one context to another can, in principle, change these contexts much faster than institutions can change.
- There would be a high degree of reconfigurability.
- There would be a high level of quality of the 'strategic conversation', and very likely at least an informal but effective 'strategic management coalition' between actors cutting across all realms of society.
- There would be several interesting experiments going on to break traditional taboos and boundaries with regard to traditionally imprisoned areas like welfare services.
- There would be a high degree of externalization of support functions for city services in infrastructure, education, healthcare, etc., as well as a certain level of 'outsourcing' of such services to international players.
- The area would be recognized as one in which aesthetic and cultural issues are particularly high on a priority list and there would be a range of people from around the world visiting for this reason. Cultural institutions would flourish.

Appendix 2
On the Use of Cases

I have used a number of case illustrations in this book, and some words about the principles I apply for using such cases are in place.[36] While theories, frameworks, and systemic insights can be derived – or induced – from single cases one must be weary of frameworks that build on few observations. A trap that many seem to fall into with open arms is that of using some currently successful companies to draw conclusions about the long-term factors that contribute to success. As is very clear in Part VI of this book, where I make the distinction between 'great ideas' and 'great companies', this is something I want to avoid at all cost. *The fact that something is currently successful should not bring us to the conclusion that processes and capabilities which ensure longer-term survival and success are necessarily characteristics of that institution.*

This book is not a comprehensive story about how the conceptual framework presented has emerged as a process of enquiry. The attentive reader can certainly find clues about that process, but I have chosen not to specifically account for it. Instead, I hope that the validity of the framework will be apparent from its degree of internal consistency as well as with its fit with a number of diverse concrete observations of what actually happens in today's business.

It is in this vein that I use cases. While certainly many of the cases accounted for have contributed to my total understanding – as have many, many other cases and experiences that I don't mention – I use them here as *illustrations* of a framework, *not* as proof that the framework is correct or good. My narrative constantly swings between the abstracted, conceptual world (in which I strive to be systematic and consistent in the build-up) and the concrete world of observations (where I do not have the ambition to give a full account of my process for the reasons mentioned above).

Many of the companies I quote I have personally worked with, and in other instances I have only second-hand knowledge. With few exceptions I do not tell which of the two is the case. I have tried to avoid too many references to what seem to be the standard cases that appear in many books, though what is well known to many is often an economic way to make a point, so some Microsofts and IBMs have been allowed.

Whenever I had a choice I have picked the simple, less technologically spectacular in favour of the most recent, flashy, technical case. If I had done the latter many of the illustrations would have looked hopelessly out of date on the publication of the book, while – in my view – many older and less fashionable cases serve my pedagogical purposes at least as well.

There are two cases I use more than others, and on several occasions. One of these is IKEA. I like this as a dramatic example of a reconfiguration process that could have been illustrated also by other, fast-moving high-tech companies – but which does not necessarily involve high technology, yet – or perhaps therefore – illustrates the principles in all their purity. I think the reader will find that, although this is nowadays (especially since 1993 when Rafael Ramirez and I presented it in a *Harvard Business Review* article) a frequently used illustration in business literature, I have chosen to extract from it some insights other than the usual ones. For the sake of clarity I have never in my career received a single dollar of fees in any kind from IKEA.

The other case is KF, the Swedish consumer cooperative. One reason why I have chosen this company is that I have already – at the request of the company – published a book (Normann and Nordfors, 1999) on their possible futures, and some options for their current reframing process. It is thus official that I have worked with them, and they have given me permission to use the material as published in this book. KF illustrates a complex but potentially very promising reframing situation of a company which oscillates between, on the one hand, finding its future in a reinterpreted version of its original identity and, on the other, finding it in the structural manifestations that the original identity has come to take. It also allows me to illustrate, in some depth and in a coherent way, the functioning of the crane artefact to help reframing processes which is described in the latter part of this book. My deep thanks for the opportunity to use this example.

Notes

[1] A simplified version of the Lampedusa statement that will be referred to later in the book.

[2] The original title of that book (which, contrary to the present book, was originally written in Swedish) was *Skapande Företagsledning* (1975), which is strictly untranslatable into English. A pre-edition in English was called *Management and Statesmanship*, a title which was unfortunately abandoned for the much more banal and less pointed *Management for Growth* (Wiley, 1977).

[3] My colleagues Rafael Ramirez and Johan Wallin recently published a study of the characteristics of such organizations (Ramirez and Wallin, 2000).

[4] Yet one must feel highly worried about the strength of what might be an unholy coalition between politicians (who want to see happy citizens – not infrequently referred to as 'consumers' by the politicians – feeling wealthy), managers (increasingly rewarded with stock options and making acquisitions paid with their own high-valued stock), the financial services establishment (more dependent on transaction commissions as transparent markets and de-regulation take out spread income) and investor citizens (who love to get richer and who don't want to miss the train). All of these now have an enormous stake in pushing equity markets towards higher levels.

[5] Later, after additional research, I published my book *Service Management* in 1984, but many of the key concepts had been published earlier in a limited edition report and in various articles from 1977 onwards. (3rd revised edition 2000).

[6] The reader will find that I have used IKEA to illustrate several principles in this book. It is a simple, pedagogical case, all the better for not being clouded by the influence of high technology. For comments on the use of cases, see Appendix 2.

[7] *Winning Strategies in Financial Services*, Richard Normann, Bengt Haikola *et al.* (1985). (The distribution of this report was limited to the some 20 corporations which financed it.)

[8] At the time of writing there are questions about the future of the Smart car. This does not change my analysis. If this attempt fails some other attempt will succeed. The logic is right; the execution in this case may or may not be sufficiently good.

[9] The notion of 'the customer's customer' has been part of SMG's framework since the early 1980s. Frank af Petersens coined the expression 'second-level customer relationship'.

[10] This concept was developed by Normann and Ramirez and published in a multi-client report of limited circulation in 1988. One spin-off of this report was the book *Designing Interactive Strategy* by Normann and Ramirez (1994; edited paperback edition 1998). Because the publication of *Designing Interactive Strategy* was delayed, the concept of the value star came to be publicly introduced in *Knowledge and Value*, by Wikström and Normann (Swedish edition 1992, English edition 1994).

[11] The notion of the almighty CEO has staying power, though. In the *Business Week* feature on '21 ideas for the 21st century' discussing management in the future and 'the leaderless corporation' one can read: 'Some companies have already gotten a jump on the process. Even General Electric Co's take-charge CEO Jack Welch makes many decisions collegially with a team of top executives. "I couldn't do this job if I didn't have them" admits Welch.' (*Business Week*, 30 August 1999, p. 46). As if this were an exceptional phenomenon!

[12] I promoted this argument at a guest lecture called 'Values and Value' at the Helsinki University of Technology in the spring of 1997.

[13] I recently read an endorsement from a well-known management guru – not the authors quoted above! – giving a belated nod to Selznick as the originator of the competence concept. His words demonstrated, with embarrassing clarity, that he had either not read Selznick or that he had completely misunderstood him.

[14] A summary of much of the work of the SIAR School, including an in-depth exposé of the business idea concept, has recently been published (Carlsson *et al.*, 2000, in Swedish).

[15] This description of Dunn's theory borrows heavily from my book *Management For Growth*, 1975–1977, p. 75.

[16] An extensive summary of complexity theory can be found, for example, in Capra (1996).

[17] This was also a key idea in my early research on innovation (cf. Normann, 1971).

[18] Ulf Mannervik and Kees van der Heijden, private conversations.

[19] For in depth analysis of the reason for using scenarios, see Peter Schwartz (1991), Kees van der Heijden (1996).

[20] These examples, however, also demonstrate that it is never clear where the end of the road is, and that the good concept must be thoroughly embraced to work. Should Xerox have thought, earlier, of the next step as the 'knowledge management company'? Or did they fail to manifest the 'document company' idea in sufficiently powerful structures and systems? Did Coca-Cola for a while in fact pay too much of lip service to the 'brand management' idea while in reality acting more as a smart capital management company?

[21] Much of this description builds on the book about KF, Samverkanspion-järerna, that I wrote with Lennart Nordfors.

[22] I use the word 'consumers' here since it is intrinsic to the identity of this organization, though the reader will hopefully recall that I throroughly dislike the concept!

[23] IKEA as a family-owned company doesn't appear on those lists.

[24] I have chosen to use 'recurrent' rather than 'continuous', to avoid the mechanistic 'push-button' connotations of the latter expression. Similarly, 'purposeful' rather than, for example, 'goal-oriented' is used in order to stress the combination of open-endedness yet well-driven characteristic of true creation.

[25] Also the wording of some concepts has been changed to better fit my current use of language, particularly as related to theories of living systems and cognition. It should be pointed out, however, that, for example, the concept of 'ecological interfacing' was highly prominent in the 1985 version.

[26] Incongruence between espoused theory and theory-in-use, as I understand it, can be the result of a more or less conscious and sometimes even deliberate strategy of a person, but it is also due to the fact that theory-in-use will inevitably involve tacit knowledge.

[27] I owe this expression to Karl Beijbom.

[28] Wally Olins has sensitized me to these and other visual image manifestations of corporate identity in speeches and private conversations.

[29] This text was kindly provided by Rolf H. Carlsson, a former colleague at SIAR (now in Gemini Consulting) at my request and after joint discussions.

[30] This figure on value-creating communication was developed together with Ulf Mannervik and Hans Strand.

[31] In its millennium issue of 31 December 1999 *The Economist* reflects over what made the western world 'take off'. It was not, the conclusion is, the state of scientific knowledge as such – other civilizations were or had been as well equipped in that domain. Rather, it had to do with values, institutions and politics. The major conclusion is that it was the emergence of a highly diverse, specialized institutional framework, knit together by values favouring progress and a political system which explained why knowledge really came to be used.

[32] Jaap Leemhuis, called my attention to these two concepts, and while I may

have abused them somewhat I think my description roughly captures the meaning he gave them.

[33] These five categories of resolution of tension and conflict are based on my earlier book *Management for Growth* (1975/1977), pp. 154ff.

[34] I identify this as a major challenge to the Japanese economy in the special foreword to the Japanese edition of Normann and Ramirez (1994/1998).

[35] This illustration case was developed by Roberto Cinquegrani in an SMG client project (not for Hamburg) led by myself in 1996.

[36] I will not go into the deeper philosophy of science and scientific method issues regarding the use of cases. A philosophy of science-based treatise of that subject made up a long and comprehensive appendix in *Management for Growth* (1975/1977), which also happens to be my doctoral dissertation.

References

Abell, A. M. (1955/1994) *Talks with Great Composers*. New York: Citadel Press.

Andersson, P. and T. Larsson (1998) *Tetra: Historien om dynastin Rausing*. Stockholm: P. A. Norstedts Förlag.

Andersson, Å. E. (1989) *Sydsvensk framtid*. Södertälje: Moraberg Förlag.

Ansoff, H. I. (1965) *Corporate Strategy*. New York: McGraw-Hill.

Argyris, C. (1990) *Overcoming Organizational Defenses*. Needham Heights, MA: Allyn and Bacon.

Argyris, C. (1993) *Knowledge in Action*. San Francisco, CA: Jossey-Bass.

Argyris, C. (1994) 'Good Communication That Blocks Learning'. *Harvard Business Review* (January).

Argyris, C. and D. A. Schön (1974) *Theory in Practice: Increasing Professional Effectiveness*. San Fransisco, CA: Jossey-Bass.

Ashby, R. (1956/1964) *An Introduction to Cybernetics*. London: University Paperbacks.

Barnard, C. I. (1938) *The Function of the Executive*. Cambridge, MA: Cambridge University Press.

Barnes, J. (1998) *England, England*. London: Jonathan Cape.

Berger, P. L. and T. Luckman (1967) *The Social Construction of Reality*. Anchorage: Doubleday.

Bernstein, P. L. (1996) *Against the Gods*. New York: Wiley.

Brand, S. (1994/1995) *How Buildings Learn*. New York: Penguin Books.

Buckley, W. (1967) *Sociology and Modern Systems Theory*. Englewood Cliffs, NJ: Prentice Hall.

Burns, T. (1961/1962) Micropolitics: Mechanisms of Institutional Change. *Administrative Science Quarterly*.

Burns, T. and G. M. Stalker (1961) *The Management of Innovation*. London: Tavistock.

Business Week (1999) '21 Ideas for the 21st Century'. 30 August.

Callon, M. and B. Latour (1981) 'Unscrewing the Big Leviathan: How Actors Macrostructure Reality and How Sociologists Help Them to Do So', in *Advances in Social Theory and Methodology*, edited by K. Knorr-Cetinn and A. V. Cicourel. London: Routledge and Kegan Paul.

Campbell, J. (1949/1973) *The Hero with a Thousand Faces*. Princeton, NJ: Bollingen.

Capra, F. (1996) *The Web of Life*. New York: Anchor Books Doubleday.

Carlsson, R. H. (2000) *Ownership & Value Creation*. Chichester: Wiley.

Carlsson, R. H. and M. Hallberg (1997) *Ägarstyrning*. Stockholm: Ekerlids Förlag.

Carlsson, R. H. *et al.* (2000) *Strategier för att tjäna pengar*. Stockholm: Ekerlids Förlag.

Carson, R. (1962/1993) *Silent Spring*. Boston: Houghton Mifflin.

Chéreau, P. (1981) *Richard Wagner: Der Ring des Niebelungen*. Baarn: Phonogram International BV.

Crichton, M. (1995) *Lost World*. New York: Random House.

Christensen, C. M. (1997) *The Innovator's Dilemma*. Boston: Harvard Business School Press.

Churchman, C. W. (1961) *Prediction and Optimal Decision: Philosophical Issues of a Science of Values*. Englewood Cliffs, NJ: Prentice Hall.

Ciborra, C. (1996) 'The Platform Organization: Strategy, Structure and Surprises'. *Organization Science* (March–April).

Claesson, C. (1994) *Mental Överlevnadsteknik*. Stockholm: Carlssons Bokförlag.

Collins, J. C. and J. I. Porras (1994) *Built to Last*. New York: HarperBusiness.

Czarniawska, B. and B. Joerges (1996) 'Travel of Ideas', in *Translating Organizational Change*, edited by B. Czarniawska and G. Sevón. Berlin: Walter de Gruyter & Co.

Danielsson, C. (1974) *Studier i företags tillväxtförlopp eller Historien om GOX, FOX, POX och de fyra telefondirektörerna*. Stockholm: SIAR Dokumentation AB.

Davis, S. (1987) *Future Perfect*. New York: Addison-Wesley Longman.

Davis, S. and C. Meyer (1998) *Blur: The Speed of Change in the Connected Economy*. Reading, MA: Addison-Wesley.

de Geus, A. (1988) 'Planning as Learning'. *Harvard Business Review*, 2: 70–74 de Geus, A. (1997) *The Living Company*. Boston, MA: Harvard Business School Press.

de Vries, M. F. R. K. and D. Miller (1987) *Unstable at the Top*. New York: NAL.

Dennett, D. C. (1995) *Darwin's Dangerous Idea*. New York: Simon & Schuster.

Dunn, E. S. Jr (1971) *Economic and Social Development – A Process of Social Learning*. Baltimore, MD: Johns Hopkins University Press, for Resources for the Future Inc.

Dyson, E. (1998) *Release 2.1: A Design for Living in the Digital Age*. New York: Broadway Books.

Edvinsson, L. and M. S. Malone (1997) *Intellectual Capital*. New York: HarperBusiness.

Eiglier, P. and E. Langeard (1987) *Servuction*. Paris: McGraw-Hill.

Emery, F. and E. Trist (1965) 'The Causal Texture of Organizational Environments'. *Human Relations*, 18.

Farrell, W. (1998) *How Hits Happen*. New York: HarperCollins.

Gagliardi, P. (1990) *Symbols and Artifacts: Views of the Corporate Landscape*. Berlin: Walter de Gruyter & Co.

Gershuny, J. and I. Miles (1983) *The New Service Economy: The Transformation of Employment in Industrial Societies*. London: Frances Pinter.

Ghoshal, S. and C. A. Bartlett (1997) *The Individualized Corporation*. New York: HarperCollins.

Giarini, O. and W. R. Stahel (1993) *The Limits to Certainty*. Dordrecht: Kluwer.

Grove, A. S. (1996) *Only the Paranoid Survive: How to Exploit the Crisis Points That Challenge Every Company and Career*. New York: Currency Doubleday

Habermas, J. (1972) *Knowledge and Human Interests*. London: Heinemann.

Hamel, G. and C. K. Prahalad (1994) *Competing for the Future*. Boston, MA: Harvard Business School Press.

Hampden-Turner, C. and A. Trompenaars (1993) *The Seven Cultures of Capitalism*. New York: Doubleday.

Hillman, J. (1995) *Kinds of Power*. New York: Currency Doubleday.

Horowitz, J. (1982) *Conversations with Arrau*. New York: Alfred A. Knopf.

Ingvar, D. (1985) 'Memory of the Future: An Essay on the Temporal Organization of Conscious Awareness'. *Human Neurobiology*.

International Herald Tribune (1998) 'In Our Pages 100, 75 and 50 Years Ago', 23 March.

Jaworski, J. (1998) *Synchronicity*. San Francisco, CA: Berett-Koehler Publishers Inc.

Johnsen, E. (1993) *Strategisk Analyse og syntese*. Copenhagen: Handelshøjskolens Forlag

Kelly, K. (1997) 'New Rules for the New Economy'. *Wired* (September).

Kersting, J. (1992) 'The Suffering in the Life of a Musician', in *Claudio Arrau: the Final Sessions, Volume 1 Schubert*. Philips Digital Classics.

Kets de Vries, M. F. R. (1989) *Prisoners of Leadership*. New York: Wiley.

Koestler, A. (1969) *The Act of Creation*. London: Hutchinson.

Kuhn, T. S. (1962) *The Structure of Scientific Revolutions*. Chicago, IL: University of Chicago Press.

Lampedusa, G. T. (1958/1991) *The Leopard*. New York: Alfred A. Knopf, Everyman's Library.

Latour, B. (1998) *Artefaktens återkomst*. Stockholm: Fakta Info Direkt N&S.

Lawrence, P. R. and J. W. Lorsch (1967) *Organization and Environment. Managing Differentiation and Integration*. Boston, MA: Harvard University Press.

Levin, B. and L. Nordfors (1999) *Internetrevolutioner*. Stockholm: Ekerlids Förlag.

Levin, B. and R. Normann (2000) *Vårdens chans*. Stockholm: Ekerlids Förlag

Levitt, T. (1960) 'Marketing Myopia'. *Harvard Business Review* (July–August).

Levitt, T. (1972) 'Production-line Approach to Service'. *Harvard Business Review* (September–October).

Libet, B. (1989) 'Conscious Subjective Experience vs. Unconscious Mental Functions: A Theory of the Cerebral Processes Involved', in *Models of Brain Function*, edited by R. M. J. Cotterill. Cambridge: Cambridge University Press.

Lovelock, J. (1978) *Gaia*. New York: Oxford University Press.

Luhmann, N. (1990) 'The Autopoiesis of Social Systems', in *Essays on Self-Reference*. New York: Columbia University Press.

Maccoby, M. (1988) *Why Work*. New York: Touchstone.

Marcuse, H. (1969) 'Repressive Tolerance', in *A Critique of Pure Tolerance*, edited by R. P. Wolff, B. Moore Jr and H. Marcuse. London: Cape.

Maturana, H. R. and F. J. Varela (1987/1998) *The Tree of Knowledge*. Boston & London: Shambhala.

May, R. (1975) *The Courage to Create*. New York: Bantham Books.

McGregor, D. (1960) *The Human Side of Enterprise*. New York: McGraw-Hill.

Morris, D. (1967) *The Naked Ape*. London: Cape.

Michael, D. N. (1973/1997) *Learning to Plan – and Planning to Learn*. Alexandria: Miles River Press.

Mintzberg, H. (1976) 'Planning on the Left Side and Managing on the Right'. *Harvard Business Review* (July–August).

Mintzberg, H. (1979) *The Structuring of Organizations: A Synthesis of the Research.* Englewood Cliffs, NJ: Prentice Hall.

Mintzberg, H. (1994) *The Rise and Fall of Strategic Planning.* Hemel Hempstead: Prentice Hall.

Modigliani, F. (1994) 'Reflections on the Past and Present of the Problems of the South', in *Naples and Southern Italy: History, Culture, Economics.* Naples: IASM and Sergio Civita.

Morgan, G. (1986) *Images of an Organization.* Beverly Hills, CA: Sage Publications.

Moore, J. F. (1996) *The Death of Competition and Strategy in the Age of Business Ecosystems.* Chichester: Wiley.

Negroponte, N. (1995) *Being Digital.* New York: Alfred A. Knopf.

Nonaka, I. and H. Takeuchi (1995) *The Knowledge-Creating Company.* Oxford: Oxford University Press.

Nordfors, L. and B. Levin (1998) *Vem tar makten – fyra scenarier med vinnare och förlorare i Norden 2008.* Stockholm: Ekerlids Förlag.

Normann, R. (1969) *Variation och omorientering. En studie av innovationsförmåga.* PhD dissertation, University of Lund.

Normann, R. (1970) *A Personal Quest for Methodology.* Stockholm: SIAR Dokumentation AB.

Normann, R. (1971) 'Organizational Innovativeness: Product variation and Reorientation'. *Administrative Science Quarterly* (June).

Normann, R. (1975/1977) *Management for Growth.* Chichester: Wiley.

Normann, R. *et al.* (1978) 'Development Strategies for Swedish Service Knowledge', *Report from Multi-client Study.* Stockholm: SIAR.

Normann, R. (1980) *Förbättrad Samhällsservice* (Better Public Service). Stockholm: SAF (The Swedish Employers' Confederation).

Normann, R. (1984/2000) *Service Management*, 3rd edition. Chichester: Wiley.

Normann, R. (1985) 'Developing Capabilities for Organizational Learning', in Johannes M. Pennings & Associates: *Organizational Strategy and Change.* San Francisco, CA: Jossey-Bass.

Normann, R. (1994) 'Naples: A City in Search of its Strategic Identity', in *Naples and Southern Italy: History, Culture, Economics.* Naples: IASM and Sergio Civita.

Normann, R. (1999) 'Patienter – eller Gakkar?' *Läkartidningen* 46/99 (November).

Normann, R., J. Cederwall, L. Edgren and A. Holst (1989) *Invadörernas Dans* (The Dance of the Invaders). Malmö: Liber AB.

Normann, R., B. Haikola *et al.* (1985) *Winning Strategies in Financial Services*. Stockholm: SMG. (Restricted circulation)

Normann. R. and L. Nordfors (1999) *Samverkanspionjärerna*. Stockholm: Prisma.

Normann, R. and R. Ramirez (1993) 'Designing Interactive Strategy: From Value Chain to Value Constellation'. *Harvard business Review* (July–August).

Normann, R. and R. Ramirez (1994/1998) *Designing Interactive Strategy*. Chichester: Wiley.

Nørretranders, T. (1998) *The User Illusion*. New York: Viking

Olins, W. (1978) *The Corporate Personality*. London: Design Council.

Olins, W. (1995) *The New Guide to Identity*. London: Design Council.

Olins, W. (1999) *Trading Identities*. London: The Foreign Policy Centre, Panton House.

Polanyi, M. (1969) *Knowing and Being*. London: Routledge & Kegan Paul.

Porter, M. E. (1980) *Competitive Strategy*. New York: Free Press.

Porter, M. E. (1990) *The Competitive Advantage of Nations*. London: Macmillan.

Porter, M. E. (1996) 'What is Strategy?' *Harvard Business Review* (November–December).

Prahalad, C. K. and G. Hamel (1990) 'The Core Competences of the Corporation'. *Harvard Business Review* (January–February).

Prigogine, I. and I. Strengers (1984) *Order of Chaos: Man's New Dialogue With Nature*. London: Bantam Books.

Putnam, R. D. (1993) *Making Democracy Work: Civic Traditions in Modern Italy*. Princeton, NJ: Princeton University Press.

Rachline, F. (1992) *De zéro à epsilon*. Paris: First.

Ramírez, R. (1987) *Towards an Aesthetic Theory of Social Organization*. PhD dissertation, University of Pennsylvania.

Ramírez, R. and J. Wallin (2000) *Prime Movers*. Chichester: Wiley.

Rhenman, E. (1964) *Företagsdemokrati och företagsorganisation*. Stockholm: Norstedt & Söners Förlag.

Rhenman, E. (1964) *Företaget som ett styrt system*. Stockholm: PA Norstedt & Söners Förlag.

Rhenman, E. (1973) *Organization Theory for Long-range Planning*. London: Wiley.

Sasser, E. W., P. R. Olsen and D. D. Wykoff (1978) *Management of Service Operations*. Boston, MA: Alleyn & Bacon.

Schama, S. (1995) *Landscape and Memory*. London: HarperCollins.

Schön, D. A. (1963) *Displacement of Concepts*. London: Tavistock.

Schön, D. A. (1967) *Technology and Change*. Oxford: Pergamon Press.

Schön, D. A. (1971) *Beyond the Stable State*. New York: Random House.

Schrage, M. (2000) *Serious Play*. Boston, MA: Harvard Business School Press.

Schumpeter, J. (1950) *Capitalism, Socialism, and Democracy*. New York: Harper & Row.

Schwarz, P. (1991) *The Art of the Long View*. New York: Doubleday.

Selznick, P. (1957) *Leadership in Administration*. New York: Harper & Row.

Senge, P. (1990) *The Fifth Discipline: The Art and Practice of Organizational Learning*. New York: Doubleday.

Simon, H. A. (1947) *Administrative Behaviour*. New York: Macmillan.

Sloan, A. P. Jr (1963) *My Years with General Motors*. New York: Doubleday.

Stymne, B. (2000) 'Särpräglad kompetens, en teori om företagsledning och konsultation', in *Strategier för att tjäna pengar*, edited by R. H. Carlsson. Stockholm: Ekerlids Förlag.

Szasz, T. S. (1973/1991) *Ideology and Insanity*. Syracuse, NY: Syracuse University Press.

The Economist (1999) 'The Road to Riches'. 31 December.

Toffler, A. (1980) *The Third Wave*. New York: Collins.

Tolstoy, L. (1869/1968) *War and Peace*. Oxford World's Classics.

Törnqvist, G. (1993) *Sverige i nätverkens Europa – Gränsöverskridandets former och villkor*. Malmö: Liber-Hermods AB.

Van Den Toorn (2000) 'Esa-Pekka Salonen Los Angeles Philharmonic', in *Bach Transcriptions*. Sony Music Entertainment.

van der Heijden, K. (1996) *Scenarios: The Art of Strategic Conversation*. New York: Wiley.

Wheatley, M. J. (1992/1994) *Leadership and the New Science*. San Francisco, CA: Berrett-Koehler Publishers.

Wichmann Matthiessen, C. (1998) *Öresundsområdet*. Malmö: IK Foundation & Company.

Wikström, S. and R. Normann (1992) *Kunskap och värde*. Stockholm: CE Fritzes AB.

Wikström, S. and R. Normann (1994) *Knowledge and Value*. London: Routledge.

Womack, J. P., D. T. Jones and D. Roos (1990) *The Machine That Changed the World*. New York: HarperCollins.

Index